Studying
Ethnic Identity

Studying Ethnic Identity

Methodological and Conceptual Approaches Across Disciplines

EDITED BY

Carlos E. Santos
Adriana J. Umaña-Taylor

AMERICAN PSYCHOLOGICAL ASSOCIATION

WASHINGTON, DC

Published by
American Psychological Association
750 First Street, NE
Washington, DC 20002
www.apa.org

To order
APA Order Department
P.O. Box 92984
Washington, DC 20090-2984
Tel: (800) 374-2721; Direct: (202) 336-5510
Fax: (202) 336-5502; TDD/TTY: (202) 336-6123
Online: www.apa.org/pubs/books
E-mail: order@apa.org

In the U.K., Europe, Africa, and the Middle East, copies may be ordered from
American Psychological Association
3 Henrietta Street
Covent Garden, London
WC2E 8LU England

Typeset in Goudy by Circle Graphics, Inc., Columbia, MD

Printer: Edwards Brothers, Inc., Lillington, NC
Cover Designer: Beth Schlenoff Design, Bethesda, MD

The opinions and statements published are the responsibility of the authors, and such opinions and statements do not necessarily represent the policies of the American Psychological Association.

Library of Congress Cataloging-in-Publication Data

Santos, Carlos E.
  Studying ethnic identity : methodological and conceptual approaches across disciplines / Carlos E. Santos & Adriana J. Umaña-Taylor.
    pages cm
  Includes bibliographical references and index.
  ISBN 978-1-4338-1979-7 — ISBN 1-4338-1979-1 1. Social sciences—Research—Methodology. 2. Ethnicity—Study and teaching. I. Umaña-Taylor, Adriana J. II. Title.
  H62.S3353 2015
  155.8'2072—dc23
                                2014039934

British Library Cataloguing-in-Publication Data

A CIP record is available from the British Library.

Printed in the United States of America
First Edition

http://dx.doi.org/10.1037/14618-000

To my loving family, Erin Godfrey, Sarah McConnell,
and Amanda Roy.
—*Carlos E. Santos*

In loving memory of Zandra Yolima Lozada.
—*Adriana J. Umaña-Taylor*

CONTENTS

CONTRIBUTORS

Sara Douglass, PhD, Arizona State University, Tempe
Annette Hemmings, PhD, Edgewood College, Madison, WI
Olga Kornienko, PhD, Arizona State University, Tempe
Irene López, PhD, Kenyon College, Gambier, OH
Patricio Ortiz, PhD, Madison College, Madison, WI
Stephen M. Quintana, PhD, University of Wisconsin, Madison
Leoandra Onnie Rogers, PhD, University of Washington, Seattle
Wendy D. Roth, PhD, University of British Columbia, Vancouver, Canada
Carlos E. Santos, PhD, Arizona State University, Tempe
Melek Yildiz Spinel, BA, Kenyon College, Gambier, OH
Moin Syed, PhD, University of Minnesota, Twin Cities
Adriana J. Umaña-Taylor, PhD, Arizona State University, Tempe
Kimberly A. Updegraff, PhD, Arizona State University, Tempe
Lovey H. M. Walker, MA, University of Minnesota, Twin Cities
Niobe Way, EdD, New York University, New York, NY
Guillermo Williamson, PhD, Universidad de la Frontera, Temuco, Chile
Tiffany Yip, PhD, Fordham University, Bronx, NY

FOREWORD

STEPHEN M. QUINTANA

This book is an exciting work of scholarship on ethnic and racial identity. It brings together a diverse collection of approaches, definitions, and measurement strategies pertaining to the topic. Reading each of the different chapters might evoke the "blind men and the elephant" parable, in which several blind men, each touching different parts of the same elephant, come to reasonable but completely disparate conclusions about the animal they're experiencing. In one version of the story, it's only after the blind men put all their perceptions together that they realize the animal is an elephant. The moral, of course, is that integrating diverse perspectives can yield a richer and more accurate understanding of a subject. The readers of this book, like the individual inspectors of the elephant, will benefit from its multiple perspectives and insights into ethnic and racial identity.

I seek to prime readers of the book by identifying some of the many frameworks that the chapter authors use to conceptualize and investigate ethnic and racial identity. The astute reader will undoubtedly be able to identify additional frameworks with a close reading of the book. Because of the richness and innovative nature of the seven chapters reporting original research, there are considerably more than seven different perspectives of the ways in which ethnic and racial identify form and function.

The chapter authors explore ethnic and racial identity, for example, from demographic, sociological, and psychological perspectives. Important to ethnic and racial identity are the demographic contexts reflecting the nature and composition of populations and subpopulations within the societies in which ethnic and racial identities develop. That is, demographic perspectives are sometimes expressed through labels and descriptors attached to groups and subgroups of a society. Issues of ethnic and racial identity can be raised unexpectedly when children and adolescents are asked to respond to forms soliciting demographic identifications. Conversely, sociological dimensions of ethnic and racial identity reflect the sociological or broad makeup of communities of social groups and reflect group-level, sometimes society-level, dynamics among subgroups. As effectively demonstrated in the following chapters, the broad composition of social groups within a society provides a critical ecological context with which individual members make sense of their connection to, or disconnection from, subgroups within a society. Although the sociological contexts provide the landscape external to individuals, psychological perspectives describe the dynamics operating within individuals' interior, as they mentally reflect on and make sense of the demographic labels ascribed to them as they are embedded in a matrix of group interactions. Relatedly, ethnic–racial identity is construed in different ways in this book's chapters, with some authors defining identity as being self-contained within the individual and others drawing on more extended self-concepts as a way to conceptualize how ethnic–racial identity operates in social groups and contexts.

Another important set of perspectives presented in this collection relates to the different markers used to establish ethnic and racial identity. Many of the popular and standard markers of ethnic–racial identity are grounded in interracial as well as intraracial attitudes and affiliations. These affective valences or orientations toward racial in-groups and out-groups are efficiently measured using self-report measures. Often the response formats used to index these self-report measures of ethnic and racial identity are forced choice, with researchers determining the specific dimensions to which participants respond. Within this book, however, there are important measurement strategies that allow for children, youth, and young adults to elaborate on the idiographic meaning and significance of their ethnic and racial self-defining experiences. Closely related to the attitudinal dimensions are the social connections in which these interracial and intraracial affiliations are expressed. Alternatively, the authors of this book's chapters represent ethnic and racial identity in complex and dynamic ways, with some using narrative structures to index the meaning of ethnic and racial identifications.

Most previous studies of ethnic and racial identity have examined the *outcome* of ethnic and racial identity formation. This collection, however, provides important insights into the dynamic *process* of identity formation—

an important distinction in identity development made by psychologist Erik Erikson, who differentiated self-identity, or self-concepts, from ego identity, the process of integrating and synthesizing information and feedback relevant to the adolescent's self (Erikson, 1968).[1] By examining the process of identity formation, rather than merely what identity had been formed or achieved, the authors of this book shed important light on the developmental processes involved in identity formation.

The chapter authors also examine another important dimension in understanding ethnic and racial identity: primary and secondary cultural characteristics (Ogbu, 1989).[2] *Primary* cultural characteristics refer to the cultural traditions and practices indigenous to a cultural group and that evolved within the culture of origin, including language, spiritual practices, social norms, and other conventions characteristic of specific cultural groups. Primary cultural characteristics are most prominent in immigrant or first-generation groups, with these characteristics being more diffused across subsequent generations. Conversely, Ogbu differentiated *secondary* cultural characteristics as those practices that developed in response, or were secondary, to contact with another cultural group. In essence, ethnic or racial identity is a secondary cultural characteristic, as humans need to identify their ethnic or racial group only in the context of other groups. More generally, secondary cultural characteristics usually developed as ways to cope with pressures to assimilate or be marginalized from another, usually powerful or dominant, group. Secondary cultural characteristics are often more, not less, prominent in later generations, often as primary cultural characteristics are being lost in response to pressures to assimilate to dominant host culture.

I hope this brief listing of these very different dimensions and components of ethnic–racial identity whet the reader's appetite to read closely the wonderful array of chapters included herein. Earlier I used a metaphor to characterize the chapters as alternative perspectives of a phenomenon, as if there were a singular phenomenon underlying the different constructions of ethnic–racial identity. However, in the last chapter, Santos invokes what may be a more apt metaphor, *dialogue*, to represent the collection of readings contained in this book. Indeed, the chapters provide a rich dialogue, each with its own unique and compelling story to share. It may be overly provincial to try to integrate into a single entity all the expressions and forms that ethnic–racial identities may take. If within physics, light can be represented with a wave–particle duality, then surely ethnic–racial identity is best appreciated from a diverse array of perspectives.

---

[1]Erikson, E. H. (1968). *Identity: Youth and crisis*. New York, NY: Norton.

[2]Ogbu, J. U. (1989). The individual in collective adaptation: A framework for focusing on academic underperformance and dropping out among involuntary minorities. In L. Weis, E. Farrar, & H. G. Petrie (Eds.), *Dropouts from school: Issues, dilemmas and solutions* (pp. 181–204). Albany: State University of New York Press.

Studying
Ethnic Identity

INTRODUCTION: ETHNIC IDENTITY RESEARCH ACROSS DIVERSE PERSPECTIVES

CARLOS E. SANTOS AND ADRIANA J. UMAÑA-TAYLOR

Social scientists have long explored the meaning, process, and content of social identities (Côté, 2006; Vignoles, Schwartz, & Luyckx, 2011). Given that humans have a desire to belong, affiliate, and individuate (Fiske, 2010), even if to varying degrees and differentially across contexts, it is not surprising that identity remains one of the most extensively studied topics among social scientists. As societies and cultures have become more interconnected, in part because of increased racial and ethnic intergroup contact and migration processes, ethnic identity has surfaced as an important facet of the human experience worthy of the attention of research scientists. Indeed, over the last 3 decades, we have seen rapid growth in research on ethnic identity (Schwartz et al., 2014). But despite this growing body of research, there remain fundamental gaps in our understanding of this critical aspect of the human experience.

http://dx.doi.org/10.1037/14618-001
Studying Ethnic Identity: Methodological and Conceptual Approaches Across Disciplines, C. E. Santos and A. J. Umaña-Taylor (Editors)

Most strikingly, the field has grown fragmented, and there is a limited understanding of how ethnic identity is conceptualized or measured within and across disciplinary and methodological perspectives (Schwartz et al., 2014). The burgeoning interest in studying ethnic identity, coupled with innovative advances in research design and statistics in social science research, has resulted in rapid advances in the methods and approaches used to study ethnic identity. This volume is intended to increase the transdisciplinary discourse on ethnic identity and to expose ethnic identity researchers to diverse perspectives and innovative methods in the field. To accomplish this goal, we invited chapters from social and applied scientists in diverse fields such as educational anthropology; developmental, community, and social psychology; and sociology. As the chapters of this volume reveal, the result is a collection of articles that serve as a methodological and conceptual toolbox intended to aid those who are conducting the next generation of research focused on ethnic identity.

VOLUME ORGANIZATION

The chapters in this volume were ordered in a particular fashion. In Chapter 1, Umaña-Taylor presents a detailed account of how conceptualizations of ethnic identity have evolved over time, as well as opportunities afforded by measurement and methodological advances in research on ethnic and racial identity. She traces the progression of ethnic and racial identity theory and measurement and discusses new directions in the field. For example, she discusses how a recent collaboration among leading ethnic identity and racial identity scholars resulted in the proposal of the metaconstruct ethnic–racial identity to reflect an individual's ethnic background, as well as the racialized experiences associated with membership in a particular group (Umaña-Taylor et al., 2014). Furthermore, Umaña-Taylor reveals how the focus on measurement of ethnic and racial identity over the last few decades has been critical in framing the perspective that ethnic identity is a multidimensional construct consisting of both process and content. In a recent review of the literature on positive development of minority youth, Cabrera and colleagues (2013) stated that "new findings in the literature show that, overall, minority children show strengths in at least three domains of development: social, language, and ethnic identity" (p. 10). The burgeoning body of work linking ethnic identity to a host of adjustment indices underscores the importance of this topic to the study of socioemotional development, and Umaña-Taylor's chapter helps us to understand the progression of conceptual and methodological advances in the past several decades that have enabled these insights.

In Chapter 2, Syed underscores methodological opportunities but also discusses limitations resulting from an overreliance on a small number of rating scales designed to capture ethnic identity. Syed states that opportunities have been afforded by these measurement advances, namely, the development of a foundational body of research on ethnic identity. However, he also argues that we must move beyond rating scales to capture the complexities of ethnic identity. Syed then presents a narrative approach to the study of ethnic identity and uncovers voices and stories of individuals related to the experience of ethnicity and race. He notes that this method is particularly apt at giving voice to members of marginalized groups whose voices have not always been reflected in developmental science. Finally, his research persuasively underscores the strength of having individuals define their own contexts and the ability to note which contexts are important to them by use of a narrative approach.

In Chapter 3, Ortiz et al. present a historical account of ethnographic methods and their application to the study of ethnic identity. The authors present a critical ethnography of an intercultural bilingual education classroom that aims to promote indigenous knowledge and traditional schooling within the context of a Chilean elementary school serving rural indigenous Mapuche children. Their results reveal a complexity in youths' ethnic identity as they express pride in their Mapuche culture but also identify with elements of Eurocentric Chilean culture. Through observations and interviews with Kimche Painemilla, a teacher and community sage, the authors reveal his commitment to promoting indigenous culture, language, and knowledge despite resistance from some students and parents. Using the methodological and analytical lens of critical ethnography, Ortiz et al. reveal a transformative experience of ethnic identity within a school setting. Painemilla raised Mapuche youths' historical and political consciousness through the use of counternarratives that challenged conventional epistemologies and, as a result, empowered students and allowed them to reconstruct their ethnic identity.

In Chapter 4, Roth introduces yet another method. Using photo elicitation techniques, Roth challenges the emphasis on identity and instead emphasizes the need to consider cognitive structures or ethnic and racial schemas that individuals use in dividing themselves and others into racial and ethnic groups. To elicit these cognitive ethnic and racial schemas, Roth presents photographs of people of different ethnicities to her participants and asks them to identify and group these individuals according to ethnicities. She then delves into an in-depth discussion with the participants exploring the classifications they made, why they made them, and where they see themselves relative to the groupings they created. Her work nicely illustrates an approach that can be used to gain a more nuanced understanding of participants' ethnic identities by taking into account their understanding and interpretations of phenotype combined with sociohistorical contextual factors, particularly as they relate to race, ethnicity, and culture.

Similarly, in Chapter 5, López et al. explore the visual experience of ethnicity, but in relation to phenotype. In particular, the authors explore the association between phenotype and ethnic identity among Puerto Rican women. Using purely quantitative as well as a mixed method approach across three different studies, the authors demonstrate that one's physical appearance affects how accepted and embedded one might feel in one's ethnic group and that others' reactions to one's physical appearance can influence how one labels and sees oneself in terms of ethnicity. The authors underscore the need for triangulation in the study of physical appearance and ethnic identity, and they emphasize that researchers should rely on multiple measures in their assessment of appearance (self-report, observational, and quantifiable appearance data, e.g., by use of a spectrophotometer to measure skin pigmentation). In the qualitative component of their study, López et al. discuss that participants thought a great deal about their physical appearance in relation to their ethnic identity, further elucidating the linkages between how one looks and how one experiences one's ethnic identity.

In Chapter 6, Rogers and Way use qualitative methods but focus on the use of semistructured interviews to examine ethnic identity development among African American boys. The authors highlight, similar to Syed's narrative approach, that semistructured interviews privilege the knowledge and perspective of participants (Marecek, Fine, & Kidder, 2001). They note that this approach involves a standardized set of questions but also allows for follow-up questions and probes to capture participants' understanding of their ethnic identity. They highlight the diverse methods that exist to analyze semistructured interview data (e.g., open coding, content analysis, grounded theory, constant comparison, case studies). They then present findings from their own research on ethnic and racial identity conducted with African American adolescent boys using grounded theory/content analysis (Strauss & Corbin, 1990) and the Listening Guide method (Gilligan, Spencer, Weinberg, & Bertsch, 2003). These analytic methods were implemented via an interpretive community, a diverse group of scholars who read and coded interview excerpts. Their findings reveal how resistance and accommodation to racial stereotypes intersected with gender stereotypes in the context of a single-gender and single-race charter school and shaped these boys' experience of ethnic and racial identity.

In Chapter 7, Kornienko et al. also emphasize context, but here they emphasize the peer context of how ethnic identities develop using quantitative methods. Their approach relies on advances afforded by social network analysis (SNA) to the study of peer selection and influence. SNA is a type of systems science methodology that allows for the examination of reciprocated and nonreciprocated ties among peers in a given ecology (Urban, Osgood,

& Mabry, 2011). In their study, they focus on friendships formed within the ecology of a middle school. Their method consists of asking youth to nominate peers who are friends within their grade. Because these nominations are obtained from most students at the school, SNA allows these scholars to closely examine friendship ties, their structure, and their position (e.g., network centrality) that individuals occupy within their peer network. Unlike sociometric approaches, which rely on nominations by participants whom they perceive to possess certain qualities (e.g., popularity), SNA enables scholars to arrive at indices of network position (e.g., popularity) by using actual data on friendship ties reported by students. This approach is uniquely equipped to account for selection factors in how ties are formed among peers and consequently affords unique measurement of peer influence on ethnic identity processes over time. In this longitudinal study, the authors reveal that, over the span of 8 months, adolescents tended to become similar to their friends in terms of how central they considered their ethnic identity to their sense of self. This evidence of peer influence on changes in ethnic identity centrality was ascertained while controlling for initial selection into friendship networks on the basis of race and ethnicity (i.e., static race/ethnic attributes of one's peers), as well as similarity on ethnic identity centrality.

Similarly, in Chapter 8, Douglass and Yip highlight the role of context in shaping ethnic identity processes by using quantitative methods. The authors introduce the multilevel integration method, which consists of the integration of daily diaries, longitudinal surveys, and large-scale data (e.g., school-level data) to understand ethnic identity among youth. Their empirical illustration reveals how analytic advances in multilevel modeling afford a unique opportunity to understand ethnic identity as a dynamic aspect of the self, how it changes across days and over time, and how these processes are sensitive to stable aspects of contexts (e.g., school ethnic/racial composition) in which youth are embedded.

Thus, the volume begins with a historical account of the field of ethnic identity (Chapter 1); moves into a series of chapters that illustrate contextually rich, predominantly qualitative approaches to study and conceptualize ethnic identity using diverse methods (Chapters 2–6); and then transitions into the illustration of two cutting-edge quantitative approaches for studying ethnic identity (Chapters 7 and 8), which provide innovative examples of how quantitative methods can be used to capture contextually rich accounts of ethnic identity. The closing chapter (Chapter 9) summarizes key advances presented in each chapter and discusses future directions for research on ethnic identity. We felt that this structure would reveal the ways in which diverse methodologies can be put to use to get at contextually rich accounts of ethnic identity, rather than to rely on the juxtaposition of one method's presumed limitations as the rationale for using an alternate method.

Although the chapters in this volume do not represent an exhaustive collection of all methods used to study ethnic identity, they highlight several major innovations and underscore important directions in the area of study. These innovative methods and approaches are fundamentally changing how we measure and conceptualize ethnic identity.

INTENDED AUDIENCE

Given the interdisciplinary perspective assumed in this volume, the chapters will appeal to a diverse audience of scholars, students, and the general public. Readers in the following areas of focus may find the ideas in these pages appealing and useful: developmental psychology, especially those interested in self-concept and personal identity; social psychology, especially social identities; cultural, clinical, and counseling psychology, in particular, how social identities influence health; human development and family studies, principally including the study of adolescents' and emerging adults' socioemotional development, and the interface of context and development; sociology, especially identity research from a sociological lens; cultural anthropology, in particular, the study of immigration, acculturation, and cultural change; ethnic studies, including issues related to cultural identification; education, mainly in terms of how social identities may shape educational experiences and affect educational outcomes; and communication studies, primarily the study of language use and linguistic acculturation. This volume will be useful to instructors of courses on adolescence, emerging adulthood, broader developmental and educational psychology, counseling and therapy, sociology and psychology of race, ethnicity and race relations, among others.

We learned a great deal from planning, pursuing, and reviewing the work presented herein. It is our hope that the information in this volume will contribute to exciting opportunities for new scholars embarking on this topic as well as for seasoned scholars interested in transforming their lines of research.

REFERENCES

Cabrera, N., Beeghly, M. J., Brown, C., Casas, J., Palacios, N., Phinney, J., . . . Witherspoon, D. (2013). Positive development of minority children. *Social Policy Report*, 27(2), 3–22.

Côté, J. E. (2006). Identity studies: How close are we to developing a social science of identity? An appraisal of the field. *Identity: An International Journal of Theory and Research*, 6, 3–25. http://dx.doi.org/10.1207/s1532706xid0601_2

Fiske, S. T. (2010). *Social beings: A core motives approach to social psychology* (2nd ed.). New York, NY: Wiley.

Gilligan, C., Spencer, R., Weinberg, M. K., & Bertsch, T. (2003). On the listening guide: A voice-centered relational model. In P. M. Camic, J. E. Rhodes, & L. Yardley (Eds.), *Qualitative research in psychology: Expanding perspectives in methodology and design* (pp. 157–172). Washington, DC: American Psychological Association.

Marecek, J., Fine, M., & Kidder, L. (2001). Working between two worlds: Qualitative methods and psychology. In D. L. Tolman & M. Brydon-Miller (Eds.), *From subjects to subjectivities: A handbook of interpretive and participatory methods* (pp. 29–41). New York, NY: New York University Press.

Schwartz, S. J., Syed, M., Yip, T., Knight, G. P., Umaña-Taylor, A. J., Rivas-Drake, D., . . . Ethnic and Racial Identity in the 21st Century Study Group. (2014). Methodological issues in ethnic and racial identity research with ethnic minority populations: Theoretical precision, measurement issues, and research designs. *Child Development, 85,* 58–76. http://dx.doi.org/10.1111/cdev.12201

Strauss, A., & Corbin, J. (1990). *Basics of qualitative research: Grounded theory procedures and techniques.* Thousand Oaks, CA: Sage.

Umaña-Taylor, A. J., Quintana, S. M., Lee, R. M., Cross, W. E., Rivas-Drake, D., Schwartz, S. J., . . . Ethnic and Racial Identity in the 21st Century Study Group. (2014). Ethnic and racial identity during adolescence and into young adulthood: An integrated conceptualization. *Child Development, 85,* 21–39. http://dx.doi.org/10.1111/cdev.12196

Urban, J. B., Osgood, N. D., & Mabry, P. L. (2011). Developmental systems science: Exploring the application of systems science methods to developmental science questions. *Research in Human Development, 8,* 1–25. http://dx.doi.org/10.1080/15427609.2011.549686

Vignoles, V. L., Schwartz, S. J., & Luyckx, K. (2011). Introduction: Toward an integrative view of identity. In S. J. Schwartz, K. Luyckx, & V. L. Vignoles (Eds.), *Handbook of identity theory and research* (pp. 1–27). New York, NY: Springer. http://dx.doi.org/10.1007/978-1-4419-7988-9_1

1

ETHNIC IDENTITY RESEARCH: HOW FAR HAVE WE COME?

ADRIANA J. UMAÑA-TAYLOR

Identity formation is an important developmental task that can continuously evolve throughout the life span (Erikson, 1968). Individuals' identities are made up of multiple social identities, and in ethnically diverse societies such as the United States, ethnic identity is a salient social identity (Umaña-Taylor, 2011). Ethnic identity is recognized as a complex, multifaceted, and dynamic process (Phinney & Ong, 2007). From a social psychological and developmental perspective, ethnic identity generally refers to individuals' feelings about their ethnic group membership (e.g., positive affect, pride, attachment), as well as the extent to which individuals have engaged in a process to gain knowledge about their ethnic group (i.e., ethnic identity exploration) and have come to a resolution or sense of clarity regarding the meaning that their ethnicity has in their lives (i.e., ethnic identity resolution; Umaña-Taylor, Yazedjian, & Bámaca-Gómez, 2004). Although this definition is extensive, it is not exhaustive, and there are various additional

http://dx.doi.org/10.1037/14618-002
Studying Ethnic Identity: Methodological and Conceptual Approaches Across Disciplines, C. E. Santos and A. J. Umaña-Taylor (Editors)

dimensions or aspects of ethnic identity that have been the focus of empirical research on ethnic identity in previous work (see Rivas-Drake et al., 2014, for a review). Indeed, one of the most challenging aspects of studying ethnic identity in the past several decades has centered on gaining conceptual clarity regarding this construct.

Furthermore, because the conceptualization of a construct has a direct bearing on its operationalization, issues of measurement have introduced unique challenges for researchers attempting to synthesize the literature on ethnic identity (Schwartz et al., 2014). Indeed, the past decade has been characterized by a lively and productive debate focused on gaining greater conceptual clarity and methodological precision with respect to the construct of ethnic identity (e.g., Cokley, 2005; Helms, 2007; Ponterotto & Mallinckrodt, 2007; Schwartz et al., 2014; Trimble, 2007; Umaña-Taylor et al., 2014). In an effort to contribute to this important discourse, the purpose of this book is to highlight diverse conceptual and methodological approaches to studying ethnic identity. Together, the chapters in this book provide readers with a diverse set of methodological tools that can move the study of ethnic identity forward in important ways. In the current chapter, I review the recent conceptual and methodological advances (relative to where the field stood in the early 1990s) that have been made in the study of ethnic identity and briefly note how the current chapters offer additional approaches to consider in advancing research on ethnic identity.

CONCEPTUALIZATION AND MEASUREMENT OF ETHNIC IDENTITY—THEN AND NOW

In their review of existing theory and empirical work on identity processes among ethnic and racial minority children, Spencer and Markstrom-Adams (1990) identified several significant challenges that plagued the literature on ethnic minority youths' identity and, specifically, ethnic and racial identity at that time. They specifically noted the lack of frameworks featuring normative developmental models of ethnic and racial minority individuals' identity processes and, instead, the abundance of pathology-driven models that permeated the literature. To move this area of research forward, they called for alternative conceptual approaches that accounted for the multifaceted nature of identity formation, considered the implications of various social identities for later life outcomes, and advanced our understanding of the processes or mechanisms by which identity may evoke certain coping responses to mitigate the association between identity-related stress and later outcomes (Spencer & Markstrom-Adams, 1990).

Since their review, there have been considerable advances in ethnic identity theory and empirical research, which have answered this call by moving the field toward understanding ethnic identity from a normative developmental framework. Specifically, more elaborate theoretical models have been presented to explain the processes by which ethnic identity develops (e.g., Bernal, Knight, Garza, Ocampo, & Cota, 1990; Phinney, 1992; Quintana, 1994; Umaña-Taylor et al., 2004), which account for the multifaceted nature of ethnic identity. This has also led to more refined scales to assess the construct of ethnic identity. Furthermore, an abundance of empirical work has followed these conceptualizations and measurement advances, with some studies examining how ethnic identity changes over time (e.g., French, Seidman, Allen, & Aber, 2006; Pahl & Way, 2006; Umaña-Taylor, Gonzales-Backen, & Guimond, 2009) and others examining how ethnic identity is associated with various indices of adjustment (for reviews, see Rivas-Drake et al., 2014; Umaña-Taylor, 2011). In addition, scholars have advanced complex models describing possible mechanisms by which ethnic identity can serve as a resource that can mitigate the negative impact of ethnic and racial adversity (e.g., Neblett, Rivas-Drake, Umaña-Taylor, 2012). These advances are significant and, by providing greater conceptual clarity and methodological precision, have positioned us well to push further and identify novel ways to gain an even more nuanced understanding of the construct of ethnic identity and its implications for psychological adjustment. Accordingly, the current chapter is organized as follows: (a) An overview of the progression of the conceptualization of ethnic identity is presented, including a brief overview of the prominent theoretical models that have guided ethnic identity research; (b) the progress that has been made with respect to measurement and research design in the study of ethnic identity since the 1990s is discussed; and (c) concluding comments regarding future directions that will continue to move this important area of research forward are presented.

Conceptualization of Ethnic Identity

Early work on ethnic identity tended to equate one's ethnic group identification label (e.g., Latino, African American, Chinese) with one's ethnic identity (Umaña-Taylor, Diversi, & Fine, 2002). Not only did this approach mask the tremendous within-group variability that existed among individuals with respect to their sense of belonging to an ethnic group and the process by which they had arrived at their identity, it also failed to acknowledge the multifaceted and complex nature of this construct. In the 1980s, definitions of ethnic identity broadened in the literature, with some studies emphasizing feelings of belonging and commitment to the group, others focusing on ethnic knowledge and behaviors, and yet others still focusing simply on identification labels (see Phinney, 1990, for a review). In the early 1990s, however, a more focused shift occurred among scholars studying young children (e.g., Bernal et al., 1990; Quintana, 1994), as well as those interested in adolescents and adults (e.g., Phinney, 1990).

With a focus on young children, Bernal and colleagues (1990) presented a conceptual model of ethnic identity development, which provided an in-depth definition of ethnic identity, including self-identification choices, knowledge of one's ethnic group, positive feelings and preferences toward the behaviors and traditions of one's ethnic group, and a developmentally salient cognitive component of ethnic constancy. Their model identified multiple ecological factors that influenced young children's understanding of and attachment to their ethnic group membership (Bernal et al., 1990). Quintana (1994, 1998) also contributed significantly to the discourse on ethnic identity during this time, focusing even more specifically on children's sociocognitive abilities and further delineating the developmental progression of individuals' understanding of ethnicity from early childhood through adolescence. Many empirical studies followed, providing support for these conceptual models that acknowledged the complex and multifaceted nature of ethnic identity development during childhood (e.g., Knight, Bernal, Garza, Cota, & Ocampo, 1993; Quintana, Castañeda-English, & Ybarra, 1999; Quintana & Vera, 1999).

During this same time, Phinney (1993) advanced her theoretical model of ethnic identity development focused largely on the developmental period of adolescence and grounded in social identity theory (Tajfel & Turner, 1986) and an Eriksonian perspective (Erikson, 1968). Phinney (1990, 1993) posited that ethnic identity reflects a process that takes place over time as individuals explore and make decisions regarding the meaningfulness of their ethnicity. She presented a model that characterized individuals into one of three stages: "ethnic identity diffused/foreclosed" (aka "unexamined"), "ethnic identity search/moratorium," or "ethnic identity achievement." Classification into the stages was determined by the degree to which individuals had explored their ethnicity, resolved uncertainties about their ethnicity, and accepted and internalized their ethnicity. The stages followed closely from Marcia's (1980) operationalization of Erikson's ego identity theory, in which individuals with low exploration and low commitment were considered "diffused," those with high exploration and low commitment were considered to be in a state of moratorium, and those with high levels of both dimensions were considered to have an achieved identity.

It is important that, in addition to presenting her conceptual model, at this time Phinney also developed and published the Multigroup Ethnic Identity Measure (MEIM; Phinney, 1992). The introduction of this measure was critical to the advancement of ethnic identity research, as it provided scholars with an easy-to-self-administer measure of ethnic identity. To date, this has been the most widely used measure of ethnic identity (Phinney & Ong, 2007) and was likely one of the most substantial factors that led to the exponential growth in empirical work on ethnic identity that took place in the late 1990s and continues today. The MEIM enabled researchers to examine adolescents' and adults' *degree* of ethnic identification in a relatively standardized manner, without having to assume that a person's self-identification label (e.g., checking the box "African American") was a direct indicator of the individual's sense of belonging and attachment to a particular group. Related to conceptualization, this tool enabled the theoretical discourse on ethnic identity to expand, as scholars began to more intricately examine and evaluate the meaning of a *strong* versus *weak* ethnic identity and the implications it had for individuals' psychological adjustment (e.g., Juang, Nguyen, & Lin, 2006; Romero & Roberts, 2003). Furthermore, scholars began to more closely examine the structure of ethnic identity and how the different components informed the broader construct (e.g., Roberts et al., 1999). These developments were critical to advancing ethnic identity theory.

In 2004, Umaña-Taylor and colleagues suggested a revision to ethnic identity theory and, perhaps more accurately, to the common operationalization of ethnic identity that pervaded the empirical literature at that time. Umaña-Taylor and colleagues (2004) argued that the existing empirical literature relied largely on a composite score across the subscales in Phinney's MEIM, which obscured important distinctions between the various components that composed individuals' ethnic identities, and resulted in scholars not attending to the theoretical distinctions that guided ethnic identity research (i.e., developmental components of ethnic identity exploration and resolution/commitment, affective component of ethnic identity affirmation). Umaña-Taylor and colleagues noted that the MEIM conflated ethnic identity affirmation (i.e., positive feelings about one's ethnic group membership) with one's sense of commitment (i.e., resolution and sense of clarity regarding the meaning of one's ethnicity) in the affirmation and belonging subscale, which included items capturing both affirmation and resolution/commitment. In an effort to resolve this, the Ethnic Identity Scale (EIS) was developed (Umaña-Taylor et al., 2004), which enabled ethnic identity theory to be more accurately reflected in the measurement of ethnic identity via the examination of affirmation and resolution/commitment as distinct components of this process.

The notion that individual components of ethnic identity should be examined as unique contributors to adjustment expanded scholars' understanding of the implications of specific ethnic identity components for individuals' adjustment, because scholars increasingly started separating the dimensions of ethnic identity and finding that, indeed, individual components of ethnic identity differentially predicted outcomes (e.g., French et al., 2006; Gaylord-Harden, Ragsdale, Mandara, Richards, & Petersen, 2007; Supple, Ghazarian, Frabutt, Plunkett, & Sands, 2006; Umaña-Taylor & Updegraff, 2007). In addition, scholars started to examine how individual components of ethnic identity developed over time (e.g., French et al., 2006; Pahl & Way, 2006; Umaña-Taylor et al., 2009) and the factors that predicted changes in specific aspects of ethnic identity (e.g., Umaña-Taylor & Guimond, 2010), thereby explicitly acknowledging the developmental foundation on which theory rested. In addition, the introduction of new measures and more refined measurement of the individual ethnic identity components also enabled scholars to examine the potential multidimensional nature of individual components of ethnic identity. As an example, Syed and colleagues (2013) conducted detailed analyses using both the MEIM and the EIS and discovered that each scale was assessing a distinct aspect of ethnic identity exploration (i.e., *search* vs. *participation*). After a careful examination of the exploration items in the MEIM and EIS, Syed et al. (2013) proposed theoretically supported explanations that advanced our understanding of why the different aspects of ethnic identity exploration, during particular developmental periods, could be adaptive versus maladaptive.

Together, these examples demonstrate how methodological advances have been critical in shaping the field's conceptual understanding of ethnic identity; namely, how and why specific ethnic identity components may change over time, the intricate nature of individual ethnic identity components, and why they may be linked to outcomes in a certain manner. These conceptual advances also significantly contributed to an expansion of ethnic identity theory as scholars started to consider how the individual ethnic identity components mapped onto individual components of a closely related construct: racial identity.

Over the years, many scholars have noted the conceptual overlap that ethnic identity has with racial identity (e.g., Casey-Cannon, Coleman, Knudtson, & Velazquez, 2011; Cokley, 2005; French, Coleman, & DiLorenzo, 2013) and have voiced frustration about the misuse of these terms in the literature (e.g., Helms, 1990). As scholars increasingly unpacked the components of ethnic identity in their theoretical and empirical work, however, it became easier to draw parallels between the constructs of ethnic identity and racial identity and to more comprehensively consider the ways in which individuals' identities are informed by both racialized experiences in a particular sociohistorical context and their socialization experiences grounded in a specific cultural or ethnic heritage (see Cross & Cross, 2008, for a discussion of the parallels). Interestingly, as explained next, the introduction of a new measure of racial identity (and its relevance to ethnic identity theory and research) also made it possible to understand the parallels between ethnic and racial identity.

While research on ethnic identity was rapidly increasing in the 1990s, Sellers and colleagues were also advancing the multidimensional model of racial identity (MMRI), which focused specifically on African Americans' racial identity (Sellers, Smith, Shelton, Rowley, & Chavous, 1998). Similar to the progression that took place with the advancement of ethnic identity theory and the introduction of Phinney's MEIM, Sellers and colleagues developed the Multidimensional Inventory of Black Identity (MIBI; Sellers, Rowley, Chavous, Shelton, & Smith, 1997), which was designed to assess three of the four dimensions of racial identity outlined in the MMRI: centrality, regard (private and public), and ideology. Sellers and colleagues' conceptualization and measurement drew on prior racial identity theory, such as Cross's model of nigrescence (Cross, 1971, 1991), but also on social psychological perspectives focused on social group identity (e.g., Luhtanen & Crocker, 1992). Sellers et al. (1998) noted that there are universal properties associated with ethnic and racial identities and that there are also unique cultural and historical experiences associated with being African American; the MMRI was developed to represent a synthesis of these two perspectives (Sellers et al., 1998), and the MIBI was presented as a method to measure key dimensions of the model (Sellers et al., 1997). The integration of ethnic identity theory (e.g., Phinney, 1992) and social group perspectives (e.g., Luhtanen & Crocker, 1992) into the conceptualization of the MMRI and the subsequent development of the MIBI likely facilitated scholars' adaptation of the MIBI for use with other ethnic groups (e.g., Latinos, Asian Americans), and not just with African Americans. Indeed, numerous scholars adapted items from the MIBI to be relevant to other ethnic groups (e.g., Rivas-Drake, Hughes, & Way, 2009; Yip, 2005), and the MIBI is the second most commonly used measure to assess ethnic and racial identity (Schwartz et al., 2014). The use of the MIBI to study ethnic identity (e.g., Rivas-Drake et al., 2009) and the use of the MEIM to study racial identity (e.g., Mandara, Gaylord-Harden, Richards, & Ragsdale, 2009; Murray, Neal-Barnett, Demmings, & Stadulis, 2012) clouded the distinctions between the constructs of ethnic and racial identity but also helped to pave the way for future developments (discussed next) in which scholars would devote significant time to synthesizing empirical and theoretical work on these constructs and proposing a construct that could capture individuals' identity in a meaningful way.

In early 2012, a study group (i.e., Ethnic and Racial Identity in the 21st Century Study Group) was convened to bring scholars together to discuss the theoretical complexities of these two constructs, synthesize the existing theoretical and empirical work, and offer specific recommendations for how the field could move forward with respect to achieving greater clarity regarding the distinctions and similarities among these constructs. After extensive deliberation, members of the study group proposed that scholars consider using the metaconstruct ethnic-racial identity (ERI) when referring to ethnic or racial identity with the intention of capturing the components of individuals' identities that are informed by both their ethnic/cultural heritage and their racialized experiences in a specific sociohistorical context (see Umaña-Taylor et al., 2014). Umaña-Taylor and colleagues (2014) also provided a much-needed synthesis of how components from prominent racial identity theories (e.g., Cross, 1971; Sellers et al., 1998) mapped onto components of ethnic identity theory, how they complemented one another, and how considering them in tandem helped to provide a more nuanced understanding of ERI development throughout the life span. Indeed, several chapters in the current book (e.g., Kornienko et al., Chapter 7; Rogers & Way, Chapter 6; Roth, Chapter 4; López et al., Chapter 5) exemplify this approach, such that the discussion and assessment of ethnic identity in these chapters consider both ethnic (e.g., cultural traditions) and racial (e.g., phenotype) experiences in a specific social context, and how the interface of these aspects of identity inform human development and adjustment.

In sum, since the early 1990s, theoretical and empirical work on ethnic identity has mushroomed, and the plethora of studies and conceptual pieces published during this period have significantly advanced the conceptualization of the construct and provided a greater understanding of ethnic identity as a normative developmental process that can serve as an important resource for ethnic and racial minority youth. The section that follows provides a historical overview of how ethnic identity has been assessed and current trends and advances in measurement and research design in studies of ethnic identity. Similar to the previous discussion regarding the impact that the introduction of the MEIM, the EIS, and the MIBI had on advancing the conceptualization of ethnic identity, the discussion that follows highlights instances in which methodological advances and new trends in research design have further advanced ethnic identity theory and research.

Measurement of Ethnic Identity and Recent Methodological Advances

As previously mentioned, early work on ethnic identity relied largely on identification labels to assess one's ethnic identity, assuming that an individual's ethnic group membership defined his or her ethnic identity (Umaña-Taylor et al., 2002). As noted by Helms (2007), the development of scales to assess ethnic and racial identity emerged from the need to move away from using one-item measures (i.e., racial categories) and toward instruments that would capture individual differences in these important constructs. With the introduction of assessment tools that enabled an examination of a continuum of attachment and sense of belonging to a particular group membership (e.g., the MEIM; Phinney, 1992), the field increasingly moved toward considering ethnic identity on a continuum, rather than as a categorical dimension. This resulted in significant gains in ethnic identity theory because of the rapid increase in empirical work examining ethnic identity and scholars' greater attention to gaining greater conceptual clarity about the associations that were emerging in new empirical studies.

Although the MEIM provided a relatively more fine-grained approach to assessment than the use of identification labels, scholars typically used composite scores of the pooled subscales within the MEIM, and the multifaceted nature of ethnic identity was rarely acknowledged initially (Schwartz et al., 2014; Umaña-Taylor et al., 2004). This obscured important associations, as recent research has demonstrated that the components of ethnic identity are differentially associated with predictors and outcomes (e.g., Pahl & Way, 2006; Supple et al., 2006). In the past decade, however, the field experienced a marked shift such that the specific dimensions of ethnic identity are increasingly examined as unique components, which enables greater conceptual clarity of ethnic identity as a multidimensional continuum and a more refined understanding of the associations between ethnic identity and extant constructs.

The increased discourse on specificity and attention to the multifaceted nature of ethnic identity in the past decade also has resulted in greater attention to the distinction between the *content* of ethnic identity versus the *process* of ethnic identity (e.g., Helms, 2007; Schwartz et al., 2014; Syed & Azmitia, 2008; Yip, 2014). Ethnic identity content captures factors such as the behaviors individuals may practice, or individuals' affect toward the group, whereas ethnic identity process refers to the mechanisms involved in learning about one's identity and forming and maintaining the identity (Umaña-Taylor et al., 2014). Scholars have suggested that because ethnic identity theory is guided largely by developmental models, ethnic identity measures tend to focus more heavily on process than content, and that an important area for future research will be to design studies in a manner that enables an examination of the interplay of process and content (e.g., Schwartz et al., 2014). Indeed, several chapters in this book illustrate methodological approaches that capture this more discrete operationalization. In his chapter, Syed describes how a qualitative design (i.e., a narrative approach) can achieve this goal. Interestingly, Douglass and Yip's chapter, which describes findings from a study relying on multiple quantitative methods, also provides a compelling approach to addressing this important research question. For example, by combining data from annual youth surveys, daily diary data, and quantitative school-level data, they were able to examine how ethnic identity processes at the individual level (one's level of exploration and commitment) interacted with contextual factors (school-level characteristics) to predict adolescents' daily ethnic identity salience (i.e., content). These examples nicely demonstrate that both qualitative and quantitative approaches can be used to address this important future area of research.

Turning to a discussion of quantitative versus qualitative approaches to studying ethnic identity, a majority of research on ethnic identity has been conducted using quantitative survey research methods (Schwartz et al., 2014). As noted by Syed (Chapter 2, this volume), and discussed previously, this work has led to important findings that have advanced the field; however, survey research methods in isolation will not be sufficient to address the more complicated questions that have yet to be answered with respect to intricacies that drive ethnic identity development. As discussed next, several chapters in this book highlight the value of qualitative approaches for moving forward research and theory on ethnic identity.

First, Syed's chapter provides an excellent overview of how a narrative approach can provide a more nuanced understanding of how ethnic identity develops, the role of context in ethnic identity development, and the multidimensional nature of ethnic identity. Focusing more specifically on the intersection of social identities, Rogers and Way's chapter provides an excellent illustration of how in-depth qualitative approaches via semistructured interviews can advance ethnic identity theory by more thoroughly addressing how social identities (e.g., ethnicity and gender) can interact to inform identity development. Similarly, in their chapter, López and colleagues present findings from a mixed method study focused on phenotype and ethnic identity in which they examine findings from their quantitative data in tandem with findings from in-depth interviews and note the discrepancies that emerge when considering the findings across the different methods; indeed, the discrepancies they identify illustrate the value added by using both qualitative and quantitative approaches in a single project. Roth's chapter also nicely illustrates how the flexibility of her qualitative method (photo elicitation combined with open-ended categorization and in-depth discussion) resulted in findings that highlighted the complexity of the intersection of race and ethnicity among Puerto Ricans and Dominicans (both in Puerto Rico/ Dominican Republic and in the mainland United States), though this was not an intention of her research at the onset of her study. Finally, Ortiz and colleagues underscore the importance of considering a more macro perspective in understanding the development and meaning of an ethnic identity. Their ethnographic study uniquely situates the construct of ethnic identity in a rural indigenous Chilean community. Together, these chapters illustrate the complexities of studying and understanding ethnic identity around the globe and also demonstrate how qualitative approaches are uniquely poised to uncover important intricacies in the process of ethnic identity development.

An additional major methodological shift in ethnic identity research in the past decade has been the noticeable increase in the number of longitudinal studies focused on ethnic identity. These studies have significantly increased our understanding of how specific components of ethnic identity change throughout adolescence (e.g., French et al., 2006; Huang & Stormshak, 2011; Kiang, Witkow, Baldelomar, & Fuligni, 2010; Pahl & Way, 2006; Umaña-Taylor et al., 2009; Yip, 2014) and into young adulthood (e.g., Syed, Azmitia, & Phinney, 2007; Umaña-Taylor, Zeiders, & Updegraff, 2013). Moreover, advances in statistical modeling techniques (e.g., latent growth curve modeling, latent transition analysis) have enabled researchers to analyze their longitudinal data in innovative ways that help answer important questions about patterns of change in ethnic identity over time, as well as common trajectories of change in ethnic identity over time (Schwartz et al., 2014). It is important that, as exemplified by the findings presented in the chapter by Douglass and Yip, there is much to be gained from detailed measures of multiple components of ethnic identity (e.g., exploration, commitment, salience) and continuous assessments of these constructs over short (i.e., daily diary) and long (i.e., annual surveys) periods of time. Their findings considerably advance the field's understanding of the nuances of ethnic identity development by demonstrating one way in which ethnic identity processes can interact with features of the social context to inform the content of individuals' ethnic identity. Although these designs are time- and cost-intensive, the benefits (in terms of the knowledge to be gained) of embarking on in-depth longitudinal studies are far reaching.

CONCLUSION AND DIRECTIONS FOR FUTURE RESEARCH

Although there have been numerous conceptual and methodological contributions to the field's understanding of ethnic identity in the past several decades, the latest research on ethnic identity, as exemplified by the chapters in the current book, presents another burst of growth in both conceptual and methodological advances. The collection of chapters in this book, and in particular the diverse methodologies they represent, demonstrates that advances in ethnic identity theory and research will only be achieved with methods that enable a relatively more nuanced examination of the construct. In some cases, the nuance can only be captured with in-depth qualitative approaches; in other cases, the nuance can be captured with detailed data on the social network characteristics of individuals' proximal surroundings, as illustrated in Kornienko and colleagues' chapter. The chapters in this book provide numerous and varied examples of the diverse methodologies and conceptualizations that can be implemented to propel this important area of research forward.

Finally, in addition to the methodological advances they represent, a strikingly common theme that emerged throughout all chapters in this book was the notion that ethnic identity cannot be fully understood without attention to context; indeed, specific empirical illustrations of this notion are provided with respect to the school (e.g., Douglass & Yip, Chapter 8; Kornienko et al., Chapter 7) and broader sociohistorical community context (e.g., Ortiz et al., Chapter 3; Roth, Chapter 4). Thus, to move ethnic identity theory and research forward, not only must scholars continue to pursue innovative and flexible methodological approaches, they must also ensure that such approaches are capable of capturing how context can introduce variability into the process and content of ethnic identity. The chapters in the current book provide examples of novel approaches that are currently moving this area of research forward and, ideally, will serve as a useful blueprint for scholars interested in taking a new approach to the study of ethnic identity.

REFERENCES

Bernal, M. E., Knight, G. P., Garza, C. A., Ocampo, K. A., & Cota, M. K. (1990). The development of ethnic identity in Mexican American children. *Hispanic Journal of Behavioral Sciences, 12*, 3–24. http://dx.doi.org/10.1177/07399863900121001

Casey-Cannon, S. L., Coleman, H. L. K., Knudtson, L. F., & Velazquez, C. C. (2011). Three racial and ethnic identity measures: Concurrent and divergent validity for diverse adolescents. *Identity: An International Journal of Theory and Research, 11*, 64–91. http://dx.doi.org/10.1080/15283488.2011.540739

Cokley, K. O. (2005). Racial(ized) identity, ethnic identity, and Afrocentric values: Conceptual and methodological challenges in understanding African American identity. *Journal of Counseling Psychology, 52*, 517–526. http://dx.doi.org/10.1037/0022-0167.52.4.517

Cross, W. E., Jr. (1971). The Negro-to-Black conversion experience: Toward a psychology of Black liberation. *Black World, 20*(9), 13–27.

Cross, W. E., Jr. (1991). *Shades of Black: Diversity in African-American identity*. Philadelphia, PA: Temple University Press.

Cross, W. E., & Cross, T. B. (2008). Theory, research, and models. In S. M. Quintana & C. McKown (Eds.), *Handbook of race, racism, and the developing child* (pp. 154–181). Hoboken, NJ: Wiley.

Erikson, E. H. (1968). *Identity: Youth and crisis*. New York, NY: Norton.

French, S. E., Coleman, B. R., & DiLorenzo, M. L. (2013). Linking racial identity, ethnic identity, and racial-ethnic socialization: A tale of three race-ethnicities. *Identity: An International Journal of Theory and Research, 13*, 1–45. http://dx.doi.org/10.1080/15283488.2012.747438

French, S. E., Seidman, E., Allen, L., & Aber, J. L. (2006). The development of ethnic identity during adolescence. *Developmental Psychology, 42*, 1–10. http://dx.doi.org/10.1037/0012-1649.42.1.1

Gaylord-Harden, N. K., Ragsdale, B. L., Mandara, J., Richards, M. H., & Petersen, A. C. (2007). Perceived support and internalizing symptoms in African American adolescents: Self-esteem and ethnic identity as mediators. *Journal of Youth and Adolescence, 36*, 77–88. http://dx.doi.org/10.1007/s10964-006-9115-9

Helms, J. E. (1990). *Black and White racial identity: Theory, research, and practice.* Westport, CT: Greenwood Press.

Helms, J. E. (2007). Some better practices for measuring racial and ethnic identity constructs. *Journal of Counseling Psychology, 54*, 235–246. http://dx.doi.org/10.1037/0022-0167.54.3.235

Huang, C. Y., & Stormshak, E. A. (2011). A longitudinal examination of early adolescence ethnic identity trajectories. *Cultural Diversity and Ethnic Minority Psychology, 17*, 261–270. http://dx.doi.org/10.1037/a0023882

Juang, L. P., Nguyen, H. H., & Lin, Y. (2006). The ethnic identity, other-group attitudes, and psychosocial functioning of Asian American emerging adults from two contexts. *Journal of Adolescent Research, 21*, 542–568. http://dx.doi.org/10.1177/0743558406291691

Kiang, L., Witkow, M. R., Baldelomar, O. A., & Fuligni, A. J. (2010). Change in ethnic identity across the high school years among adolescents with Latin American, Asian, and European backgrounds. *Journal of Youth and Adolescence, 39*, 683–693. http://dx.doi.org/10.1007/s10964-009-9429-5

Knight, G. P., Bernal, M. E., Garza, C. A., Cota, M. K., & Ocampo, K. A. (1993). Family socialization and the ethnic identity of Mexican-American children. *Journal of Cross-Cultural Psychology, 24*, 99–114. http://dx.doi.org/10.1177/0022022193241007

Luhtanen, R., & Crocker, J. (1992). A collective self-esteem scale: Self-evaluation of one's social identity. *Personality and Social Psychology Bulletin, 18*, 302–318. http://dx.doi.org/10.1177/0146167292183006

Mandara, J., Gaylord-Harden, N. K., Richards, M. H., & Ragsdale, B. L. (2009). The effects of changes in racial identity and self-esteem on changes in African American adolescents' mental health. *Child Development, 80*, 1660–1675. http://dx.doi.org/10.1111/j.1467-8624.2009.01360.x

Marcia, J. E. (1980). Identity in adolescence. In J. Adelson (Ed.), *Handbook of adolescent psychology* (pp. 159–187). New York, NY: Wiley.

Murray, M. S., Neal-Barnett, A., Demmings, J. L., & Stadulis, R. E. (2012). The acting White accusation, racial identity, and anxiety in African American adolescents. *Journal of Anxiety Disorders, 26*, 526–531. http://dx.doi.org/10.1016/j.janxdis.2012.02.006

Neblett, E. W., Jr., Rivas-Drake, D., & Umaña-Taylor, A. J. (2012). The promise of racial and ethnic protective factors in promoting ethnic minority youth development. *Child Development Perspectives, 6,* 295–303. http://dx.doi.org/10.1111/j.1750-8606.2012.00239.x

Pahl, K., & Way, N. (2006). Longitudinal trajectories of ethnic identity among urban Black and Latino adolescents. *Child Development, 77,* 1403–1415. http://dx.doi.org/10.1111/j.1467-8624.2006.00943.x

Phinney, J. S. (1990). Ethnic identity in adolescents and adults: Review of research. *Psychological Bulletin, 108,* 499–514. http://dx.doi.org/10.1037/0033-2909.108.3.499

Phinney, J. S. (1992). The Multigroup Ethnic Identity Measure: A new scale for use with diverse groups. *Journal of Adolescent Research, 7,* 156–176. http://dx.doi.org/10.1177/074355489272003

Phinney, J. S. (1993). A three-stage model of ethnic identity development in adolescence. In M. E. P. Bernal & G. P. Knight (Eds.), *Ethnic identity: Formation and transmission among Hispanics and other minorities* (pp. 61–79). New York, NY: State University of New York Press.

Phinney, J. S., & Ong, A. D. (2007). Conceptualization and measurement of ethnic identity: Current status and future directions. *Journal of Counseling Psychology, 54,* 271–281. http://dx.doi.org/10.1037/0022-0167.54.3.271

Ponterotto, J. G., & Mallinckrodt, B. (2007). Introduction to the special section on racial and ethnic identity in counseling psychology: Conceptual and methodological challenges and proposed solutions. *Journal of Counseling Psychology, 54,* 219–223. http://dx.doi.org/10.1037/0022-0167.54.3.219

Quintana, S. M. (1994). A model of ethnic perspective-taking ability applied to Mexican-American children and youth. *International Journal of Intercultural Relations, 18,* 419–448. http://dx.doi.org/10.1016/0147-1767(94)90016-7

Quintana, S. M. (1998). Children's developmental understanding of ethnicity and race. *Applied and Preventive Psychology, 7,* 27–45. http://dx.doi.org/10.1016/S0962-1849(98)80020-6

Quintana, S. M., Castañeda-English, P., & Ybarra, V. C. (1999). Role of perspective-taking abilities and ethnic socialization in development of adolescent ethnic identity. *Journal of Research on Adolescence, 9,* 161–184. http://dx.doi.org/10.1207/s15327795jra0902_3

Quintana, S. M., & Vera, E. (1999). Mexican-American children's representations of ethnic prejudice. *Hispanic Journal of Behavioral Sciences, 21,* 387–404. http://dx.doi.org/10.1177/0739986399214001

Rivas-Drake, D., Hughes, D., & Way, N. (2009). A preliminary analysis of associations among ethnic-racial socialization, ethnic discrimination, and ethnic identity among urban sixth graders. *Journal of Research on Adolescence, 19,* 558–584. http://dx.doi.org/10.1111/j.1532-7795.2009.00607.x

Rivas-Drake, D., Seaton, E. K., Markstrom, C., Quintana, S., Syed, M., Lee, R. M., . . . Ethnic and Racial Identity in the 21st Century Study Group. (2014). Ethnic and racial identity in adolescence: Implications for psychosocial, academic, and health outcomes. *Child Development, 85,* 40–57. http://dx.doi.org/10.1111/cdev.12200

Roberts, R. E., Phinney, J. S., Masse, L. C., Chen, Y. R., Roberts, C. R., & Romero, A. (1999). The structure of ethnic identity of young adolescents from diverse ethnocultural groups. *The Journal of Early Adolescence, 19*, 301–322. http://dx.doi.org/10.1177/0272431699019003001

Romero, A. J., & Roberts, R. E. (2003). The impact of multiple dimensions of ethnic identity on discrimination and adolescents' self-esteem. *Journal of Applied Social Psychology, 33*, 2288–2305. http://dx.doi.org/10.1111/j.1559-1816.2003.tb01885.x

Schwartz, S. J., Syed, M., Yip, T., Knight, G. P., Umaña-Taylor, A. J., Rivas-Drake, D., . . . Ethnic and Racial Identity in the 21st Century Study Group. (2014). Methodological issues in ethnic and racial identity research with ethnic minority populations: Theoretical precision, measurement issues, and research designs. *Child Development, 85*, 58–76. http://dx.doi.org/10.1111/cdev.12201

Sellers, R. M., Rowley, S. A., Chavous, T. M., Shelton, J. N., & Smith, M. (1997). Multidimensional Inventory of Black Identity: Preliminary investigation of reliability and construct validity. *Journal of Personality and Social Psychology, 73*, 805–815. http://dx.doi.org/10.1037/0022-3514.73.4.805

Sellers, R. M., Smith, M. A., Shelton, J. N., Rowley, S. A. J., & Chavous, T. M. (1998). Multidimensional model of racial identity: A reconceptualization of African American racial identity. *Personality and Social Psychology Review, 2*, 18–39. http://dx.doi.org/10.1207/s15327957pspr0201_2

Spencer, M. B., & Markstrom-Adams, C. (1990). Identity processes among racial and ethnic minority children in America. *Child Development, 61*, 290–310. http://dx.doi.org/10.2307/1131095

Supple, A. J., Ghazarian, S. R., Frabutt, J. M., Plunkett, S. W., & Sands, T. (2006). Contextual influences on Latino adolescent ethnic identity and academic outcomes. *Child Development, 77*, 1427–1433. http://dx.doi.org/10.1111/j.1467-8624.2006.00945.x

Syed, M., & Azmitia, M. (2008). A narrative approach to ethnic identity in emerging adulthood: Bringing life to the identity status model. *Developmental Psychology, 44*, 1012–1027. http://dx.doi.org/10.1037/0012-1649.44.4.1012

Syed, M., Azmitia, M., & Phinney, J. S. (2007). Stability and change in ethnic identity among Latino emerging adults in two contexts. *Identity: An International Journal of Theory and Research, 7*, 155–178. http://dx.doi.org/10.1080/15283480701326117

Syed, M., Walker, L. H., Lee, R. M., Umaña-Taylor, A. J., Zamboanga, B. L., Schwartz, S. J., . . . Huynh, Q. L. (2013). A two-factor model of ethnic identity exploration: Implications for identity coherence and well-being. *Cultural Diversity and Ethnic Minority Psychology, 19*, 143–154. http://dx.doi.org/10.1037/a0030564

Tajfel, H., & Turner, J. (1986). The social identity theory of intergroup behavior. In W. Austin & S. Worchel (Eds.), *Psychology of intergroup relations* (2nd ed., pp. 7–24). Chicago, IL: Nelson-Hall.

Trimble, J. E. (2007). Prolegomena for the connotation of construct use in the measurement of ethnic and racial identity. *Journal of Counseling Psychology, 54,* 247–258. http://dx.doi.org/10.1037/0022-0167.54.3.247

Umaña-Taylor, A. J. (2011). Ethnic identity. In S. J. Schwartz, K. Luyckx, & V. L. Vignoles (Eds.), *Handbook of identity theory and research* (pp. 791–809). New York, NY: Springer. http://dx.doi.org/10.1007/978-1-4419-7988-9_33

Umaña-Taylor, A. J., Diversi, M., & Fine, M. A. (2002). Ethnic identity and self-esteem among Latino adolescents: Making distinctions among the Latino populations. *Journal of Adolescent Research, 17,* 303–327. http://dx.doi.org/10.1177/0743558402173005

Umaña-Taylor, A. J., Gonzales-Backen, M. A., & Guimond, A. B. (2009). Latino adolescents' ethnic identity: Is there a developmental progression and does growth in ethnic identity predict growth in self-esteem? *Child Development, 80,* 391–405. http://dx.doi.org/10.1111/j.1467-8624.2009.01267.x

Umaña-Taylor, A. J., & Guimond, A. B. (2010). A longitudinal examination of parenting behaviors and perceived discrimination predicting Latino adolescents' ethnic identity. *Developmental Psychology, 46,* 636–650. http://dx.doi.org/10.1037/a0019376

Umaña-Taylor, A. J., Quintana, S. M., Lee, R. M., Cross, W. E., Rivas-Drake, D., Schwartz, S. J., . . . Ethnic and Racial Identity in the 21st Century Study Group. (2014). Ethnic and racial identity during adolescence and into young adulthood: An integrated conceptualization. *Child Development, 85,* 21–39. http://dx.doi.org/10.1111/cdev.12196

Umaña-Taylor, A. J., & Updegraff, K. (2007). Latino adolescents' mental health: Exploring the interrelations among discrimination, ethnic identity, cultural orientation, self-esteem, and depressive symptoms. *Journal of Adolescence, 30,* 549–567. http://dx.doi.org/10.1016/j.adolescence.2006.08.002

Umaña-Taylor, A. J., Yazedjian, A., & Bámaca-Gómez, M. Y. (2004). Developing the Ethnic Identity Scale using Eriksonian and social identity perspectives. *Identity: An International Journal of Theory and Research, 4,* 9–38. http://dx.doi.org/10.1207/S1532706XID0401_2

Umaña-Taylor, A. J., Zeiders, K. H., & Updegraff, K. A. (2013). Family ethnic socialization and ethnic identity: A family-driven, youth-driven, or reciprocal process? *Journal of Family Psychology, 27,* 137–146. http://dx.doi.org/10.1037/a0031105

Yip, T. (2005). Sources of situational variation in ethnic identity and psychological well-being: A Palm Pilot study of Chinese American students. *Personality and Social Psychology Bulletin, 31,* 1603–1616. http://dx.doi.org/10.1177/0146167205277094

Yip, T. (2014). Ethnic identity in everyday life: The influence of identity development status. *Child Development, 85,* 205–219. http://dx.doi.org/10.1111/cdev.12107

2

THEORETICAL AND METHODOLOGICAL CONTRIBUTIONS OF NARRATIVE PSYCHOLOGY TO ETHNIC IDENTITY RESEARCH

MOIN SYED

Two decades of research on ethnic identity development has yielded some important findings (Quintana, 2007; Rivas-Drake, Seaton, et al., 2014). Recent meta-analyses have indicated that ethnic identity is consistently, although modestly, associated with positive well-being, psychological distress, and academic attitudes (Rivas-Drake, Syed, et al., 2014; Smith & Silva, 2011). Other research has suggested that ethnic identity contributes to the ability to cope with the harmful effects of discrimination (Yip, Gee, & Takeuchi, 2008; but see Yoo & Lee, 2008). In addition to gaining knowledge of the correlates of ethnic identity, we now also have a clearer picture of the longitudinal course of ethnic identity from early adolescence into emerging adulthood. Taken together, these studies suggest that ethnic identity waxes and wanes across school transitions but generally increases over time (French, Seidman, Allen, & Aber, 2006; Pahl & Way, 2006; Syed & Azmitia, 2009). Thus, it is safe to say that we have learned many things about ethnic identity development.

http://dx.doi.org/10.1037/14618-003
Studying Ethnic Identity: Methodological and Conceptual Approaches Across Disciplines, C. E. Santos and A. J. Umaña-Taylor (Editors)

But there are many things we do not know. For example, we know that change in ethnic identity occurs throughout adolescence and emerging adulthood, but we know little to nothing about why or how that change comes about.

In general, there has been a dearth of analyses focusing on the lived experiences that constitute one's ethnic identity and contribute to its development. The primary reason for this is that research on ethnic identity development has relied heavily on quantitative, rating-scale instruments (Phinney, 1992; Sellers, Smith, Shelton, Rowley, & Chavous, 1998). These instruments are exceptionally valuable—indeed, they have led to all of the discoveries that I listed at the outset. However, our ability to answer complex questions about the process, content, and structure of ethnic identity development has been constrained by a narrow methodological repertoire (Schwartz et al., 2014).

The purpose of this chapter is to showcase how narrative, or the stories that people tell about their experiences, is a useful theoretical and methodological tool for understanding ethnic identity development. To do so, I synthesize a series of published and ongoing studies on ethnic identity using narrative and survey approaches to demonstrate that the use of an alternative method has opened the door for deeper theorizing on the nature and consequences of ethnic identity development.

CONCEPTUALIZATION OF ETHNIC IDENTITY

There are three primary conceptions of ethnic or racial identity represented in the psychological literature, each associated with a different psychological tradition: Phinney's (1990) developmental model, Sellers and colleagues' (1998) multidimensional model of racial identity (MMRI; social psychology), and Cross's (1971) nigrescence theory (personality psychology). The work described in this chapter is situated within Phinney's developmental model of ethnic identity. This is the case for a very simple reason: I am a developmental psychologist, and Phinney's model is the only one that I consider developmental. The MMRI is a social psychological model and as such does not include any theoretical propositions pertaining to change in its core dimensions (Syed, 2013). Although there are longitudinal studies using dimensions of the MMRI (e.g., Hughes, Way, & Rivas-Drake, 2011), a longitudinal design is not a sufficient condition for a developmental perspective (Wohlwill, 1973). Nigrescence theory includes articulated mechanisms of change, but the proposed stage theory is idiosyncratic rather than age graded. Additionally, there are no longitudinal studies demonstrating hypothesized movement through the stages. Finally, in the revised version of nigrescence theory, Cross and colleagues have moved away from the stage aspect of the theory and recast the stages as "attitudes" that can be arranged in different configurations at any given time (Cross & Cross, 2008).

As a developmental theory, Phinney's has roots in Erikson's (1950) life span psychosocial theory of development and, more directly, in Marcia's (1966; Kroger & Marcia, 2011) identity status model. Fundamentally, ethnic identity is viewed as an evolving developmental process that involves the coordination of cognitive, affective, and behavioral dimensions of identification with an ethnic group: the *cognitive* dimension refers to the clarity and resolution of the meaning of ethnicity, the *affective* dimension is the emotional significance and pride associated with ethnicity, and the *behavioral* dimension is the degree to which individuals engage in a process of exploring and learning about their ethnicity. These three dimensions underlie the current measurement of ethnic identity from a developmental perspective, although not always in the same way. Some measures combine the affective and cognitive components into a single *commitment* dimension, complemented by an *exploration* dimension to capture the behavioral component (Phinney & Ong, 2007; Roberts et al., 1999). Other measures retain the three dimensions as separate (Juang & Nguyen, 2010; Lee & Yoo, 2004; Umaña-Taylor, Yazedjian, & Bámaca-Gómez, 2004). Regardless of the way in which it is measured, under the developmental model, ethnic identity is presumed to have roots in childhood but emerges as a salient developmental task in early adolescence that continues into emerging adulthood and beyond (Umaña-Taylor et al., 2014). Through a period of exploration, youth come to a sense of resolution about the role of ethnicity for their identities, whether it is positive or negative.

My own working conception of ethnic identity is heavily rooted in Phinney's model but is more Eriksonian in nature. That is, many neo-Eriksonian researchers, Phinney included, take Marcia's identity status model as their starting point (see Schwartz, 2001). The identity status model relies on the processes of exploration and commitment to assign individuals to one of four identity statuses: *achieved* (high past exploration, high commitment), *foreclosed* (low past exploration, high commitment), *moratorium* (high current exploration, low commitment), or *diffused* (low exploration, low commitment). Within this model, diffusion and foreclosure are viewed as less-mature identity statuses, and the developmental prerogative is for individuals to move to a period of moratorium and ultimately to achievement (Kroger & Marcia, 2011). Although this model has been used extensively, it has also been criticized as not being an accurate representation of Erikson's theorizing (Côté & Levine, 2002).

In response, there is a recent movement within the identity field to go back to Erikson's original works to further refine theories of identity development (e.g., Hammack, 2008; McLean, Syed, Yoder, & Greenhoot, in press; Schachter, 2004; Syed, 2012b). The direction I have taken such efforts is to move away from the Marcian characterization of development as progression from foreclosure to achievement in favor of a characterization of development as an increasing sense of *integration*. This characterization is consistent with Erikson (1968), who described a healthy identity as one in which individuals integrate disparate aspects of the self (e.g., ethnic, gender) and integrate themselves through time (past, present, and future).

Taking this approach has several benefits. First, it brings attention beyond the heavy focus on identity *processes* found in the literature. The process of identity development—how individuals arrived at where they are—has long been viewed as more important than the *content* of identities, what those identities actually look like (Syed & Azmitia, 2010). In addition to process and content are identity *structures*, the configuration of relevant identities within a particular person (Schachter, 2004). Thus, ethnic identity—and identity more broadly—can be thought of as consisting of process, content, and structure (Hammack, 2008). Second, this approach allows room for heterogeneity in the identity process, content, and structure rather than mandating a particular developmental sequence (e.g., Cross, 1971; Phinney, 1993). Third, and most pertinent to the task at hand, locating my conceptualization of ethnic identity largely within an Eriksonian versus neo-Eriksonian perspective permits flexibility in the types of research questions I pursue and the methods through which I pursue them. That is, the identity status model is rather limited in scope vis-à-vis the universe of the identity concept. Erikson has been accused of many things, but "limited in scope" is certainly not among them. In this chapter, I highlight how narrative psychology helps to realize these benefits, focusing on (a) how ethnic identity develops, (b) the role of context in development, and (c) the dimensionality of ethnic identity. But first, we need to know about the narrative approach to identity.

OVERVIEW OF NARRATIVE APPROACHES TO IDENTITY

McAdams' (2001) autobiographical life-story model focuses on how individuals construct their identities through the process of creating and telling their life stories. McAdams argued that individuals' stories from the past are integrated into an evolving and internalized *narrative identity*. From this perspective, stories are not only representations of identity, but *stories are the identity*. That is, whether they are conscious of it, people see their lives in storied terms, viewing themselves as the authors of a life consisting of multiple chapters, highs and lows, turning points, heroes and villains, and various settings (McAdams, 2013). Moreover, the life story is constantly being written and revised, as past experiences are subject to reinterpretation to fit with individuals' current beliefs and goals for the future.

McAdams' model draws on Eriksonian theory and thus has strong developmental underpinnings. The life story does not begin to develop in earnest until adolescence, when youth develop advanced cognitive skills that allow them to reflect on their lives in sophisticated ways. These skills include the ability to recognize and reconcile contradictions in their beliefs and behaviors, to link different aspects of their lives in causal terms, and to achieve a sense of thematic coherence that unites disparate aspects of the self (Habermas & Bluck, 2000; Harter & Monsour, 1992). These cognitive advances facilitate adolescents' ability to make *meaning* of their past experiences, a key element of the narrative identity model. *Meaning making* is defined as reflecting on past events to see how individuals have changed over time (McLean, Pasupathi, & Pals, 2007). It serves as a core psychological process in connecting memories to identities and therefore is a driving force for identity development (McLean, 2005; Thorne, 2000; Thorne & McLean, 2003).

Within the narrative identity approach, the term *narrative* represents both the theory and the method. This is one of the major distinctions between narrative and other methods that rely on open-ended data. As described previously, narrative is the theory or, more accurately, the metaphor (Sarbin, 1986) that guides the approach to identity. Narrative also represents the method, as the data gathered in narrative studies are stories or episodic memories from the past. Thus, rather than requesting participants to talk about how they think or how they feel about a particular topic, narrative studies request specific memories of events. Stories are a natural way for humans to communicate (Bruner, 1990) and therefore provide an easy and familiar way for individuals to discuss their experiences. Because all stories are filtered through individuals' current context, respondents indirectly and unknowingly reveal how they are thinking and what is important to them at that time. This approach has a long history in psychology, going back to Henry Murray (1938), the development of the Thematic Apperception Test, and the personological tradition (Hogan, 1976).

EXISTING RESEARCH HIGHLIGHTING THE USE OF NARRATIVE TO STUDY ETHNIC IDENTITY

Despite the promise, there has not been a whole lot of research using an explicitly narrative approach to study ethnic identity development, particularly from a psychological perspective. There are, however three strands of related work. First, there is some narrative research in education (Nasir & Saxe, 2003), discourse studies (Malhi, Boon, & Rogers, 2009), communication (Gudykunst, 2003), and cultural studies (Langellier, 2010), but they define ethnic identity in very different ways. Second, within psychology, there has been an increasing number of ethnic identity studies using qualitative methods, such as interviews (Rogers & Way, Chapter 6, this volume; Charmaraman & Grossman, 2010), journaling (Vo-Jutabha, Dinh, McHale, & Valsiner, 2009), ethnography (Ortiz et al., Chapter 3, this volume), and participant observation (Way, Santos, Niwa, & Kim-Gervey, 2008). None of these studies, however, are *narrative* per se, in that they are not informed by models of narrative identity and do not explicitly examine participants' stories. That is, although stories may be told in the course of the interviews or other open-ended data, stories tend not be directly requested, and the analytic approach is not narrative. Finally, there are many narrative studies of cultural identity (e.g., Gone, Miller, & Rappaport, 1999; Hammack, 2006), which tend to focus on values, beliefs, and behaviors rather than the subjective importance of one's cultural background. For example, Wang (2008) examined how Asian American participants' memories were influenced by a prime that made salient their Asian versus American identities. The focus of the analysis was the degree to which the memories contained elements that were personal focused or social focused, consistent with the dichotomous independent–interdependent model of self-construal widespread in the cross-cultural literature (Markus & Kitayama, 1991).

There are, however, some studies that used a narrative approach to understand the psychological aspects of ethnic identity. In one of the first of those studies, Syed and Azmitia (2008) collected survey-based data on ethnic identity exploration and commitment using the Multigroup Ethnic Identity Measure (MEIM; Roberts et al., 1999) and narratives about ethnicity-related experiences. Through an iterative and interactive process, the research team inductively generated a coding system that identified the main themes in the data (see Syed & Azmitia, 2008, for more detail). The coding system resulted in four narrative themes that captured 95% of the stories: (a) experiences of prejudice, racism, discrimination, or oppression (*experiences of prejudice* stories); (b) feelings of connection, closeness, or belongingness to their ethnic and/or cultural background (*connection to culture* stories); (c) a time when they became aware that they were different ethnically, either from those in other ethnic groups or their own group (*awareness of difference* stories); and (d) a time when they were in the numerical minority in a particular context (*awareness of underrepresentation* stories). Turning to the survey data, we then used cluster analysis, a person-centered statistical procedure, to create identity status categories on the basis of participants' reported levels of exploration and commitment on the MEIM (see Phinney, 1993). This provided us with a content measure of ethnic identity (the narrative themes) and a process measure of ethnic identity (statuses) that could then be compared. The results indicated that those in the achieved status (high levels of exploration and commitment) were most likely to tell experience of prejudice or connection to culture stories, whereas those in the unexamined status (low levels of exploration and commitment) were more likely to tell awareness of difference and awareness of underrepresentation stories. In a subsequent longitudinal study (Syed & Azmitia, 2010), we found that respondents who increased in ethnic identity exploration over 18 months were more likely to change their story theme, particularly to experience of prejudice or connection to culture. In contrast, those who decreased or remained stable were more likely to tell a story with a similar theme at both time points. Moreover, 18% of respondents told the same story at both time points, with all of those being participants who decreased or remained stable.

Taking these findings together suggests that a more developed ethnic identity is associated with a broader and more personalized repertoire of ethnicity-related experiences. For those who are actively engaged with their ethnic identities, the focus seems to be *personal*, and when asked to recount an ethnicity-related memory, they select one of many available such memories. In contrast, individuals who are not actively involved with their ethnic identities seem to focus more on *difference*, and this focus is maintained across multiple requests for a memory. The personal experiences of prejudice and connections to culture are thus indicative of what it means to identify with one's ethnic background.

Thus, drawing on a narrative model of identity, and integrating findings from narrative research with survey-based research, can lead to greater insights about ethnic identity *development* than we have seen with much of the extant research. I provide three examples in the next section of this chapter.

EMPIRICAL ILLUSTRATIONS:
THREE INSIGHTS FROM NARRATIVES

In selecting the insights to describe in detail, I elected not to simply reiterate the findings from my published narrative research (Syed, 2010a, 2010b, 2012a; Syed & Azmitia, 2008, 2010). The interested reader can consult those papers directly. Rather, I opted to highlight insights that I have gleaned through doing narrative research. The three insights described next speak to theoretical issues of major importance to the study of ethnic identity: (a) how ethnic identity develops, (b) the role of context in development, and (c) the dimensionality of ethnic identity. In describing these insights, I review studies that are based on both narratives and surveys and report on some emerging findings from our unpublished work. The reason I am including survey work in a chapter on narrative methods is because I never would have thought to do the particular survey research that I discuss if not for my work with narratives. Thus, I highlight not only what can be learned through narrative research, but also how "narrative thinking" can inform subsequent survey-based work.

Encounters, Triggers, and Turning Points: All Misleading vis-à-vis Identity

The words *encounters*, *triggers*, and *turning points* invoke similar imagery: Speed. Abrupt change. These words were not selected at random. Encounter is one of the stages in Cross's (1971) nigrescence theory, and trigger has been used by Phinney and other researchers using her model (Pahl & Way, 2006; Phinney & Rosenthal, 1992; Quintana, 2007; Syed & Azmitia, 2009; Yip, 2005). Turning points are frequently used in narrative research to designate memories that reflect a change or reorientation in how one views the self (McLean & Pratt, 2006). These terms suggest that ethnic identity can change quickly as a result of some singular event or series of events and that one day, an individual who never thought much about his or her identity may have an experience (e.g., discrimination) and BAM!—that person is set on a course to become strongly ethnically identified.

To be fair, so far as I am aware, no one actually believes that. However, it is important to note that these heavily used terms suggest it, and such a suggestion has real impact on both theory and research. Conceptualizing time is a major task of the developmental scientist (Wohlwill, 1973), and the manner in which we do so can affect our interpretations of how time plays a role in psychological phenomena (Lerner, Schwartz, & Phelps, 2009). Thus, it seems important that we take a closer look at these dominant speed metaphors and how well they fit with how ethnic identity actually develops.

The findings from narrative studies have suggested that the abrupt change suggested by the terms encounter and trigger is unlikely to be a frequent experience. I provide two examples using different methodological approaches. These examples make use of the narrative concept of *meaning*, or reflecting on past events and connecting them to self. When we examine the meaning-making process in detail, a different picture of the speed of identity development begins to emerge.

When recounting stories of their past experience, individuals talk about both "what happened" at the time of the event itself (from their current perspective, of course), as well as how they think about that event at the time of the telling. Thus, an element of time is embedded within the stories. We recently began work on understanding this construction of time in narratives by separating stories into immediate (at the time of the event) and delayed (after the event itself) components (Walker & Syed, 2011). We then coded these segments for the presence of markers that indicate affective (emotions), behavioral (did they "do" anything?), and cognitive (meaning-making) processes, as these have been identified as the three broad domains of ethnic identity (Ashmore, Deaux, & McLaughlin-Volpe, 2004; Phinney, 1993). This resulted in a "deconstructed" narrative in which we create a 2 (time) × 3 (dimension) matrix to represent the stories. That is, each of the three dimensions (affective, behavioral, and cognitive) could be located in each of two temporal spaces (immediate and delayed). Although affective and behavioral components were most frequently located in the immediate events, the cognitive component—meaning making—was much more likely to occur in the delayed segment. This finding indicates that meaning making is not occurring immediately following an event, as would be suggested by encounter and trigger. Rather, meaning making takes place after a period of time in which individuals have had time to think about the experience, to talk to others, or to have subsequent experiences that led them to rethink the original event (McLean et al., 2007; Thorne, 2000).

A limitation of the previously described study—and the vast majority of narrative research—is that it is cross-sectional and retrospective. What we need are longitudinal studies of meaning making, wherein individuals talk about the same event both when it is relatively recent and after a period of time. In other words, the study needs to be both prospective and retrospective. Such studies are hard to come by, but there is one that is useful to consider. This study was not about ethnic identity development per se, but rather was about how college students integrate their ethnic and academic identities over time (Syed, 2010a). One particular case is germane to the current topic. During her sophomore year, a student discussed participating in an ethnic-based educational activity. At that time, she described it as fun and interesting, but not much more. When we spoke to her in her senior year of college, she targeted that experience as a "turning point" for her identity. That may very well be the case, but that is not the way she viewed it at the time. Retrospectively, however, that singular experience has been identified as the primary source of identity change. It may have been a turning point, but she did not know that when it was happening. It is likely quite rare for individuals to be conscious of their own identity-related turning points. On the occasions when they are, it may be best referred to as an epiphany (see Cross & Cross, 2008).

In sum, narrative research has suggested that identity is generally a slow process that unfolds over time (see also Josselson, 2009). Moreover, notions of abrupt identity change are likely to be a product of retrospective construction of past experiences, rather than the way in which identities actually change in response to life experiences. Thus, there is a distinction between how identities change and how we construct and situate those changes within our life stories.

Social Context: Cold and Hot

A small wave of research several years ago began to investigate the degree to which ethnic density, or the relative proportion of coethnics in a given geographical area, may be associated with ethnic identity development (Juang, Nguyen, & Lin, 2006; Syed, Azmitia, & Phinney, 2007; Umaña-Taylor, 2004). On the one hand, Eriksonian identity theory, which stresses the importance of resources and opportunities from which individuals can draw on their identities, suggests that individuals in contexts with high ethnic representation should have stronger and more fully developed ethnic identities. Social identity theory, on the other hand, specifies that group identification is heightened and subsequently strengthened when that group is in the minority (Tajfel & Turner, 1986). Thus, from this perspective, it is contexts with very low representation that should give rise to stronger ethnic identities.

The findings on the role of ethnic density reflect these theoretical contradictions, sometimes finding differences in levels of ethnic identity but not links to mental health (Umaña-Taylor, 2004), differences in links to mental health but not in levels (Juang et al., 2006), and no differences in levels or developmental trajectories (Syed et al., 2007). Thus, the role of social context—as defined by ethnic density—for ethnic identity development is far from clear.

At the 2008 Society for Research on Adolescence meeting, Andrew Fuligni served as a discussant for a symposium on ethnic identity process and content. In his comments, he drew on the distinction between cold cognition and hot cognition (Abelson, 1979). *Cold cognition* refers to basic information processing, such as learning and memory. *Hot cognition*, however, refers to how those cognitive processes are influenced by the emotional and motivational contexts in which they are performed. Fuligni made a connection between the cold/hot cognition distinction and the way in which contexts are conceptualized in ethnic identity research. He suggested that ethnic density is "cold context" because it relies purely on the relative proportion or representation of a particular group in a particular geographical area (typically ill-defined; see Syed & Juan, 2012). The context can be understood through looking up the appropriate figures on the U.S. Census website. What is lacking in this approach is how individuals personally *experience* these social contexts, which is the core idea of "hot context." I have frequently made a similar distinction between objective (e.g., density) and subjective contexts (Syed, 2010a; Syed & Juan, 2012; see also Juang & Alvarez, 2011; Way et al., 2008). Past research has indicated that the same "context" is not perceived similarly for different individuals who are a part of it (Syed, 2010a). That is, the same level of density in the same geographical location can be viewed as "diverse" by one individual and "not very diverse" by another. Although research directly comparing the two is minimal, the existing research has suggested that subjective assessments of context have more predictive power than objective assessments (Juang & Alvarez, 2011; Syed & Juan, 2012; Way et al., 2008; Yip, Seaton, & Sellers, 2006).

Bringing awareness of this distinction to ethnic identity scholars paves the way for asking new questions about how contexts matter for ethnic identity development. Way et al. (2008) provided a useful example of this point through their ethnographic study of ethnic identity of Puerto Rican, Dominican, Chinese American, and African American high school students. The Chinese American students were well represented in the schools (cold context) but were at the bottom of the peer social hierarchy (hot context). In contrast, the Puerto Rican students were fewer in number but enjoyed the highest social status. Through their interviews and observations, Way et al. determined that the peer social context played a much bigger role in the students' ethnic identity experiences than did their raw numerical representation. Thus, rather than focusing on "how many," a greater consideration of the hot context allows for questions about how individuals directly engage with their contexts, both actively and passively. Narratives may have some advantages relative to rating-scale surveys for addressing these questions. I provide two empirical examples next.

In addition to contributing to an understanding of development, narrative meaning making may be one route for assessing the hot context of ethnic identity. Two types of stories that repeatedly appear in my narrative studies are awareness of difference stories and awareness of underrepresentation stories (Syed & Azmitia, 2008, 2010; Walker & Syed, 2011). Awareness of difference stories are about times in which individuals become aware that they are ethnically different from others. There is an inherent element of meaning making, as the tellers often observed something (e.g., different food practices) and subsequently gained some insights about their ethnic identity (e.g., the food of my culture is considered "weird" by others). In contrast, awareness of underrepresentation stories are commentaries on the relative diversity in a particular context (e.g., I went to a party, looked around, and saw that I was the only Asian guy there). No meaning is made of the experience, it is simply a story about a time the teller realized that he or she was in the minority (or in some cases majority) and is thus an example of cold ethnic context. An important—and still yet unanswered—question is why do some individuals attach meaning to the experience and others not? Both types of stories are related to lower levels of ethnic identity, assessed via survey measures. It is possible, however, that the awareness of difference stories are told by individuals who are primed for development. They may not have thought much about their ethnicities, but they are beginning to and thus have thought enough about their experiences to imbue them with meaning. These two story types, largely differentiated by meaning, show how individuals differently engage with their cold contexts. Knowing simply that they were in a situation where they *noticed* a difference may not be as useful for understanding ethnic identity as knowing the meaning they made about the difference.

Another way to think about the hot context of ethnic identity is how individuals talk about race and ethnicity with others. The dominant focus in the literature in this regard is research on racial and cultural socialization (Hughes et al., 2006). Racial socialization is the process through which individuals convey messages about the role and meaning of race in society. One form of racial socialization is *preparation for bias*, where individuals communicate the potential for institutional and personal racism and discrimination. In contrast, cultural socialization is the process through which individuals are exposed to the history, traditions, and practices associated with their ethnic or cultural group (Umaña-Taylor, 2001). Both racial and cultural socialization have been positively linked to ethnic identity (Hughes et al., 2006). The majority of the literature has relied on rating-scale instruments and has identified parents as the primary socialization agents. One narrative study, however, suggests a more dynamic view of socialization.

In a recent study, I had college students first write down an ethnicity-related memory, then write down a memory about telling that memory to someone else (Syed, 2012a). This is referred to as a *telling memory*—a memory about telling a memory (McLean, 2005; Thorne & McLean, 2003). First of all, only 60% of the stories had been told to others at all; the remaining 40% had never been told. Of the stories that were reported to have been told, I analyzed the data for what the story was about and to whom they told it. One of the key findings is that stories about discrimination were most likely to be told to peers, whereas stories about learning about one's cultural background were most likely to be told to parents. This distinction in story content aligns with the distinction between racial socialization and cultural socialization, respectively, and suggests that peers may be important agents of racial socialization, whereas parents may be important agents of cultural socialization. This "division of labor" regarding socialization had not been previously recognized or discussed, in part because peer ethnic socialization has scantly been investigated in past research. These findings led me to do just that, assessing both racial and cultural socialization from peers and parents using rating-scale instruments (Syed & Hu, 2013). The results dovetailed with the narrative observations: Greater ethnic identity exploration and commitment were associated with higher levels of parental cultural socialization and higher levels of peer preparation for bias (see Figure 2.1). Thus, this example illustrates how by understanding the ways individuals interact with their contexts—to whom they tell different life experiences—we can develop new empirical and theoretical ideas about how identities are managed and the specific sources of their development.

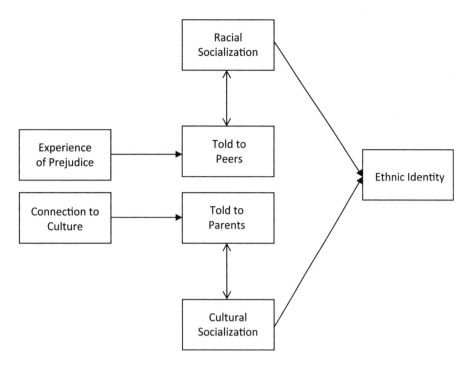

Figure 2.1. Model showing peer and parent socialization patterns to ethnic identity.

Exploration Is Not Exploration Is Not Exploration

Ethnic identity exploration is a critical component of ethnic identity development (Phinney, 1990). Exploration has traditionally been conceptualized as a unidimensional construct. My narrative research, however, made it clear to me that there are likely different ways of "doing" exploration. This observation dovetails with the relatively low alpha for the MEIM exploration scale (in comparison with the MEIM commitment scale). Someone might talk to others about ethnicity, for example, but that does not necessarily mean that they will attend ethnicity-related events. Thus, there is some evidence that ethnic identity exploration may be a multidimensional construct.

My final illustration is a more direct example of how narrative research can contribute to more traditional forms of ethnic identity research. Conducting narrative research is not for everyone, but such research should not be considered as a "separate stream" from research based on survey measures. My narrative work is what motivated me to think of exploration as a multidimensional process, that there may be distinct forms of exploration with which individuals engage. I then returned to survey data to examine whether ethnic identity exploration, as currently measured with rating scales, has multiple subdimensions. Along with several of my colleagues, I used the MUSIC data set (an online survey of over 10,000 college students from across the United States; see Weisskirch et al., 2013, for a detailed description of method and sample), which has both a very large number of ethnic minority participants ($N > 3,000$) and contains the two leading measures of ethnic identity exploration, the MEIM and the Ethnic Identity Scale (EIS; Umaña-Taylor et al., 2004). We factor analyzed the two scales together to test whether exploration made up a single latent factor or could be conceptualized as multidimensional. The results were rather striking (Syed et al., 2013).

As I suspected, there were multiple factors, but not exactly in the way I had imagined. Each scale, in fact, constituted its own factor. This could be dismissed as due to method factors, but that does not appear to be the case. Close inspection of the items from each scale suggests that they may actually be tapping into different exploratory processes and outcomes. The EIS items pertain to concrete behaviors in which the individuals learned something about their identities ("participation"). The MEIM items, on the other hand, generally tap into exploratory processes that have less clear of an outcome ("search"). That is, those items about talking to people, attending events, and readings books do not explicitly state that anything was learned. It becomes clear that these two scales are tapping into different forms of exploration when using them as simultaneous predictors of well-being. Participation (via the EIS) positively predicted higher well-being, whereas search (via the MEIM) negatively predicted well-being. Note that the zero-order correlation between the MEIM exploration scale and well-being is zero. Thus, the potentially negative impact of search-related exploration is being suppressed until the positive impact of participation is removed. Search on its own is not a bad thing, but search outside of participation appears to be negative. Further models we tested revealed why this is the case: Participation leads to identity coherence, which leads to higher well-being. In contrast, search leads to identity confusion, which leads to lower well-being (see Syed et al., 2013).

The point of this example is to illustrate that my narrative research led to this analysis. Reading and analyzing individuals' stories about their ethnicity-related experiences broadened my thinking about constructs such as exploration and commitment. I was then able to cycle back and bring this new thinking to analyses on the basis of rating-scale instruments. Indeed, this new lens allowed me to interpret and synthesize the existing research in new ways and to detect patterns of relations that I had not previously noticed (see Syed et al., 2013, for more details). The result is a deepening of ethnic identity theory; there are (potentially) many ways that individuals "do" exploration, and these different ways may have different implications for psychological functioning. These findings open the door to new lines of inquiry in ethnic identity research. How many different types of exploration are there? What are their implications? Why do individuals engage in some rather than others? Is there a normative developmental pattern? At this time, these questions have no answers. Nevertheless, we should feel good about the fact that we are asking them.

STRENGTHS OF USING A NARRATIVE APPROACH TO STUDY ETHNIC IDENTITY

Although I believe there are numerous strengths to using a narrative approach in the study of ethnic identity, I highlight just two here. First, as I hope I have illustrated, a narrative approach can lead to new insights that may be very difficult to achieve—impossible even—using rating-scale instruments. For new insights and discovery, it is hard to argue against the value of listening to and reading about individuals' everyday life experiences (Arnett, 2005; Charmaz, 2006; Thorne, 2000). This is particularly true for underrepresented and marginalized groups. Indeed, narrative figures prominently within the field of critical race theory as it gives voice to individuals who are largely silenced within the mainstream culture (see Duncan, 2005). Relying solely on rating-scale instruments—particularly those that have not been subject to psychometric rigor (e.g., the multitrait-multimethod matrix, Campbell & Fiske, 1959; invariance testing, Knight, Roosa, & Umaña-Taylor, 2009)—could result in overlooking constructs or dimensions that are important to the group of interest.

The second strength of the narrative approach to ethnic identity is that it allows individuals to specify their own context. That is, through telling their stories, individuals communicate what is important about themselves and their surrounding environment. Not only do you often get information about where they were, who they were with, and what they were doing, but you also get information about their subjective evaluation of the situation. On a related note, narratives can often reveal links across different life domains or areas of functioning, even if you were not looking for them. In some of our work on identity development more broadly, we have begun to examine the degree to which domains of identity tend to co-occur within a single narrative and whether certain identity domains surface when respondents are recounting stories about different domains (McLean et al., in press). If asked for a memory about politics, do they also tend to weave in discussions of values and occupation? This work is ongoing, so as yet we do not have definitive answers. These are the kinds of questions, however, that narratives are well positioned to address.

CHALLENGES OF USING A NARRATIVE APPROACH TO STUDY ETHNIC IDENTITY

Despite the strengths associated with adopting a narrative approach to the study of ethnic identity, there are, of course, some challenges as well. Here I review some of the conceptual challenges. The more procedural challenges are discussed in the subsequent section on best practices in narrative research. Many researchers who study ethnic identity do so because they believe it has relevance to the psychosocial functioning of ethnic minority youth (see Quintana, 2007). Accordingly, many studies seek to connect dimensions of ethnic identity to important indicators such as well-being, distress, and academic functioning (see Rivas-Drake, Seaton, et al., 2014; Rivas-Drake, Syed, et al., 2014). This goal, in general, will be more easily accomplished using survey-based approaches than narrative approaches for three reasons. First, using narrative elements to predict psychosocial outcomes means that shared survey method variance will be removed from the analysis, as most psychosocial outcomes are measured via survey. Given that the effect sizes are small to moderate when this shared variance is present (Rivas-Drake, Syed, et al., 2014; Smith & Silva, 2011), the reduction of method variance will likely attenuate effect sizes to triviality.

Second, narrative research is sometimes based on a single memory at a time (e.g., Syed & Azmitia, 2008, 2010). It may be asking quite a lot to expect elements of a single memory to be associated with more generalized ratings of psychosocial functioning. Indeed, narrative research has the potential to be heavily affected by demand characteristics, as a number of situational and life factors could influence the memory that comes to mind in the lab. For this reason, narrative research outside of ethnic identity tends to collect several memories at a time from participants, typically between three and 10, which could either be of the same type (e.g., self-defining memories; McLean, 2005) or a variety of types (e.g., low point, high point, turning point; McAdams et al., 2006). Collecting numerous memories allows for the extraction of consistent elements that cut across individual memories and thus provides insights into reminiscing that is more dispositional than situational. Such an approach may be more fruitful when looking for links to psychosocial functioning. Thus, depending on the research question, collecting a single narrative may not yield sufficient data. It is critical that the number and types of narratives requested appropriately match the goals of the research.

Finally, in narrative research you have little control over the nature of the responses. This is because the "questions" asked in narrative research are for types of memories that can range in specificity. A typical prompt that I use is, "Please describe an experience, either positive or negative, in which you became particularly aware of your race/ethnicity." This prompt is very open-ended and can lead to a wide variety of memory types. This can be a good thing or a bad thing, depending on the research question. For example, at first glance, such a prompt may not seem advantageous if a researcher was specifically interested in experiences of discrimination, as the prompt requested an experience in which the participants "became aware" of their ethnicity and did not explicitly request a discrimination story. However, this prompt may actually yield stronger data by paradoxically generating a greater number of discrimination stories compared with a prompt that specifically requests an experience of discrimination. When describing experiences of discrimination, many participants do not use the words *racism*, *discrimination*, *prejudice*, or any other similar terms, and it is very likely that many of them would not readily label their experience of discrimination as such (see Syed & Azmitia, 2008). Thus, directly requesting stories about discrimination could actually lead to lower rates of telling such stories. This suggestion is supported by past research. For example, when Pituc, Syed, and Lee (2010) specifically requested a memory about discrimination, over half of the participants responded that they had never had such an experience. Pasupathi, Wainryb, and Twali (2012) requested a memory of "a time when you felt singled out or treated differently, in a negative way, because of your ethnicity" (p. 59). They did not use the word discrimination in their prompt and yet still had 30% of the sample state that they had never experienced discrimination. Juang and Syed (2014) used the prompt "Please describe a time when you were a child or teenager when you felt treated differently because of your racial/ethnic/cultural background," and had only 14% of the sample report not having such an experience. Although similar to the Pasupathi et al. (2012) prompt, the Juang and Syed (2014) prompt did not include any valence, which could potentially have accounted for the greater compliance. The bottom line is one of great simplicity and immense importance: The way the question is phrased will impact the nature of the responses.

BEST PRACTICES IN NARRATIVE RESEARCH

When discussing narrative research with my more quantitatively oriented colleagues, I get a very consistent response: They think it is fascinating and relevant to what they do, but they have no idea how to do it. In this section, I briefly sketch a road map of crucial steps in the process of executing a narrative study and offer some best practices for going about the work. This is by no means an exhaustive list of concerns, and the depth of the exposition will not be sufficient for someone interested in planning a study. Rather, this section should be viewed as a starting point from which further education and training can be pursued.

As with any qualitative-based methodology, narrative research requires a great investment of time and resources. Time and resources play a factor at several levels: collecting the data, transcribing the data (if necessary), developing the coding system, training coders, and coding the data. Potential pitfalls lurk at every phase of the project, which can lead to serious delays. I briefly discuss each of these phases in turn.

Collecting the Data

As with any study, considerations for data collection in narrative studies depend on the particular research question and study design. First, under no circumstances should a narrative study be launched without first conducting a pilot study. It is critical to test out the memory prompt(s) being considered to ensure that participants are responding to them as intended. In terms of sample size, narrative studies range from single-case studies (Schachter, 2005) to studies of several hundred participants (McLean & Pratt, 2006), with the optimal choice being dependent on the goals of the research. Participants can communicate their stories by writing them down on paper, typing them on the computer, or telling them orally in interviews. The selection of the method should be done carefully and is dependent on the research question and the types of memories being requested. For example, especially sensitive memories that are resistant to disclosure (e.g., discrimination) may be best requested via handwriting or typing rather than interviews. The benefit of privacy, however, must be considered in relation to the limitation of being unable to ask follow-up questions. Regardless of the method through which the stories are told, narrative data must be collected in the research lab or other monitored setting to get high-quality data. In other words, the use of online surveys that participants complete on their own time should not be used for narrative research.

Transcribing the Data

Creating verbatim transcripts is necessary for verbal and handwritten narratives. The formal transcripts become the data that are used for subsequent coding. Transcription takes an enormous amount of time—much longer than most people would think. A 1-hour interview does not take 1 hour to transcribe. A rough guide for transcribing one-on-one interviews is that every hour of interview will take approximately 4 hours to transcribe. The task can be facilitated by the use of transcription software and enlisting the services of experienced transcribers and/or skilled typists. Of course, having participants write their narratives on the computer obviates the need for this particularly onerous task.

Developing the Coding System

Collecting and transcribing the data are significant challenges, but developing the coding system can be the most daunting step in the process of narrative analysis. There are three broad approaches to developing a coding system, which range from the least to the most time intensive: (a) using an existing coding system, (b) modifying an existing coding system, and (c) creating a new coding system. I am frequently asked how many coding categories there should be within an optimal system. The answer: not too many, and not too few. More specifically, overly detailed coding systems will likely result in losing focus of the big picture and will make it difficult to achieve acceptable interrater reliability (see the next section). Having too few categories will result in coarse categories that contain too much variability to be meaningful. The optimal system balances these two poles, and the precise number will depend on the research question. That said, a survey of the narrative identity literature would show that most coding systems tend to have between three and seven categories.

Training Coders and Coding the Data

Once the coding system has been developed, coders need to be trained to follow the specified coding manual. Coders often consist of a mixture of research assistants (undergraduate or graduate students) and key personnel. The coders must go through a training period until they are able to achieve an acceptable level of interrater reliability. There are many different ways of establishing some type of reliability, ranging from qualitative, discussion-based methods such as the Listening Guide (Taylor, Gilligan, & Sullivan, 1996) to quantitative methods such as percentage of agreement and Cohen's kappa (Bakeman & Gottman, 1986). Regardless of the method, there should be some evidence that multiple perspectives were brought to bear on the narratives, both for the purpose of establishing reliability and also because differing views can lead to new insights that would not otherwise have occurred (see Taylor et al., 1996).

All of the phases described involve substantial time, but they also require extensive training. This is not only the case for research assistants who often do the coding, but for the principal investigator as well. This barrier points to the increased need for graduate training in diverse methods, as well as collaborations among researchers with varying skills. As narrative analysis is becoming increasingly prevalent within identity studies, there are greater opportunities for collaborations between narrative and nonnarrative researchers. Only good things can come from such collaborations.

FUTURE DIRECTIONS

Our collective understanding of ethnic identity development, in terms of antecedents, consequences, and trajectories, has increased substantially in recent years. These advances are reflected in the work of the Ethnic and Racial Identity in the 21st Century Study Group, which recently published a special section of *Child Development* devoted to the state of the field (see Rivas-Drake, Seaton, et al., 2014; Rivas-Drake, Syed, et al., 2014; Schwartz et al., 2014; Umaña-Taylor et al., 2014). One issue that came into relief during the work of the study group is that despite the many advances, there remain substantial gaps in our understanding of key questions pertaining to ethnic identity. These gaps include the three main topics covered in this chapter: (a) how ethnic identity develops, (b) the role of context in development, and (c) the dimensionality of ethnic identity. To be sure, there have been many studies that have addressed these topics. We would be remiss, however, to say we have firm understandings of any of them, as debates on all three continue to this day.

From my perspective, part of the reason for our limited knowledge on these important theoretical questions is our reliance on a narrow set of methodological tools. Although our methods and measures should never dictate the questions that we ask, it is the case that the methods and measures set boundary constraints of the types of questions that can be asked, as well as the nature of the answers. It can be useful to think about the five sequential steps involved in any science: observation, description, explanation, prediction, and control. What these steps suggest is that one needs to observe a phenomenon before describing, one must describe a phenomenon before seeking to explain it, one must be able to adequately explain a phenomenon before attempting to predict its occurrence, and one must be able to predict a phenomenon with regularity prior to successfully controlling or altering it. Most of the research on ethnic identity (and psychological research more broadly) has been fixated on the middle steps of explanation and prediction. This is all well and good, but I argue that we have not spent nearly enough time with observation and description. Observation and description are the bedrock of scientific knowledge, and they all but require the use of qualitative methods, including narrative, ethnography (Ortiz et al., Chapter 3, this volume), interviews (Rogers & Way, Chapter 6, this volume), and a host of other methods. Until researchers acknowledge this and diversify their methods and research questions, our explaining and predicting will continue to be plagued by inconsistencies and inaccuracies.

CONCLUDING THOUGHTS

Ethnic identity has emerged as a major topic of study in developmental psychology and related fields. This emergence has come on the backs of a small number of rating-scale instruments that have seen widespread use. Now that much of the fundamental research on ethnic identity has been conducted, it will be critical to move beyond a sole focus on rating scales of ethnic identity process and content. To contribute to further theoretical development, the study of ethnic identity must include diverse methodologies, including—but not limited to—narrative. My goal in this chapter was to make this point evident. Indeed, I hope to have demonstrated how methodological innovations can contribute to a deepening and refining of ethnic identity theory and how a continued emphasis on method and theory is critical for advances in this important domain of positive ethnic minority development.

REFERENCES

Abelson, R. P. (1979). Differences between belief and knowledge systems. *Cognitive Science, 3*, 355–366. http://dx.doi.org/10.1207/s15516709cog0304_4

Arnett, J. J. (2005). The vitality criterion: A new standard of publication for Journal of Adolescent Research. *Journal of Adolescent Research, 20*, 3–7. http://dx.doi.org/10.1177/0743558404271251

Ashmore, R. D., Deaux, K., & McLaughlin-Volpe, T. (2004). An organizing framework for collective identity: Articulation and significance of multidimensionality. *Psychological Bulletin, 130*, 80–114. http://dx.doi.org/10.1037/0033-2909.130.1.80

Bakeman, R., & Gottman, J. M. (1986). *Observing interaction: An introduction to sequential analysis.* Cambridge, England: Cambridge University Press.

Bruner, J. S. (1990). *Acts of meaning.* Cambridge, MA: Harvard University Press.

Campbell, D. T., & Fiske, D. W. (1959). Convergent and discriminant validation by the multitrait-multimethod matrix. *Psychological Bulletin, 56*, 81–105. http://dx.doi.org/10.1037/h0046016

Charmaraman, L., & Grossman, J. M. (2010). Importance of race and ethnicity: An exploration of Asian, Black, Latino, and multiracial adolescent identity. *Cultural Diversity and Ethnic Minority Psychology, 16*, 144–151. http://dx.doi.org/10.1037/a0018668

Charmaz, K. (2006). *Constructing grounded theory: A practical guide through qualitative analysis.* Thousand Oaks, CA: Pine Forge Press.

Côté, J. E., & Levine, C. G. (2002). *Identity, formation, agency, and culture: A social psychological synthesis.* Mahwah, NJ: Erlbaum.

Cross, W. E. (1971). The Negro-to-Black conversation experience: Toward a psychology of Black liberation. *Black World, 20*(9), 13–27.

Cross, W. E., & Cross, T. B. (2008). Theory, research, and models. In S. M. Quintana & C. McKown (Eds.), *Handbook of race, racism, and the developing child* (pp. 154–181). New York, NY: Wiley.

Duncan, G. A. (2005). Critical race ethnography in education: Narrative, inequality, and the problem of epistemology. In A. D. Dixson & C. K. Rousseau (Eds.), *Critical race theory in education* (pp. 191–211). New York, NY: Routledge. http://dx.doi.org/10.1080/1361332052000341015

Erikson, E. H. (1950). *Childhood and society.* New York, NY: Norton.

Erikson, E. H. (1968). *Identity: Youth and crisis.* New York, NY: Norton.

French, S. E., Seidman, E., Allen, L., & Aber, J. L. (2006). The development of ethnic identity during adolescence. *Developmental Psychology, 42,* 1–10. http://dx.doi.org/10.1037/0012-1649.42.1.1

Gone, J. P., Miller, P. J., & Rappaport, J. (1999). Conceptual self as normatively oriented: The suitability of past personal narrative for the study of cultural identity. *Culture & Psychology, 5,* 371–398. http://dx.doi.org/10.1177/1354067X9954001

Gudykunst, W. B. (Ed.). (2003). *Cross-cultural and intercultural communication.* Thousand Oaks, CA: Sage.

Habermas, T., & Bluck, S. (2000). Getting a life: The emergence of the life story in adolescence. *Psychological Bulletin, 126,* 748–769. http://dx.doi.org/10.1037/0033-2909.126.5.748

Hammack, P. L. (2006). Identity, conflict, and coexistence: Life stories of Israeli and Palestinian adolescents. *Journal of Adolescent Research, 21,* 323–369. http://dx.doi.org/10.1177/0743558406289745

Hammack, P. L. (2008). Narrative and the cultural psychology of identity. *Personality and Social Psychology Review, 12,* 222–247. http://dx.doi.org/10.1177/1088868308316892

Harter, S., & Monsour, A. (1992). Developmental analysis of conflict caused by opposing attributed in the adolescent self-portrait. *Developmental Psychology, 28,* 251–260. http://dx.doi.org/10.1037/0012-1649.28.2.251

Hogan, R. (1976). *Personality theory: The personological tradition.* Oxford, England: Prentice-Hall.

Hughes, D., Rodriguez, J., Smith, E. P., Johnson, D. J., Stevenson, H. C., & Spicer, P. (2006). Parents' ethnic-racial socialization practices: A review of research and directions for future study. *Developmental Psychology, 42,* 747–770. http://dx.doi.org/10.1037/0012-1649.42.5.747

Hughes, D., Way, N., & Rivas-Drake, D. (2011). Stability and change in private and public ethnic regard among African American, Puerto Rican, Dominican, and Chinese American urban early adolescents. *Journal of Research on Adolescence, 21,* 861–870. http://dx.doi.org/10.1111/j.1532-7795.2011.00744.x

Josselson, R. (2009). The present of the past: Dialogues with memory over time. *Journal of Personality, 77,* 647–668. http://dx.doi.org/10.1111/j.1467-6494.2009.00560.x

Juang, L. P., & Alvarez, A. N. (2011). Family, school, and neighborhood: Links to Chinese American adolescent perceptions of racial/ethnic discrimination. *Asian American Journal of Psychology, 2*, 1–12. http://dx.doi.org/10.1037/a0023107

Juang, L. P., & Nguyen, H. H. (2010). Ethnic identity among Chinese-American youth: The role of family obligation and community factors on ethnic engagement, clarity, and pride. *Identity: An International Journal of Theory and Research, 10*, 20–38. http://dx.doi.org/10.1080/15283481003676218

Juang, L. P., Nguyen, H. H., & Lin, Y. (2006). The ethnic identity, other-group attitudes, and psychosocial functioning of Asian American emerging adults from two contexts. *Journal of Adolescent Research, 21*, 542–568. http://dx.doi.org/10.1177/0743558406291691

Juang, L. P., & Syed, M. (2014). Sharing stories of discrimination with parents. *Journal of Adolescence, 37*, 303–312. http://dx.doi.org/10.1016/j.adolescence.2014.02.004

Knight, G. P., Roosa, M. W., & Umaña-Taylor, A. J. (2009). *Methodological challenges in studying ethnic minority or economically disadvantaged populations.* Washington, DC: American Psychological Association. http://dx.doi.org/10.1037/11887-000

Kroger, J., & Marcia, J. E. (2011). The identity statuses: Origins, meanings, and interpretations. In S. J. Schwartz, K. Luyckx, & V. L. Vignoles (Eds.), *Handbook of identity theory and research* (pp. 31–53). New York, NY: Springer. http://dx.doi.org/10.1007/978-1-4419-7988-9_2

Langellier, K. M. (2010). Performing Somali identity in the diaspora: 'Wherever I go I know who I am'. *Cultural Studies, 24*, 66–94. http://dx.doi.org/10.1080/09502380903200723

Lee, R. M., & Yoo, H. C. (2004). Structure and measurement of ethnic identity for Asian American college students. *Journal of Counseling Psychology, 51*, 263–269. http://dx.doi.org/10.1037/0022-0167.51.2.263

Lerner, R. M., Schwartz, S. J., & Phelps, E. (2009). Problematics of time and timing in the longitudinal study of human development: Theoretical and methodological issues. *Human Development, 52*, 44–68. http://dx.doi.org/10.1159/000189215

Malhi, R. L., Boon, S. D., & Rogers, T. B. (2009). 'Being Canadian' and 'Being Indian': Subject positions and discourses used in South Asian-Canadian women's talk about ethnic identity. *Culture & Psychology, 15*, 255–283. http://dx.doi.org/10.1177/1354067X09102893

Marcia, J. E. (1966). Development and validation of ego-identity status. *Journal of Personality and Social Psychology, 3*, 551–558. http://dx.doi.org/10.1037/h0023281

Markus, H. R., & Kitayama, S. (1991). Culture and the self: Implications for cognition, emotion, and motivation. *Psychological Review, 98*, 224–253. http://dx.doi.org/10.1037/0033-295X.98.2.224

McAdams, D. P. (2001). The psychology of life stories. *Review of General Psychology, 5*, 100–122. http://dx.doi.org/10.1037/1089-2680.5.2.100

McAdams, D. P. (2013). The psychological self as an actor, agent, and author. *Perspectives on Psychological Science, 8*, 272–295.

McAdams, D. P., Bauer, J. J., Sakaeda, A. R., Anyidoho, N. A., Machado, M. A., Magrino-Failla, K., . . . Pals, J. L. (2006). Continuity and change in the life story: A longitudinal study of autobiographical memories in emerging adulthood. *Journal of Personality, 74*, 1371–1400. http://dx.doi.org/10.1111/j.1467-6494.2006.00412.x

McLean, K. C. (2005). Late adolescent identity development: Narrative meaning making and memory telling. *Developmental Psychology, 41*, 683–691. http://dx.doi.org/10.1037/0012-1649.41.4.683

McLean, K. C., Pasupathi, M., & Pals, J. L. (2007). Selves creating stories creating selves: A process model of self-development. *Personality and Social Psychology Review, 11*, 262–278. http://dx.doi.org/10.1177/1088868307301034

McLean, K. C., & Pratt, M. W. (2006). Life's little (and big) lessons: Identity statuses and meaning-making in the turning point narratives of emerging adults. *Developmental Psychology, 42*, 714–722. http://dx.doi.org/10.1037/0012-1649.42.4.714

McLean, K. C., Syed, M., Yoder, A., & Greenhoot, A. (in press). The role of domain content in understanding identity development processes. *Journal of Research on Adolescence.*

Murray, H. A. (1938). *Explorations in personality.* New York, NY: Oxford University Press.

Nasir, N. S., & Saxe, G. B. (2003). Ethnic and academic identities: A cultural practice perspective on emerging tensions and their management in the lives of minority students. *Educational Researcher, 32*(5), 14–18. http://dx.doi.org/10.3102/0013189X032005014

Pahl, K., & Way, N. (2006). Longitudinal trajectories of ethnic identity among urban Black and Latino adolescents. *Child Development, 77*, 1403–1415. http://dx.doi.org/10.1111/j.1467-8624.2006.00943.x

Pasupathi, M., Wainryb, C., & Twali, M. (2012). Relations between narrative construction of ethnicity-based discrimination and ethnic identity exploration and pride. *Identity: An International Journal of Theory and Research, 12*, 53–73. http://dx.doi.org/10.1080/15283488.2012.632393

Phinney, J. S. (1990). Ethnic identity in adolescents and adults: Review of research. *Psychological Bulletin, 108*, 499–514. http://dx.doi.org/10.1037/0033-2909.108.3.499

Phinney, J. S. (1992). The Multigroup Ethnic Identity Measure: A new scale for use with diverse groups. *Journal of Adolescent Research, 7*, 156–176. http://dx.doi.org/10.1177/074355489272003

Phinney, J. S. (1993). A three-stage model of ethnic identity in adolescence. In M. E. Bernal & G. P. Knight (Eds.), *Ethnic identity: Formation and transmission among Hispanics and other minorities* (pp. 61–79). Hillsdale, NJ: Erlbaum.

Phinney, J. S., & Ong, A. D. (2007). Conceptualization and measurement of ethnic identity: Current status and future directions. *Journal of Counseling Psychology, 54*, 271–281. http://dx.doi.org/10.1037/0022-0167.54.3.271

Phinney, J. S., & Rosenthal, D. A. (1992). Ethnic identity in adolescence: Process, context, and outcome. In G. R. Adams, T. P. Gullotta, & R. Montemayor (Eds.), *Adolescent identity formation. Advances in adolescent development* (Vol. 4, pp. 145–172). Thousand Oaks, CA: Sage.

Pituc, S. T., Syed, M., & Lee, R. M. (2010, March). *A mixed-method approach to illustrating the racial triangulation of discrimination.* Paper presented at the biennial meeting of the Society for Research on Adolescence, Philadelphia, PA.

Quintana, S. M. (2007). Racial and ethnic identity: Developmental perspectives and research. *Journal of Counseling Psychology, 54,* 259–270. http://dx.doi.org/10.1037/0022-0167.54.3.259

Rivas-Drake, D., Seaton, E. K., Markstrom, C., Quintana, S., Syed, M., Lee, R. M., . . . Ethnic and Racial Identity in the 21st Century Study Group. (2014). Ethnic and racial identity in adolescence: Implications for psychosocial, academic, and health outcomes. *Child Development, 85,* 40–57. http://dx.doi.org/10.1111/cdev.12200

Rivas-Drake, D., Syed, M., Umaña-Taylor, A., Markstrom, C., French, S., Schwartz, S. J., . . . Ethnic and Racial Identity in the 21st Century Study Group. (2014). Feeling good, happy, and proud: A meta-analysis of positive ethnic-racial affect and adjustment. *Child Development, 85,* 77–102. http://dx.doi.org/10.1111/cdev.12175

Roberts, R. E., Phinney, J. S., Masse, L. C., Chen, Y. R., Roberts, C. R., & Romero, A. (1999). The structure of ethnic identity of young adolescents from diverse ethnocultural groups. *The Journal of Early Adolescence, 19,* 301–322. http://dx.doi.org/10.1177/0272431699019003001

Sarbin, T. R. (1986). The narrative as a root metaphor for psychology. In T. R. Sarbin (Ed.), *Narrative psychology: The storied nature of human conduct* (pp. 3–21). Westport, CT: Praeger.

Schachter, E. P. (2004). Identity configurations: A new perspective on identity formation in contemporary society. *Journal of Personality, 72,* 167–200. http://dx.doi.org/10.1111/j.0022-3506.2004.00260.x

Schachter, E. P. (2005). Context and identity formation: A theoretical analysis and a case study. *Journal of Adolescent Research, 20,* 375–395. http://dx.doi.org/10.1177/0743558405275172

Schwartz, S. J. (2001). The evolution of Eriksonian and neo-Eriksonian identity theory and research: A review and integration. *Identity: An International Journal of Theory and Research, 1,* 7–58. http://dx.doi.org/10.1207/S1532706XSCHWARTZ

Schwartz, S. J., Syed, M., Yip, T., Knight, G. P., Umaña-Taylor, A. J., Rivas-Drake, D., . . . Ethnic and Racial Identity in the 21st Century Study Group. (2014). Methodological issues in ethnic and racial identity research with ethnic minority populations: Theoretical precision, measurement issues, and research designs. *Child Development, 85,* 58–76. http://dx.doi.org/10.1111/cdev.12201

Sellers, R. M., Smith, M. A., Shelton, J. N., Rowley, S. A. J., & Chavous, T. M. (1998). Multidimensional model of racial identity: A reconceptualization of

African American racial identity. *Personality and Social Psychology Review, 2,* 18–39. http://dx.doi.org/10.1207/s15327957pspr0201_2

Smith, T. B., & Silva, L. (2011). Ethnic identity and personal well-being of people of color: A meta-analysis. *Journal of Counseling Psychology, 58,* 42–60. http://dx.doi.org/10.1037/a0021528

Syed, M. (2010a). Developing an integrated self: Academic and ethnic identities among ethnically diverse college students. *Developmental Psychology, 46,* 1590–1604. http://dx.doi.org/10.1037/a0020738

Syed, M. (2010b). Memorable everyday events in college: Narratives of the intersection of ethnicity and academia. *Journal of Diversity in Higher Education, 3,* 56–69. http://dx.doi.org/10.1037/a0018503

Syed, M. (2012a). College students' storytelling of ethnicity-related events in the academic domain. *Journal of Adolescent Research, 27,* 203–230. http://dx.doi.org/10.1177/0743558411432633

Syed, M. (2012b). The past, present, and future of Eriksonian identity research: Introduction to the special issue. *Identity: An International Journal of Theory and Research, 12,* 1–7. http://dx.doi.org/10.1080/15283488.2012.632362

Syed, M. (2013). Assessment of ethnic identity and acculturation. In K. Geisinger (Ed.), *APA handbook of testing and assessment in psychology* (pp. 393–405). Washington, DC: American Psychological Association.

Syed, M., & Azmitia, M. (2008). A narrative approach to ethnic identity in emerging adulthood: Bringing life to the identity status model. *Developmental Psychology, 44,* 1012–1027. http://dx.doi.org/10.1037/0012-1649.44.4.1012

Syed, M., & Azmitia, M. (2009). Longitudinal trajectories of ethnic identity during the college years. *Journal of Research on Adolescence, 19,* 601–624. http://dx.doi.org/10.1111/j.1532-7795.2009.00609.x

Syed, M., & Azmitia, M. (2010). Narrative and ethnic identity exploration: A longitudinal account of emerging adults' ethnicity-related experiences. *Developmental Psychology, 46,* 208–219. http://dx.doi.org/10.1037/a0017825

Syed, M., Azmitia, M., & Phinney, J. S. (2007). Stability and change in ethnic identity among Latino emerging adults in two contexts. *Identity: An International Journal of Theory and Research, 7,* 155–178. http://dx.doi.org/10.1080/15283480701326117

Syed, M., & Hu, A. (2013). *Diverging pathways of socialization from peers and parents to ethnic identity.* Manuscript in preparation.

Syed, M., & Juan, M. J. D. (2012). Discrimination and psychological distress: Examining the moderating role of social context in a nationally representative sample of Asian American adults. *Asian American Journal of Psychology, 3,* 104–120. http://dx.doi.org/10.1037/a0025275

Syed, M., Walker, L. H. M., Lee, R. M., Umaña-Taylor, A. J., Zamboanga, B. L., Schwartz, S. J., . . . Huynh, Q.-L. (2013). A two-factor model of ethnic identity exploration: Implications for identity coherence and well-being. *Cultural Diversity and Ethnic Minority Psychology, 19,* 143–154. http://dx.doi.org/10.1037/a0030564

Tajfel, H., & Turner, J. C. (1986). The social identity theory of intergroup behavior. In S. Worchel & W. G. Austin (Eds.), *Psychology of intergroup relations* (pp. 7–24). Chicago, IL: Nelson-Hall.

Taylor, J. M., Gilligan, C., & Sullivan, A. M. (1996). Missing voices, changing meanings: Developing a voice-centered, relational method and creating an interpretative community. In S. Wilkinson (Ed.), *Feminist social psychologies: International perspectives* (pp. 233–257). Buckingham, England: Open University Press.

Thorne, A. (2000). Personal memory telling and personality development. *Personality and Social Psychology Review, 4,* 45–56. http://dx.doi.org/10.1207/S15327957PSPR0401_5

Thorne, A., & McLean, K. C. (2003). Telling traumatic events in adolescence: A study of master narrative positioning. In R. Fivush & C. Haden (Eds.), *Autobiographical memory and the construction of a narrative self: Developmental and cultural perspectives* (pp. 169–185). Mahwah, NJ: Erlbaum.

Umaña-Taylor, A. J. (2001). *Ethnic identity development among Mexican-origin Latino adolescents living in the U.S.* Unpublished doctoral dissertation, University of Missouri, Columbia.

Umaña-Taylor, A. J. (2004). Ethnic identity and self-esteem: Examining the role of social context. *Journal of Adolescence, 27,* 139–146. http://dx.doi.org/10.1016/j.adolescence.2003.11.006

Umaña-Taylor, A. J., Quintana, S. M., Lee, R. M., Cross, W. E., Rivas-Drake, D., Schwartz, S. J., . . . Ethnic and Racial Identity in the 21st Century Study Group. (2014). Ethnic and racial identity during adolescence and into young adulthood: An integrated conceptualization. *Child Development, 85,* 21–39. http://dx.doi.org/10.1111/cdev.12196

Umaña-Taylor, A. J., Yazedjian, A., & Bámaca-Gómez, M. Y. (2004). Developing the Ethnic Identity Scale using Eriksonian and social identity perspectives. *Identity: An International Journal of Theory and Research, 4,* 9–38. http://dx.doi.org/10.1207/S1532706XID0401_2

Vo-Jutabha, E. D., Dinh, K. T., McHale, J. P., & Valsiner, J. (2009). A qualitative analysis of Vietnamese adolescent identity exploration within and outside an ethnic enclave. *Journal of Youth and Adolescence, 38,* 672–690. http://dx.doi.org/10.1007/s10964-008-9365-9

Walker, L. H. M., & Syed, M. (2011, October). *Emerging adults' stories of their ethnicity-related experiences: A narrative analysis of cognitive, affective, and behavioral components.* Paper presented at the 5th Conference on Emerging Adulthood, Providence, RI.

Wang, Q. (2008). Being American, being Asian: The bicultural self and autobiographical memory in Asian Americans. *Cognition, 107,* 743–751. http://dx.doi.org/10.1016/j.cognition.2007.08.005

Way, N., Santos, C., Niwa, E. Y., & Kim-Gervey, C. (2008). To be or not to be: An exploration of ethnic identity development in context. *New Directions for Child and Adolescent Development, 2008*(120), 61–79.

Weisskirch, R. S., Zamboanga, B. L., Ravert, R. D., Whitbourne, S. K., Park, I. J., Lee, R. M., & Schwartz, S. J. (2013). An introduction to the composition of the Multi-Site University Study of Identity and Culture (MUSIC): A collaborative approach to research and mentorship. *Cultural Diversity and Ethnic Minority Psychology, 19*, 123–130. http://dx.doi.org/10.1037/a0030099

Wohlwill, J. F. (1973). *The study of behavioral development*. New York, NY: Academic Press.

Yip, T. (2005). Sources of situational variation in ethnic identity and psychological well-being: A Palm Pilot study of Chinese American students. *Personality and Social Psychology Bulletin, 31*, 1603–1616. http://dx.doi.org/10.1177/0146167205277094

Yip, T., Gee, G. C., & Takeuchi, D. T. (2008). Racial discrimination and psychological distress: The impact of ethnic identity and age among immigrant and United States-born Asian adults. *Developmental Psychology, 44*, 787–800. http://dx.doi.org/10.1037/0012-1649.44.3.787

Yip, T., Seaton, E. K., & Sellers, R. M. (2006). African American racial identity across the lifespan: Identity status, identity content, and depressive symptoms. *Child Development, 77*, 1504–1517. http://dx.doi.org/10.1111/j.1467-8624.2006.00950.x

Yoo, H. C., & Lee, R. M. (2008). Does ethnic identity buffer or exacerbate the effects of frequent racial discrimination on situational well-being of Asian Americans? *Journal of Counseling Psychology, 55*, 63–74. http://dx.doi.org/10.1037/0022-0167.55.1.63

3

A CRITICAL ETHNOGRAPHIC APPROACH TO THE STUDY OF ETHNIC IDENTITY: CHILEAN MAPUCHE INTERCULTURAL BILINGUAL EDUCATION

PATRICIO ORTIZ, GUILLERMO WILLIAMSON,
AND ANNETTE HEMMINGS

Ethnographic fieldwork data collection methods and attendant analytical procedures have been used by educational researchers for decades. They are most commonly used in school ethnographies characterized by fieldwork carried out in the natural settings of classrooms, corridors, and administrative offices. Ethnography has deep roots in anthropology, and many school ethnographers situate themselves in the subfield of educational anthropology, which specializes in research on cultural processes in schools and other educational settings framed by anthropological theories and constructs.

Up until the late 1960s, most school ethnographers studied the transmission of mainstream or local cultural knowledge in schools with attention to processes of enculturation (socialization into one's own culture), acculturation (learning appropriate behaviors in a host culture), and accommodations that come about when people with new or different cultural knowledge come into contact (Singleton, 1974). This emphasis changed dramatically in the 1970s,

http://dx.doi.org/10.1037/14618-004
Studying Ethnic Identity: Methodological and Conceptual Approaches Across Disciplines, C. E. Santos and A. J. Umaña-Taylor (Editors)

when neo-Marxism, feminism, semiotics, hermeneutics, and other intellectual movements were infused with some ferment into the fields of anthropology and sociology (Anderson, 1989). School ethnographers during this period began to concentrate much more attention on the persistent academic under-achievement patterns of racial, ethnic, and immigrant minority students. Rather than endorsing the prevailing view that low-performing minority students came from culturally deficient families, they regarded the behaviors attributed to low school performance as expressions of cultural resistance to the dominant mainstream culture transmitted in schools (McDermott, 1974; Ogbu, 1978).

Ethnic identity was, and still is, emphasized in this line of inquiry as a powerful psychocultural force compelling whether or how students resist or accommodate to schooling (Dolby & Dimitriadis, 2004; Holland, Lachicotte, Skinner, & Cain, 2001; McCarty et al., 2005; Willis, 1981; Zou & Trueba, 2002). It has been honed as an analytical construct through a steady succession of theories as well as major paradigmatic shifts, especially post-modernism and poststructuralism. New approaches to ethnography also emerged. Among them is critical ethnography, which appeared on the methodological scene as an applied form of ethnography that could be used to understand and possibly alter local cultural knowledge in ways that foster social change (Creswell, 1998).

Critical ethnography is informed by versions of critical theory and critical paradigms that as a whole are concerned with how power, culture, social status, and other phenomena disempower impoverished people, racial and ethnic minorities, and other historically marginalized groups (Gulati, 2011). It is geared toward changing the conditions of stigmatized or oppressed people through critical dialogue and the demystification of cultural ideology (Quantz, 1992). The ultimate aim of critical ethnography is cultural and social transformation.

Critical ethnography is a transformative extension of traditional ethnography. The approach not only seeks to explicate cultural processes but also strives to empower marginalized groups through the power of group members' own identities and ways of life. It can be especially empowering in settings such as schools, where the transmission of culture is intentional and pedagogies can be intentionally developed to affirm, challenge, or create cultural meanings and practices aimed at freeing students from sources of domination and repression (Anderson, 1989).

The focus of this chapter is on critical ethnography as an extension of traditional ethnography and how the approach can be used to unveil and transform ethnic identities within a school setting. The methodology associated with critical ethnography is described with attention to the use of conventional fieldwork data collection methods. Also described are the overarching research purpose, intellectual orientation, and approaches to analysis and findings embraced by critical ethnographers. This description is followed by a discussion of how definitions of ethnic identity are rendered into analytical categories that enhance the ideological aspects of cultural practices and meanings. A critical ethnography is then presented of an intercultural bilingual education (IBE) program in a Chilean elementary school serving impoverished rural indigenous Mapuche children. A primary focus of the study was on how Kimche Painemilla, a local community sage, worked as an IBE teacher to facilitate the reconstruction of Mapuche ethnic identity, transmit Mapuche culture, and create an epistemological space for critical dialogue on the basis of historical and political counternarrative texts. We conclude with a discussion of the limitations of critical ethnography for studying ethnic identity, best practices, and recommendations for future research.

CRITICAL ETHNOGRAPHY

Fieldwork Data Collection Methods

Critical ethnographers use conventional ethnographic fieldwork data collection methods, which include participant observation, in-depth semistructured one-on-one interviews and focus groups, and collection of archival materials. Participant observation is a signature ethnographic method and involves prolonged observations of research participants' behaviors and verbal interactions in natural settings that are recorded in field notes or on film, videotape, or electronic digital devices (Denzin & Lincoln, 2000; Spradley, 1980). This method can provide insight into cultures that are unfamiliar to researchers or are hidden or off limits to many outsiders. The observational data it generates can also be used to corroborate or contradict what participants verbally say or write.

Semistructured interviews conducted during one-on-one sessions and focus groups are effective means for eliciting the cultural knowledge and emic perspectives of people who inhabit the settings being studied. They are often conversational in style, but open-ended questions are intentionally constructed to uncover the dimensions, boundaries, expressions and other aspects of culture from the point of view of the people who live it (Schensul, Schensul, & LeCompte, 1999; Spradley, 1979). Archival materials such as artwork, printed or handwritten texts, and photographs are also routinely collected in critical ethnography. Although data collection methods in critical ethnography are conventional, the overarching research purpose and intellectual orientation associated with the approach are quite distinctive.

Research Purpose and Intellectual Orientation

Ethnography has traditionally been geared toward investigations of a social group's culture, subculture, or particular cultural scene. The focus of fieldwork is on daily routines, behaviors, values, beliefs, norms, rituals, dress, and other practices and meanings that can be rendered into descriptions of cultural patterns in the life of the group (Fetterman, 1998; LeCompte & Schensul, 1999b; Spradley, 1980). The overarching purpose of *critical* ethnography is radically distinct. The intent of the approach is to unveil and possibly transform the practices and meanings that perpetuate inequalities and social injustices. Critical ethnography is applied research wrought with political agendas and social critiques. The intellectual orientation associated with the approach has a decidedly critical thrust with regard to the theories favored by researchers and how local cultural meanings are conceptually located in larger impersonal systems of political economy.

Critical ethnographers gravitate intellectually toward thinkers who focus attention on how cultural, social, linguistic, and other forces perpetuate social inequalities and injustices. They have embraced neo-Marxist critical thought with roots in the Frankfurt School; Pierre Bourdieu's insights on cultural reproduction resulting from the unequal distribution of power embedded in social, cultural, symbolic, and other forms of capital (Bourdieu, 1977; Bourdieu & Passeron, 1990; Bourdieu & Wacquant, 1992); the sociolinguistics of Basil Bernstein (1971), who explains how elaborated and restricted language codes contribute to social stratification; and a host of other theoreticians.

Some of the theories that are especially relevant to the study presented in this chapter explain how resistance through cultural counternarratives (narratives that counter dominant culture) can become key components of agency and identity construction in schools (Dolby & Dimitriadis, 2004; Foley, 2010; Giroux & McLaren, 1996; Levinson, Foley, & Holland, 1996; McLaren, 2006; Scott, 1992; Willis, 1981). Also influential was the work of critical educational anthropologists who promote the notion of cultural production as an orientation toward agency that moves beyond cultural reproduction (Levinson & Holland, 1996). The study was additionally informed by contemporary postmodern and poststructural insights. The rise of poststructuralism was fueled by the germinal work of Michel Foucault (1979, 1990), who construed human social systems as discursive epistemological spaces imbued with disciplinary power supported by tacit discourses (culturally constructed representations of realities) where knowledge and power are combined in ways that affect the psychology, thoughts, and identities of people (Pignatelli, 1998; Rabinow, 1984). Postmodern critical theory essentially politicizes social problems by situating them in historical and cultural contexts (Best & Kellner, 1991; Jameson, 1990).

Critical ethnographers, regardless of their theoretical leanings, politicize cultural practices and meanings as key to understanding the perpetuation of social inequalities and injustices (Carspecken, 1996). Another aspect of their intellectual orientation is the conceptual location of cultural practices and meanings within larger political and economic systems. These systems are construed as the historical and contemporary contexts within which people do what they do. The practices and meanings within these contexts are often regarded as common sense by inhabitants, but they are imbued with ideological standpoints and socioeconomic interests that affect relations of power. There are, in other words, predetermined intellectual orientations that affect how critical ethnographers construe contexts and how they study the people within these contexts. These orientations have a direct bearing on data analyses and how findings are interpreted.

Analysis and Findings

Critical ethnographers also use conventional procedures for analyzing fieldwork data. These procedures are recursive and iterative in that data analysis begins the moment the researcher enters the field and continues until the final write-up is complete. Analysis is practically accomplished through coding processes in which data are connected, broken apart, or synthesized into analytical categories and interpreted with reference to theoretical or other kinds of frameworks (LeCompte & Schensul, 1999a).

What distinguishes critical ethnography in their analyses is that the analytical categories they generate have ideological aspects. Critical ethnographers in education do not view categories such as *giftedness* or *dropouts* as nonproblematic. Rather, they locate them in larger political and economic contexts in ways that shed ideological light on whose interests are being served and how dominant groups benefit from maintaining "commonsense" meanings as they are currently defined (Anderson, 1989). Data are coded with these conceptually front-loaded analytical categories in mind, and findings are interpreted in light of researchers' critical intellectual orientations. Critical ethnographic studies are ultimately written as cultural and social critiques that ideally shed light on, guide, and/or incite transformative change. What follows are definitions of ethnic identity in educational anthropology and how critical ethnographers have rendered them into constructs that highlight ideological aspects, especially those related to political resistance and accommodation.

ETHNIC IDENTITY IN CRITICAL ETHNOGRAPHY

Ethnic identity has been traditionally defined by educational anthropologists as comprising individuals' innermost psychocultural commitments as well as their social and psychological allegiances to ethnic groups (Hoffman, 1998; Spindler & Spindler, 1992; Trueba & Zou, 1998). People who share an ethnic identity have memories of a common past, attachments to demarcated territories, cultural traditions, and folklore in which collective actions, including historical (re)enactments of important events, become central to group dynamics (Cohen, 1994). Shared ethnic identities involve perceived group boundaries that can be sustained by objective cultural characteristics such as language and religion, a more subjective sense of "groupness," or some combination of both (Barth, 1969; Edwards, 2009).

School ethnographers in the 1980s and 1990s, especially those who were drawn to the theories of John Ogbu, examined the role that racial and ethnic identity played in minority students' resistance or accommodation to schooling (Fordham, 1996; Fordham & Ogbu, 1986; Ogbu, 1978, 1987; Ogbu & Simons, 1998). Critical ethnographers enhanced the political and ideological aspects of resistance and accommodation by emphasizing how schools serving the interests of dominant groups suppress ethnic identities and how some ethnic minority students stage political opposition by reconstructing their identities in ways that are self-valorizing, that are expressed in opposition to dominant cultures, or that lead to transformative change (Foley, 2002; Levinson & Holland, 1996; Trueba & Zou, 1998).

This enhancement is evident in a study that Foley (2010) conducted in a high school located in an economically depressed, predominantly Mexican-American town in Texas. The school is portrayed as "dedicated to stripping kids of their ethnic identity and replacing it with an institutional, mainstream identity" (p. 161). Rather than have their identities stripped away, Chicano students resisted and produced their own ethnic identities through "expressive practices" as institutionally situated forms of "communicative labor" that secured their positions in "capitalist culture" (p. 161). They reconstructed their ethnic identities in ways that symbolically countered the oppressive dominant culture and stigmatization of Chicanos in their school.

Other critical ethnographers by the end of the 1990s were generating more poststructural/postmodern studies of ethnic identity. Davidson (1996), citing Foucault, observed how the cultural productions of Chicano students in a California high school were constantly reemerging in new shapes and forms. Students' ethnic identities were fluid rather than fixed, changing from one context to another, and seemingly inconsistent in how they were expressed in opposition to, or in agreement with, school expectations. Students' ethnic identity work was elastic within the institutional constraints of academic tracking, disciplinary practices, and bureaucratic relations. Hemmings (2006), in a study of the coming of age of Christina, an underachieving Mexican American girl in a predominantly White upper-middle-class school, also observed fluid expressions of ethnic identity productions. Christina's shifting identity work was quite remarkable in how it opened up "possibilities for the expression of creative agency within powerful cultural crosscurrents and institutional structures" (p. 129).

Ethnic identity as an ideologically enhanced construct has enabled critical ethnographers conducting research in schools to unveil, affirm, and occasionally transform students' innermost psychocultural commitments and social/psychological allegiances to ethnic groups. But as the following study indicates, empowering ethnic identities can also be fostered by teachers who assume "critical" instructional roles.

CRITICAL ETHNOGRAPHY IN THE STUDY OF ETHNIC IDENTITY IN AN IBE PROGRAM IN CHILE

The lead author, Patricio Ortiz, conducted a critical ethnographic study of Kimche Painemilla, a community sage teacher who taught in an elementary school serving indigenous Mapuche children living in a rural region of Chile. The school had an IBE program established to teach Mapuche children about their indigenous culture and language and bolster a positive sense of their ethnic identity. Kimche Painemilla's classroom was ideal for a study of how a politically astute teacher unveiled and, in this case, strengthened ethnic identity in ways intended to empower ethnic minority children.

Kimches are community sages who are one of three main authorities in Mapuche ancestral tradition that also includes the *Longko* (head of the community) and the *Machi* (shaman). Kimches are the keepers of Kimün indigenous knowledge; speakers of Mapuzungun, the indigenous language; and highly respected indigenous educators. Kimche Painemilla resided in the rural Pacific village of Piedra Alta in the ADI-Budi area of Chile. The majority of residents in Piedra Alta are indigenous Mapuche people, most of whom live in poverty. Historically, Mapuche ethnic groups have been politically subjugated in a country dominated by Euro-Chileans. The local elementary school in Piedra Alta has an IBE program that was implemented as a result of collective political action on the part of indigenous people throughout South America. Kimche Painemilla was employed as an IBE teacher in the school. His job was to teach Mapuche children about their culture and language and affirm their ethnic identity.

A critical ethnographic study was conducted in Kimche Painemilla's classroom for several months that focused on how, despite some community and student resistance, he strengthened Mapuche ethnic identity, transmitted Mapuche culture, and raised historical and political consciousness about Mapuche oppression. The following narrative account of what the study unveiled begins with the historical context for IBE programs.

HISTORICAL CONTEXT FOR IBE PROGRAMS

Critical ethnographers take into account the historical contexts within which ethnic group members are situated, especially the political and economic aspects of these contexts. They do so to understand the history of relations between dominant and marginalized groups and discern whose interests are currently being served in a setting. It was thus vital for the research on Kimche Painemilla to gather and critically analyze historical information.

The history of IBE programs began decades ago in colonial Latin America when indigenous people were subjected to systematic efforts on the part of the government to eradicate their traditional cultures and languages through forced assimilation into Eurocentric ways of life. Public schools were the primary institutions where policies of forced assimilation were imposed on indigenous children (Bengoa, 1998; Hornberger, 1996; López, 2008). This policy was challenged during the 1990s when indigenous people engaged in concerted political action to end forced assimilation and subjugation at international, national, and local levels. Internationally, the Declaration of Rights of Indigenous People was adopted by the United Nations General Assembly in 2007, preceded in 1989 by an avowal of indigenous people's rights by the International Labor Organization. At the national level, a number of constitutional amendments were passed in Latin American countries that officially acknowledged cultural and linguistic diversity (Stavenhagen, 1997). Indigenous people were elected to high political offices, including the president of Bolivia in 2005 and vice president of Ecuador in 1993.

Indigenous political movements at the local level incited uprisings such as the one that occurred in Chiapas, Mexico. The Chiapas uprising had a profound impact in Mexico and inspired protests in cities across Latin America. These and other events were a defining political moment for indigenous people (Bengoa, 2000; Hernández, 2003).

The actions that ignited political change in the 1990s in many respects were cultural movements aimed at addressing the cultural, linguistic, and educational needs of indigenous people. Indigenous people demanded legislation and public policies that protected their rights to maintain cultural and linguistic traditions. These movements led to the revitalization of ethnic identities that, in turn, strengthened indigenous people's allegiance to, and expressions of, indigenous knowledge, language, and traditional culture (Cajete, 2008;

Díaz-Coliñir, 1999; Macedo, 1999). Indigenous people at the most localized level of their everyday lives began to reconstruct their ethnic identities and redefine group boundaries into sociocultural spaces where they could express objective cultural characteristics (i.e., language, religion, rites) and create a subjective sense of groupness (Barth, 1969; Edwards, 2009; Williamson, 2012).

Despite the significant progress incited by political and cultural movements, Latin American countries like Chile, with low percentages of indigenous people, continued to struggle with whether or how to sustain ethnic identities and traditions in nation-states dominated by neocolonial governments and institutions that promote Eurocentric cultural commitments and privileges (Ortiz, 2009a, 2009b; Williamson, Pinkney-Pastrana, & Gomez, 2005). This is especially true in schools where dominant Eurocentric culture and languages are transmitted in ways that threaten the ethnic identities and traditional ways of life of indigenous children.

Educational initiatives have been launched in Latin America to make schools less culturally threatening and more culturally responsive. Among them are IBE programs implemented in countries with large indigenous populations, such as Bolivia, Guatemala, Ecuador, Mexico, and Peru. These programs have also been introduced in countries like Chile and Argentina with much smaller percentages of indigenous populations (Chiodi, 1990; Hornberger, 1996; López, 2008; Ortiz, 2009b; Williamson, 2012). IBE pedagogies are intended to promote the valuing of indigenous cultures and languages as a means to strengthen a positive sense of ethnic identity among indigenous school children and youth (Ortiz, 2009a, 2009b; Semali & Kincheloe, 1999). Some of the IBE programs in Chile were implemented in elementary schools serving Mapuche children.

Despite their positive billing, the outcomes of IBE programs in schools serving Mapuche children in Chile are mixed. There are inherent difficulties with developing programs that simultaneously uphold mainstream Eurocentric schooling and preserve indigenous cultural and linguistic diversity (Williamson et al., 2005). Mainstream schooling conveys the particular sets of skills, knowledge, discourses, and other cultural practices that define what it means to be an "educated person" in ways that generally exclude the point of view of indigenous people (Levinson & Holland, 1996). The curriculum in Chilean public schools defines what it means to be an educated person within European standards as someone who possesses cultural and social capital validated within the dominant culture. It is the capital that enables people to secure social mobility, lucrative jobs, and access to power and advantages in specific social contexts (Bourdieu, 1977; Durston, 2004). But in Latin America, as in other parts of the world, such schooling for success has clearly not been the one provided to indigenous people. Research studies conducted by the World Bank indicated that the marginalization, impoverishment, poor health, and inadequate schooling of indigenous people have occurred throughout the Americas (Hall

& Patrinos, 2012; Ortiz, 2009a; Saavedra, 2002; Williamson, 2012). Mapuche indigenous people in Chile are no exception to these oppressive conditions.

THE MAPUCHE PEOPLE OF CHILE

The Mapuche people are the largest indigenous group in Chile, constituting 83.5% (604,349) of the total indigenous population and 4.7% of the total Chilean population of 15,047,652 (Instituto Nacional de Estadística de Chile, 2002). There were four distinctive Mapuche cultural groups at the initial point of contact with Spanish colonizers 500 years ago and three remain: the Pehuenches, Huilliches, and Lafkenches (Bengoa, 2000, 1998). Historically, the sociopolitical dynamics of Mapuche groups have been complex. After the war with the Chilean state in 1881, they were placed on reservations and subdivided into 3,000 rural kinship-based communities that through time have developed into highly differentiated political affiliations with intricate networks of relations. Mapuzungun, the Mapuche language, was transcribed into five different alphabets within a linguistic territory that included seven dialectical regions (Bengoa, 2000, 1998).

Economic hardship became endemic in rural Mapuche communities, resulting in a steady migration of adults to the larger cities of Chile. This has rendered many Mapuche into one of the most urbanized indigenous groups in the Americas, with 80% of its population living in the main five cities of Chile. This diversity within Mapuche groups adds to the complexity of the internal cultural, linguistic, and political dynamics of this ethnic group (Ortiz, 2009a, 2009b).

In terms of educational achievement, only 69.5% of Mapuche people under the age of 39 have attained an average of 8.5 years of formal schooling. Indications of disaffection from schooling are reflected in the school dropout rate among Mapuche students, of whom 30.4% never graduate and often leave school before eighth grade (Ortiz, 2009a, 2009b; Williamson et al., 2005).

Dismal school achievement patterns, historically complex intragroup cultural dynamics, poverty, and other factors have been challenging for IBE programs. Although government policies and institutions have taken different positions through time, the concept of IBE programs has been supported by the political Mapuche urban leadership but has been contested by some Mapuche communities in rural areas. IBE programs have acquired legitimacy under the current social democratic government in Chile. Laissez-faire policies and the indirect neutrality of the Chilean state and its educational bureaucracy have opened important ideological spaces for strong indigenous commitment to IBE programs. And yet, Mapuche rural community support has not been consistent or at the level necessary for their success.

Although IBE programs are enthusiastically promoted by some members of the urban Mapuche intellectual and political elite, they are not necessarily supported by the people most directly affected by them (Ortiz, 2009a, 2009b). Many rural Mapuche parents regard IBE programs as second-class education that does not concentrate enough attention on mainstream literacy skills (Díaz-Coliñir, 1999). Parents essentially want their children to be "educated persons" like the Winkas (mainstream Euro-Chileans) who can go to the cities to pursue economic opportunities and perform with the skills and the Spanish language that social mobility requires.

IBE program personnel and curricular requirements in Chile were directly affected by a law (DS. 280) that was passed in 2009. The law mandates that schools teach indigenous languages if their indigenous student population is 20% or more. Many schools in rural Mapuche communities were already in compliance before the law was implemented because they were incorporating Kimches (community sages) as teachers in local school IBE programs. Having Kimche community sages work as teachers in IBE programs became common practice in the early 2000s. The law passed in 2009 secured Kimches' position as stable figures in schools. Their position as representatives of, and cultural advisors for, Mapuche people was solidified by being elected as teachers by the community. What follows is an account of the work of Sergio Painemilla, a Kimche teacher who worked in the Piedra Alta elementary school located in the rural ADI-Budi region of the Araucanía of Chile. We begin with a description of the fieldwork conducted for the study.

FIELDWORK

The lead author, Patricio Ortiz, is a Chilean ethnographer who conducted the fieldwork for this study using conventional ethnographic data collection methods. He spent 6 months at the elementary school site, with most of his observations taking place in Kimche Painemilla's IBE classroom. His data were augmented by the findings of other studies conducted between 2002 and 2009 with school administrators, teachers, parents, students, community members, and government officials (Fontana & Frey, 2005). Archival data were also collected from sources in Chilean universities and research centers and from audiovisual depositories in the form of film, still photography, and sound recordings.

Substantial observational field notes were taken that were supplemented by still photography, video, and tape recordings amounting to approximately 50 hours of audiovisual material. Daily classroom observations were carried out for 3 months in the school's IBE program for 4 days a week. Extensive semi-structured interviews and informal conversations were conducted with Kimche

Painemilla. The interviews were conducted in Spanish, tape recorded, and transcribed. The most relevant parts of the interviews that were transcribed amounted to 80 pages of transcriptions. Conversations were also held with a few students.

The data collected in the study were used to construct vignettes of Kimche Painemilla's learning objectives and instructional practices. Data were also coded and interpreted with reference to poststructural/postmodern, linguistic, and other critical theoretical insights in educational anthropology to discern how Kimche Painemilla worked to facilitate the reconstruction of Mapuche ethnic identity. Phenomena categorized as ethnic identity and language code switching; knowledge and epistemological conflicts; and culturally relevant teaching, resistance, and counternarratives emerged as politically and ideologically enhanced themes central to understanding what transpired in Kimche Painemilla's classroom.

Research Site: Piedra Alta School

According to a 1999 socioeconomic report, the ADI-Budi area contains one of the highest concentrations of Mapuche people in Chile. An estimated 85% of this population under the age of 34 is literate in Spanish, with basic reading and writing skills (Ministerio de Planificación de Chile, 1999). Approximately 10% have never attended school; 63% have finished elementary school; 13% have gone to high school; and only 1.6% have attended college. The older segments of this population are less schooled than the younger. The illiteracy rate among those between 35 and 59 years old is 20%, and it is 45% for those over 60.

The Piedra Alta school in the ADI-Budi area is part of a network of schools in the region of the Araucanía owned by the Catholic Church and administered by its educational wing, the Fundación del Magisterio de la Araucanía (Educational Foundation of the Araucanía). It is an elementary school with Grades 1 through 8. Schools in indigenous Chilean communities do not go beyond Grade 8, so Mapuche students must go to an urban center if they decide to attend high school (educación media) Grades 9 through 12.

The student population of the Piedra Alta school at the time of the fieldwork was 99 children (49 boys and 50 girls), 98% of whom were Mapuche. The school had five teachers including the principal, who had a double assignment as teacher and administrator. There were four Kimche teachers, including two men and two women who taught in the IBE program. The Kimche teachers sometimes team-taught with regular teachers but were mostly working independently in their own classrooms.

The school facilities consisted of a series of one-story wood buildings. There were five classrooms, a teacher lounge/meeting room, a computer lab with six computers with Internet access, a cafeteria, a playground with soccer and volleyball courts, a garage with basic mechanical facilities for maintenance of a school bus, and the only public pay phone in the Piedra Alta area served by the school. The school was a gathering point for the community and thus served an important role in the development of social capital within the community (Durston, 2004).

All five teachers in the school lived in faculty housing on school grounds, and the 2% of non-Mapuche students were their children. At the time of the study, none of the regular teachers were Mapuche. They and their families were the only non-Mapuche residents in Piedra Alta.

The Piedra Alta school became well known during the late 1990s when the National Office of Indigenous Affairs (CONADI) implemented a series of pilot IBE programs in various areas of the Araucanía. The Piedra Alta school was chosen as an experimental site in the ADI-Budi area, and it soon developed a reputation for its innovative pedagogical practices, including the hiring of Kimches as IBE instructors. Sergio Painemilla was one of the Kimches who was teaching in the school during fieldwork for the study. He became a focal point because of the reconstructive ethnic identity work he was trying to accomplish.

Ethnographic Vignette: Portrait of Kimche Painemilla at Work

Kimche Painemilla began class like most teachers by trying to establish order among the boisterous children in front of him. "Son, sit down and keep quiet!" he exclaimed. "Daughter, stop talking! Silence all, we need to begin!" Dressed in a dignified mixture of native *Campesino* dress and the typical garb of rural schoolteachers with books in his hands, he had the look of a distinguished Mapuche intellectual. His witty sense of humor and bright-eyed, full-faced smile revealed the vivacious mind of a wise and well-read man with a clear sense of the history and place of his people.

The classroom was adorned with flags, posters, decorations, and other symbolic representations of the republican nation-state, with few images of Mapuche indigenous traditions or children. This virtual exclusion of Mapuche culture in the classroom settings was rectified every day by Kimche Painemilla's lessons about the next coming Nguillatún and other local indigenous celebrations and practices linked to ancestral Kimün knowledge. He routinely switched back and forth from the Mapuche Mapudungun language to Spanish, fashioning an oral narrative of Mapuche cultural and linguistic experiences that was combined and juxtaposed with dominant culture and Spanish. The value and uniqueness of having a Kimche as a teacher became clear as Don Sergio, as he was known among students, worked to create a culturally relevant pedagogy that validated Mapuche ethnic identity and opened up a discursive epistemological space where students could negotiate "cultures in between" (Bhabha, 1998). The space was conducive for the reconstruction of ethnic identities and also for dialogues that raised critical awareness of and resistance to Eurocentric epistemologies and patterns of instruction that have historically dominated formal schooling for indigenous people (Freire & Faúndez, 1989; Giroux & McLaren, 1996). Historically silenced indigenous perspectives became a visibly important part of the foundation of knowledge, experiences, and cognitive resources used by Kimche Painemilla to foster learning among Mapuche students. They were key to how he worked to strengthen his students' Mapuche ethnic identity.

CRITICAL ETHNOGRAPHIC EMPOWERMENT

Reconstructing Mapuche Students' Ethnic Identity

The fieldwork for the study was essentially accomplished through traditional ethnographic data collection methods. Critical ethnography goes beyond conventional methodology by actively seeking ways to empower marginalized or oppressed people. In the case of Kimche Painemilla, empowerment entailed the intentional reconstruction of Mapuche ethnic identity and the preservation of traditional cultural knowledge and ways.

Mapuche children are growing up in the cultural aftermath of the forced assimilation of their ancestors over many generations. They have come to embrace Eurocentric views under the strong influence of the dominant culture. Media and digital technology have opened their formerly isolated, rural indigenous communities to global cultural and economic influences that have transformed traditional ways of life.

Although it is controversial, many Chilean scholars have argued that Mapuche youngsters have almost completely lost their ancestral culture and language (Saavedra, 2002). According to Grebe (1998), urban Mapuche youngsters face even more intense pressure for assimilation in metropolitan centers, where indigenous cultures and languages are more stigmatized. Discontinuity and asymmetric relations of power between cultures demean the value of indigenous cultures and languages with enormously negative effects on Mapuche children's perceptions of reality, personality development, and ethnic identity construction (Díaz-Coliñir, 1999). Defensive mechanisms of "ethnic masquerading" and "ethnic identity shifts" arise and may result in children denying their ethnic backgrounds and traditions in public spaces (Hernández, 2003). This can have disturbing consequences for the emotional well-being and intellectual development of Mapuche children.

Only 20% of students who were interviewed claimed Mapudungun as their native language and almost 80% declared having only a fair understanding of it. Most defined themselves as native Spanish speakers. And yet, their sense of being Mapuche was quite strong and came across as natural given the school's location in an indigenous community. A group of students expressed their identity as follows:

> We are Mapuche-Lafkenches, and we feel very happy about it because we have a different race, culture, and history, and we live in the country. But we also like the idea of being Chileans. We learned how to speak Spanish before Mapudungun, which is very different from our grandparents who learned Mapudungun first and Spanish later. I guess we can say that we are more Mapuche than Chileans, but I guess we are both.

There were no apparent conflicts or tensions between students' identity as Mapuche and schooling processes, even though their Mapudungun language skills were not strong. Identities and other messages in the school were expressed mainly through the Spanish language. The apparent lack of conflict in being immersed in the Spanish language and culture of the school was evident in the frequent use of language code-switching for communicating between and within groups.

Code switching from Spanish to Mapudungun and vice versa was a regular occurrence in IBE classrooms. Kimches, including Kimche Painemilla, created abbreviated forms of dual-immersion language practices as they code switched from one language to the other, sustaining long stretches of speech in each language. But Mapudungun language as an independent subject was not officially taught in the Piedra Alta school. Spanish was the dominant language of both instruction and spontaneous interactions among students in the classroom and school facilities. It was also the language dominant in many family and community settings (Ortiz, 2009a, 2009b).

Teaching Mapudungun as an independent subject had become controversial within some of the communities of the area, so Kimches began to use it as a complement to Spanish, the language most widely understood by students. Kimche Painemilla explained the challenges that previous Kimches had faced when they refused to speak Spanish in their classes:

> One of the main problems that the older generation of Kimches had in school with the Mapuche children was that they refused to speak and deliver their classes in Spanish. It is very sad to say, but I quickly realized that if I spoke only in Mapudungun to my Mapuche students, I would lose their attention very soon, because they clearly did not understand what I was saying.

Although the Mapuzungun language was present in the IBE program far more than in any other classes in the school, it supplemented rather than displaced Spanish as the language of the classroom. The alternating use of the two languages not only ensured that students understood what was said, but also placed Mapuzungun alongside Spanish as equally valuable, thus producing two-way linguistic avenues for the development and expression of ethnic identities. Students could learn to express their identities through code switching rather than completely deny or silence their Mapuche selves.

Preserving Traditional Cultural Knowledge and Ways of Life

Kimün indigenous knowledge and epistemologies were also transmitted by Kimche teachers as necessary for ethnic identity reconstruction and the preservation of traditional knowledge and ways of life. Kimche Painemilla worked to create a discursive epistemological space in his classroom where he could convey Kimün. But he faced fierce opposition in the community from some members, especially parents who did not see the usefulness of transmitting Kimün in school if it displaced the knowledge their children needed to compete in the cities. Knowledge is power, and many Mapuche parents feared their children would be disempowered if Kimün supplanted mainstream school curriculum and language. Although Kimches once held high status within Mapuche communities as scholars and teachers, current "school" Kimches were much less revered because some members of the community and school perceived the knowledge they were teaching as inappropriate.

Despite the conflict and loss of status, Kimche Painemilla was convinced that Kimün was and could be empowering. He and other Kimche teachers were organic intellectuals in the sense that they were local intellectuals emerging from the cultural grassroots of their communities rather than from the urban Mapuche intellectual elite schooled in Western academic institutions. There are important ideological differences between the Mapuche urbanized intellectual elite and the Mapuche rural organic intellectual who remains part of the social fabric of the rural community environment. Rural Kimches remain rooted in traditional Mapuche epistemology and are actively involved in traditional religious-ceremonial practices and political roles in their indigenous communities.

Placing organic intellectual Kimches rather than formally educated teachers in the schools of the ADI-Budi area fueled the opposition from sectors of Mapuche communities. The school of Piedra Alta was an interesting case in point. Two of the current Kimches began the IBE pilot programs in that school more than a decade ago. One of them was Sergio Painemilla, a well-respected community elder linked directly to the Painemilla lineage of Longkos community chiefs dominant in the Lof communities of Piedra Alta. The other was Roberto Millao, a Ngenpin who is the master of ceremonies of the main Mapuche ancestral ceremony called the Nguillatún. Both men were widely respected persons in their indigenous communities. But as Kimches in the school they have, according to Kimche Painemilla, encountered disapproval by some community members who argue that they have no formal teacher training and their knowledge in matters of the Winka (mainstream Chilean) world is not enough for them to be teaching their children in schools. Kimche Roberto Millao said,

> Although there is nothing personal against Kimches as members of the Mapuche communities, there is a natural lack of trust toward them as teachers in schools by some Mapuche parents. Some Kimches have definitely been viewed as unacceptable teachers by some in the community.

During a school meeting, a parent voiced her strong opinion about a prospective Kimche teacher:

> He is not a teacher; he has no educational nor pedagogical training. So why should he be teaching our children in school? We oppose him in our school as a teacher. We do not need the school to teach the Mapuche culture and language; we can do that at home. We want our children to be prepared for the Winka (mainstream) world.

Kimche Painemilla was more optimistic and felt that although there has been opposition toward Kimche teachers, there has also been slow improvement in the situation. In his words:

> At the beginning, many Mapuche parents thought that taking the Mapuche culture into the school was going to take us backwards, that Mapuche culture was not what people needed in schools, and that schools were places to learn Spanish and everything needed by Mapuche children when they move to live into the cities. But now, there are larger numbers of parents who have become enthusiastic about the idea of the Kimches. Some Mapuche people used to say that the Mapudungun language was not worth it at all, that it had no use outside of the community; now they have another opinion about it. The teaching of Mapuche culture in the school has had an important impact, even among the parents of the children in school. We are slowly reversing a situation of opposition coming from some in the Mapuche communities toward IBE programs and Kimches as teachers in schools. We are moving toward one of more acceptance and support. Things are looking better every day.

Kimche Painemilla, during interviews, offered extensive portraits of his life and the power of Kimün from a very early age when he went with his older sister into the housekeeping service of a wealthy family from Santiago, who sent him to school and gave him access to the educational resources of the household in which he lived. He told me how despite the advantages he was given in the city, he had to deal with an urban cultural environment that stigmatized and discriminated against his indigenous background and experience. He met his Mapuche wife in Santiago, and the two formed a family. In 1973, the military dictatorship seized power through a violent coup d'état. He became a labor union activist in the industrial corridor of Santiago and was forced into hiding by the political repression that struck the country. He decided to move incognito back to his isolated ancestral home in the ADI-Budi area. There he received a piece of land from his father and the protection and recognition of his Mapuche community as a man of learning. There was no turning back, only moving forward as an organic intellectual who understood the life-sustaining power of Kimün in a nation-state where political power has been violently contested.

CRITICAL PEDAGOGY

Critical ethnographers in school settings often look for or develop empowering critical pedagogies. Kimche Painemilla, a case in point, was a sage who made a conscious effort to implement critical pedagogy at the Piedra Alta school. He became a Kimche who in time became a teacher, and as a teacher, he encountered challenging classroom dynamics. He explained:

> At the beginning it is always very difficult because students are in many ways very disconnected from their own indigenous history and language. In a certain way, I have to entice them and make them understand that we are friends and we can have fun with the Mapudungun language, our past history, our traditions and knowledge as Mapuche people. I wish things would be different, but they are not. It does not happen by itself; among the young people today, there is a lot of deeply ingrained natural resistance to our own indigenousness. Today, one needs to convince the children of the importance of becoming Mapuche again.

The learning objectives and sequence of Kimche Painemilla's instruction were not based on externally designed or mandated curriculum, but rather on the Mapuche calendar of ritual events celebrated by communities in the ADI-Budi area. Kimche Painemilla's primary focus of instruction was on the cosmology and Kimün indigenous knowledge connected to community celebrations. His instructional strategies were based on traditional oral transmission practices among Mapuche people. His approach linked ethnohistorical facsimiles of past events with current events in the community. He accomplished this in part by weaving his own life experiences into his teachings. Kimche Painemilla explained how he became a Kimche:

> It was many years ago, when I had just returned from Santiago, that I was asked to deliver an eulogy in a Eluwün (funeral) of a respected and beloved member of the community. Mapuche Eluwüns have long dis-

courses and sometimes become an event that lasts for several days. They become a historical and personal reflection for the family and the community of the deceased. I gave a really heartfelt eulogy in Mapudungun delivered in a Ngütram format (dialogues from which children learn indirectly about events) of what I thought the deceased had contributed to his family and to our Mapuche community. When I finished, to my surprise, I could see that people were very impressed with my delivery, and my words had deeply touched them to the heart to a point where they even applauded my performance. This was something I did not expect at all as it is something very unusual in a solemn occasion such as a funeral. It is not customary for Mapuche people to applaud at a funeral, but there it was. They applauded and this event really became a turning point for me, in terms of my standing within the community. I was asked to become a Kimche when the time arrived.

The main learning objectives defining Kimche Painemilla's curriculum was the strengthening of Mapuche ethnic identity, transmission of Kimün, Mapuche indigenous knowledge and cosmology, and other traditions. In the classroom discursive epistemological space, he organized his teaching around perennial community events such as the Nguillatún (thanksgiving to the Gods) taking place in December; the Mapuche New Year celebration Wachipantu in June; and the Mingaco and Kelluwün, which entailed cooperative work related to agricultural activities of planting, harvesting, and threshing. Other important community ceremonies that did not have fixed dates—such as Machitúns healing ceremonies done by Machis shamans, Palín sport/ritual games similar to hockey on grass, Mafüns weddings, Eluwüns burials, Rucan community construction of houses, and other unexpected community events—were incorporated into his IBE curriculum as they took place in the Lof group of communities served by the school.

Referring in class to the Nguillatún, the main thanksgiving ceremony for Gnechen, the main Mapuche deity, Kimche Painemilla explained to his students:

> In the case of the Nguillatún, we see that there has been a big change between what the Spanish chroniclers such as Ercilla and others reported from a long time ago, to what we can find in the stories of Pascual Coña from the last century and what we live today here in the ADI-Budi. I remember my grandfather telling me something he saw was similar to what I saw when I was very young. But that is clearly not what we always see that exists today as the Nguillatún in many of our communities. Things have changed very much. But evidence that Kimün still exists is that the Nguillatún still exits, because we believe in it. It is our main thanksgiving event to our ancestral gods.

Mapuche communities and people are linked together through highly interconnected and extended kinship-based networks that transmit Mapuche historical memory and Kimün indigenous knowledge and language. Mapuche ethnic identity relies heavily on these links, and Kimche Painemilla constantly tapped into them during his classes as a way to produce meanings for personal and group identity reconstruction. "Who were your grandfather and grandmother, and who were your great-grandfather and great-grandmother?" asked Kimche Painemilla as he assigned students to draw genealogical trees mapping their ancestral interconnections as branches of a Foye cinnamon tree, the sacred ritual tree of the Mapuche. Students linked the names and histories of their grandparents (*Folil-melche* or four roots) as the foundational components of their Mapuche identity during classroom recognition of local community events in the present and Mapuche historical events of the past. The Mapuche concepts of *Tuwün* as the maternal line of descent, *Küpan* as the paternal line, and *Küpalme* as the community line also played central roles in classroom conversations as Kimche Painemilla constructed knowledge and meaning of past events linked to the present as a form of culturally relevant pedagogy and identity construction processes.

Kimche Painemilla, during the course of his teaching, not only facilitated the reconstruction of Mapuche ethnic identity and transmission of traditional knowledge and ways of life but also attempted to introduce historical and political counternarratives that challenged the power and privilege of dominant groups and their perceptions about Mapuche people. He used indigenous texts for these counternarratives, such as the autobiographical work of Pascual Coña (1984), *Testimonio de un Cacique Mapuche* (Testimony of a Mapuche Chief), considered a key ethnographic document during the late 19th and early 20th century. Coña was a resident of Piedra Alta and a distant relative of Kimche Painemilla. His memoir is the only ethnographic account written by a Mapuche on the life of the Mapuche-Lafkenches in the ADI-Budi area. It was an important source of curriculum material that Kimche Painemilla used for the construction of counternarratives such as the story of a trip that Coña took to Argentina. Kimche Painemilla told his students:

> Longko (Chief) Pascual Painemilla, who was the organizer of the famous 1882 expedition to Buenos Aires in which Pascual Coña and a group of Mapuche leaders went to visit Argentina's President Roca to negotiate the release of Mapuche prisoners of war in that country, had a son named Pascual Segundo Painemilla, who created the current Lof communities of Piedra Alta in 1903 after the war of conquest waged by the Chilean state and army against the Mapuche, following the great Malón uprising of 1881. Pascual Segundo Painemilla had a son named Esteban, and Esteban had a son named Sergio, and that is obviously me. Therefore I am a great-grandson of Pascual Painemilla, who was a close friend and relative of Pascual Coña, who, with a Capuchin monk, wrote the famous book about his life. Many years ago, once I knew about the book of Coña, I began investigating his life, and I discovered that he had been born and

raised here in the Lof of Piedra at that time called Reuquenhue. We can read in Coña's introduction to his book: The old Mapuche knew how to name the stars, the birds and all creatures that fly in the air. The animals that walked over the surface of the earth and the insects over the plants. They had a name, even for the rocks. I know very well the human beings that live in Reuquenhue and in other regions because through traveling I have gone around half of the world.

Kimche Painemilla added, "We will see how Coña tells us about the stories of our Mapuche communities in his book written a long time ago, and we will try to compare them with how we see them today."

Kimche Painemilla also used some biographical materials of early colonial Spanish chroniclers of Mapuche life, such as the *Cautiverio Feliz* of Nuñez de Pineda and F. Bascuñan (1673), clearly sympathetic to the Mapuche cause. Reinterpreting the meanings of the Spanish colonial texts through his oral narratives coming from his Mapuche-Lafkenche tradition, Kimche Painemilla continually portrayed the events depicted by these Spanish chronicles as counternarratives to the official Chilean mainstream historiography. In this way, he was reinforcing Vanciana's (1985) concept of oral tradition as an alternative form of historical reconstruction. In relation to *Cautiverio Feliz*, Kimche Painemilla explained:

> Students, you realize the image we Mapuche get from mainstream history books is that we as indigenous people in the past were savage and violent people. But we must also realize that not all Spaniards and Europeans thought that to be the truth at that time. We must look into the story of Nuñez de Pineda, an upper class Spanish soldier, who in his book "Cautiverio Feliz" tells his story after being captured in battle by a Mapuche Longko chief and held prisoner for many years. During this time, he was adopted by his captors, married the daughter of the Longko, and is said to have lived some of the best years of his life in a Mapuche community. We need to look at these stories of the past and compare them to what people think of us today.

Alongside the use of a few bibliographical colonial materials as written texts, Kimche Painemilla was very vocal about the need to maintain an oral tradition for knowledge construction and transmission through some of the nine varieties of Mapuche oral discursive practices (Relmuán, 2001). Kimches at Piedra Alta school strongly resisted the idea of using a written curriculum and textbooks to organize their courses. Although they recognized the written word as part of the dominant literacy practices leading to social mobility and status acquisition in mainstream Chilean culture and the need for their students to master reading and writing skills, their IBE courses were deliberately organized and based on validating the oral Mapuche mode of knowledge construction and transmission. Consequently, reading and writing skills were not the main instructional focus. Although students took notes occasionally, and Kimches frequently wrote on the blackboard in both languages (Spanish and Mapudungun), most of the instruction was intentionally based on oral transmission of events in a storytelling format using Mapuche discursive formats such as Pentukún greetings, Ngülam advice, Gnütram long stories and conversations with a pedagogical content, and Epew short stories of wise and devious animal characters. Kimche Painemilla described his teaching methodology this way:

> In many ways, we like the idea that we have not been given much direction on how to teach our classes by the school authorities because that would have brought us the Winka (mainstream Chilean) way of teaching, which is completely based on reading and writing and disregards the Mapuche oral tradition, which is so varied and rich. But on the other hand, we have also been forced to work with the written text, especially because of the demands of some Mapuche parents that have complained that we do not teach their children how to read and write in our classes like all teachers must. We have not completely discarded reading and writing from our classes, but it is certainly not the main mode of instruction that we propose.

Kimche Painemilla also created an active learning environment through field projects in which groups of students gathered knowledge through data collection in the school and community. Activities were organized into cohorts by age and gender in keeping with Mapuche tradition (Díaz-Coliñir, 1999; Ortiz, 2009a, 2009b). One student explained her experience in this type of learning environment very positively:

> One of the projects that I really liked was to go and interview people of the communities on many issues of the past and the present. It was fun to talk with people and see what they thought about many things. That was at a time when we had a Mapuche principal in the school, and the community radio program transmitting from the school was growing strong. I began feeling very good about being Mapuche during that time. Now we have a new principal who is not Mapuche, and the radio no longer transmits, but I still like Kimche Painemilla's classes.

Classroom relations were also generally positive. Kimche Painemilla was a member of the tightly interwoven community networks from which the children came. He was directly related to some of the students. Therefore, the level of familiarity between him and the students, who in some cases also had his last name, created a strong bond and a highly protective learning environment, enabling easy, free-flowing interaction among participants in class. A powerful relationship of trust and respect, based on kinship, was defined in classroom interactions between Kimche Painemilla and his students. He always addressed his students as *hijo* or *hija* (Spanish for "son" or "daughter"), and students were quite comfortable with this. Although some students did not always agree with all his stories and sometimes showed little interest in them, there were never gestures of disrespect. Kimche Painemilla's pedagogical style in the classroom flowed naturally in a synchronized, culturally relevant manner as the students had the same cultural codes and background knowledge as he.

Nevertheless, there was some resistance among some students. One of the strongest oppositional statements was from a student who complained that to be Mapuche from Kimche Painemilla's perspective was to learn how to do lots of crafts and wood carvings and "I really don't want to have anything to do with that in my life." He was not convinced that ethnic reconstruction processes were useful.

For many people in the communities of the ADI-Budi area, the lack of interest in learning the Mapudungun language and Mapuche traditions shown by many youths was evidence of a generational breakdown in the transmission of the indigenous culture and language which, according to Kimche Painemilla, had become more evident in the last 2 decades. Some among the younger Mapuche generation saw this not so much as a lack of interest on their part but as a consequence of the older generation's not taking the time or making the effort to teach them the Mapudungun language or their ancestral culture and knowledge.

Another reason for resistance was the powerful impact of global popular culture conveyed through television, the Internet, cell phones, and marketing devices. This contributed to a significant movement toward hybrid identity work threaded with indigenous, Chilean, and popular cultural meanings (Larraín, 2004). Hybrid identities were pulling Mapuche children and youths further and further away from their traditional indigenous ethnic identities.

The following emphatic statement of a Machi shaman, Carmen Curín, on a television program in 1995 revealed the complexity of the current challenges faced by Mapuche educators in trying to reverse the high levels of assimilation and cultural and linguistic identity loss among Mapuche youth:

> Young people who have grown up lately have begun learning Spanish and have learned how to read. Their teachers taught them how to speak Spanish, so they have forgotten their own Mapuche language. I often think and I get sad because my work as a Machi (Shaman) is no longer understood by the young. The girls that have grown up do not dress as I do anymore; they dress like the Winka. I bring health to the sick. I call the father God and the mother Goddess to cure the ill, so they will be in good health on earth, so their children yet to be born will also be in good health. That is the matter that concerns me. Now the young people do not consider when prayers to the gods are needed, and secretly they mock these beliefs. Behind my back they are mocking me. They do not listen to my words; they despise my words; and they prefer the Spanish language they have learned with their teachers. That is what they have in their hearts and minds.

Kimche Painemilla persevered despite the challenges. He was convinced on the basis of the history of the Mapuche people and his own personal experiences in the external Eurocentric world that it was vitally important that Mapuche children and youth listen to and learn from him and other community sages. He stayed true to his teaching for their sake.

CONCLUSION

The critical ethnographic study conducted in Kimche Painemilla's IBE classroom in the Piedra Alta school produced a mixed account. Students expressed pride in their Mapuche ethnic identities, and Mapuche culture was transmitted and affirmed. The usefulness of code switching between Mapudungun and Spanish languages was evident. Students learned a great deal about the history of Mapuche people in relation to dominant groups.

Yet, it was also the case that students identified with the people and lifestyles of Eurocentric Chile and global popular culture sometimes to the point of out-and-out resistance to Mapuche identity. The Kimün knowledge that Kimche Painemilla tried to teach was strongly opposed by some Mapuche parents and also by some students who recognized the social and economic power of dominant school knowledge. Schools from their point of view were inappropriate sites not only for the transmission of Kimün knowledge but also for Mapuche cosmology, ceremonial rituals, and other traditions.

Kimche Painemilla answered the resistance in part by calling attention to the historical costs of forced and voluntary accommodation to dominant Eurocentric Chilean culture and groups. His most critically courageous lessons were based on counternarrative texts intended to infuse critical consciousness into the classroom discourse in an effort to raise awareness about the inequalities, injustices, and violent suppressions that Mapuche people have endured for centuries in Chile. Mapuche people have been historically marginalized in Chilean institutions, especially Chilean schools. Mapuche children in Kimche Painemilla's classroom were brought in from the margins and placed squarely at the center, where they came into direct contact with their indigenous ethnic identity, culture, language, and history.

Kimche Painemilla held fast to his educational agenda despite resistance to it. He believed his brand of critical pedagogy using ancestral patterns of instruction would strengthen Mapuche ethnic identities. He held fast to a curriculum that grounded students in Kimün knowledge, enabled students to express themselves in Mapuzungun as well as in Spanish, and forged community bonds and relations through indigenous cosmology and ceremonies. Kimche Painemilla raised historical and political consciousness through illuminating counternarratives. He created a discursive epistemological space in his classroom with cultural practices and meanings students could use to reconstruct their ethnic identities and become empowered through indigenous knowledge and traditions as well as dominant school knowledge. His teaching was thus critical for the future of Mapuche children and the Mapuche community.

LIMITATIONS

The study of ethnic identity, Mapuche cultural transmission, and the raising of historical and political consciousness in Kimche Painemilla's classroom showcases the conventional and distinguishing methodological elements of critical ethnography. Data were collected through well-established ethnographic fieldwork methods of participant observation, semistructured interviews, and the gathering of archival material. Data analysis involved standard coding procedures. A distinctive element of this research was how constructs like ethnic identity were rendered into critical analytical categories with ideologically enhanced aspects such as identity-driven resistance and accommodation to dominant group culture. Analytical categories were conceptually and politically front-loaded and thus conducive for interpretations of findings grounded in an intellectual orientation that locates cultural practices and meanings in larger political and economic systems. The methodological strengths of the critical ethnographic approach used to study Kimche Painemilla's classroom were the use of conventional fieldwork data collection methods and coding procedures, and the analytical power of the approach was how it unveiled the potentially transformative practices and meanings inherent in Kimche Painemilla's pedagogy.

However, there are limitations to this approach that are endemic to ethnography in general and critical ethnography in particular. Because all ethnographic studies rely on prolonged fieldwork, they often take a long period of time to produce reliable findings. Successful fieldwork depends on the interpersonal skills of researchers who are the primary instruments of data collection. There is a great deal of writing in ethnographic research that begins with the transcription of data into texts for coding and continues to the production of final write-ups. Ethnography is time-consuming, socially intense, and labor intensive.

Having the time, interpersonal acumen, and writing skills necessary to conduct and complete a rigorous ethnographic study can place logistical, relational, or literacy limitations on critical ethnography. Other limitations are related to trustworthiness, the term commonly used in ethnography for validity and reliability. Like all ethnographic approaches, critical ethnography typically relies on the observations of one person or a few people who do much of the data analysis and interpretation of findings. Interpretations are affected by researcher biases, which in the case of critical ethnographers, are influenced by their political stances. Ethnographers try to balance their personal involvement and feelings for people in research settings with some measure of objectivity (Woods, 1986). Critical ethnographers lean heavily toward personal and political involvement, which can make them less objective when it comes to interpreting the function and value of cultural practices and meanings. Whereas in much ethnographic research participants' own emic accounts and points of view are regarded as essential for making sense of data, participants' perspectives in critical ethnography are viewed as permeated with ideologies that perpetuate inequalities and social injustices (Anderson, 1989). This standpoint, along with researchers' political biases, has led to the questioning of the trustworthiness of critical ethnography. Such questioning along with other limitations are best addressed by best methodological practices.

BEST PRACTICES IN CRITICAL ETHNOGRAPHY

Despite the intensiveness of rigorous fieldwork, participant observation, semistructured one-on-one interviews and focus groups, and the gathering of archival materials are the best practices or methods for collecting ethnographic data. They yield the most optimal data for the most plausible findings. The use of these methods is crucial in ethnography focusing on ethnic identity. They are the surest means for collecting adequate kinds and amounts of data on the identities of people associated with a particular ethnic group or a more broadly defined group and also data on the cultural knowledge, practices, languages, and linguistic codes through which, among other ways, identities are expressed. Critical ethnographers use these methods, but they render them into techniques that enable them to gather data conducive for the analytical unveiling of the meanings and practices that perpetuate inequality and social injustices. They seek data on how ethnic identities are openly expressed, forcibly suppressed, catalysts for resistance, forces for accommodation, or otherwise factor into the oppression and empowerment of individuals and groups.

Among the best practices for gathering data on ethnic identity is autobiographical interviewing, a method used in the study of Kimche Painemilla. Munoz (1995) characterized this type of interviewing as "stories of identity where we tell ourselves and others who we are, where we came from, and where we are going" (p. 46). Ethnographers ask questions in semistructured one-on-one interviews or focus groups that invite people to talk about themselves, their pasts and their present circumstances, relations within their families and social groups, relations with outside groups, aspirations, and future plans. Critical ethnographers in their own renditions of this technique ask research participants to share tales of their past and present political involvements, relations of power within their ethnic groups and with dominant groups, the obstacles or opportunities they have encountered to social or economic advancement, the violence or imprisonment they have endured, and other autobiographical accounts of their struggles. The questions critical ethnographers ask are aimed at amassing autobiographical stories of identity with political overtones.

Critical ethnographers studying ethnic identity also use the best practices of participant observation. But in their observations they look for expressions of resistance that can be overt, such as a child telling a teacher her curriculum is worthless, or passive, such as a student with his head down on his desk feigning sleep. There are expressions of accommodation, such as visible engagement in classroom activities, that can be fairly constant or more sporadic. Critical ethnographers embracing poststructural and postmodern perspectives look for how cultural productions as expressions of ethnic identity constantly emerge and reemerge in new images and forms (Davidson, 1996). They observe and record how research participants' resistance and accommodation change from one context to another and are otherwise fluid in how they enable people to project who they are or want to be especially in opposition to dominant groups. Critical ethnographers are very much on the lookout for ethnic identity expressions that enable individuals and groups to assert themselves and effectively navigate situations through code switching or other strategies, as was the case in Kimche Painemilla's classroom. Such observations coupled with data gleaned from interviews or other data sources are the stuff of new knowledge and/or theories that can hopefully be applied in ways that foster cultural and social change.

Rigor in ethnography also involves best analytical practices, especially those that ensure trustworthiness—validity and reliability—in findings. Trustworthiness depends on the truth value or credibility of findings (internal validity); applicability or transferability of findings to other settings or situations (external validity); consistency where findings are dependable and defensible enough to draw plausible conclusions (internal reliability); and neutrality or objectivity where findings are or can be confirmed by research participants, other researchers, and/or outside sources (external reliability; Guba, 1981; Shenton, 2004).

In critical ethnography, as is the case in all ethnographic approaches, trustworthiness can be enhanced through a variety of practices. One of the most common practices is *triangulation*, in which multiple and different data collection methods, sources, theories, and/or researchers are used to corroborate findings (Creswell, 1998). Triangulation enhances the credibility and consistency of findings. Ethnographers can also engage in *reflexivity*, in which they reflect in their written reports on how their backgrounds, viewpoints, and interests influenced their research (Krefting, 1991). Reflexivity reveals how neutral or objective a researcher is or can be. Another practice that enhances truth-value is *member checking*, in which research participants are asked to review the accuracy of findings and interpretations (Creswell, 1998). Trustworthiness is also supported by rich, thick descriptions of research settings, participant demographics, and what happened in the field that allowed others to determine credibility and the transferability of findings to other settings (Creswell, 1998). Critical ethnographers bolster the integrity of their research when they use these practices, as well as confidence that their findings may actually promote the kind of change that alleviates, ameliorates, or eradicates oppression.

RECOMMENDATIONS FOR FUTURE RESEARCH

This chapter focuses on critical ethnography as an applied approach to the study of ethnic identity and transformative change, especially in school settings. This approach could also be used to study ethnic identity in non-school settings that serve or are inhabited by ethnic minority groups, such as health care facilities, rehabilitation programs, juvenile justice systems, neighborhoods, and community programs for children and youths. The expansion of critical ethnography into a variety of settings is recommended for future research because of the conduciveness of the approach for studying how the identities, cultures, and subcultures of ethnic groups affect the extent to which children, youths, and adults resist or comply with treatments, interventions, and well-intentioned initiatives.

Other recommendations for research are related to the vexing challenges of how to apply study findings in a manner that actually transforms the lives and conditions of oppressed or marginalized ethnic groups. Applying findings in critical ethnography is often conceived as forms of praxis in which practices are combined with new knowledge or theory in ways that yield real-world change. Praxis can be the practical application of new knowledge in a setting, the application of theory to a set of practices, or the translation of new ideas into action (Greenwood & Levin, 2005). *Ethnic identity praxis* is the process of combining cultural practices and new knowledge and theory through psychocultural identity work that leads to self-determination, creative self-transformation, or personal and group empowerment. In critical ethnography, this kind of praxis is political, and ethnic identity work is a process in which people become critically aware of who they are, what has been done to them, and what they can become (Quantz, 1992).

There are challenges associated with fostering this kind of praxis. One challenge is the extent to which individuals and ethnic groups can or want to undergo critical ethnic identity work. There are ethical considerations involved in whether researchers ought to encourage people to become critically aware beings. Another challenge is how to render knowledge gathered in fieldwork into discrete practices that people can use if they do want to engage in critical ethnic identity work. There are inherent problems with turning complex cultural processes shaped by the exigencies of local contexts into a clear set of practices that people can use in any or all situations. And yet, the hope is that such practices can be generated and somehow combined with knowledge and theories that truly empower people. These and other challenges are critical topics for future research.

REFERENCES

Anderson, G. L. (1989). Critical ethnography in education: Origins, current status, and new directions. *Review of Educational Research, 59*, 249–270. http://dx.doi.org/10.3102/00346543059003249

Barth, F. (1969). *Ethnic groups and boundaries*. London, England: Allen and Unwin.

Bengoa, J. (1998). *Historia del pueblo Mapuche* [History of the Mapuche people]. Santiago, Chile: LOM Ediciones.

Bengoa, J. (2000). *La emergencia indígena en América-Latina* [The indigenous emergence in Latin-America]. Santiago, Chile: Fondo de Cultura Económica.

Bernstein, B. (1971). *Class, codes, and control* (Vol. 1). London, England: Routledge and Kegan Paul. http://dx.doi.org/10.4324/9780203014035

Best, S., & Kellner, D. (1991). *Postmodern theory*. New York, NY: Guilford Press.

Bhabha, H. (1998). Culture is in between. In D. Bennett (Ed.), *Multicultural states: Rethinking difference and identity* (pp. 29–36). New York, NY: Routledge.

Bourdieu, P. (1977). *Outline of a theory of practice*. London, England: Cambridge University Press. http://dx.doi.org/10.1017/CBO9780511812507

Bourdieu, P., & Passeron, J. C. (1990). *Reproduction in education, society and culture* (2nd ed.). London, England: Sage.

Bourdieu, P., & Wacquant, L. J. D. (1992). *An invitation to reflexive sociology*. Chicago, IL: University of Chicago Press.

Cajete, G. (2008). Seven orientations for the development of indigenous science education. In N. K. Denzin, Y. S. Lincoln, & L. T. Smith (Eds.), *Critical and indigenous methodologies* (pp. 487–496). London, England: Sage.

Carspecken, P. (1996). *Critical ethnography in educational research: A theoretical and practical guide*. New York, NY: Routledge.

Chiodi, F. (Ed.). (1990). *La educación indígena en América Latina: México, Guatemala, Ecuador, Perú, Bolivia* [Indigenous education in Latin America: Mexico, Guatemala, Ecuador, Peru, Bolivia]. Santiago, Chile: UNESCO.

Cohen, A. P. (1994). *Self-consciousness: An alternative anthropology of identity*. London, England: Routledge. http://dx.doi.org/10.4324/9780203418987

Coña, P. (1984). *Testimonio de un cacique Mapuche* [Testimony of a chief Mapuche] (4th ed.). Santiago, Chile: Pehuén.

Creswell, J. W. (1998). *Qualitative inquiry and research design: Choosing among five traditions*. Thousand Oaks, CA: Sage.

Davidson, A. L. (1996). *Making and molding identity in schools: Student narratives on race, gender and academic engagement*. New York, NY: State University of New York Press.

Denzin, N. K., & Lincoln, Y. S. (2000). Introduction: The discipline and practice of qualitative research. In N. K. Denzin & Y. S. Lincoln (Eds.), *Handbook of qualitative research* (pp. 1–28). Thousand Oaks, CA: Sage.

de Pineda, N., & Bascuñan, F. (1673). *Cautiverio feliz. Edición resumida de Lipschutz y Jara, 1973* [Happy captivity. Abridged edition of Lipschutz and Jara, 1973]. Santiago, Chile: Editorial Universitaria.

Díaz-Coliñir, M. (1999). *El Proceso de enseñanza aprendizaje en el Lof Mapuche y en la escuela rural* [The teaching learning process in the Lof Mapuche and in the rural school]. Temuco, Chile: Instituto de Estudios Indígenas, Universidad de la Frontera.

Dolby, N., & Dimitriadis, D. (2004). *Learning to labor in new times*. New York, NY: Routledge.

Durston, J. (2004). *Social capital: Part of the problem or part of the solution. How can it perpetuate or deter poverty in Latin America and the Caribbean?* Santiago, Chile: ECLAC/CEPAL.

Edwards, J. (2009). *Language and identity*. Cambridge, England: Cambridge University Press. http://dx.doi.org/10.1017/CBO9780511809842

Fetterman, D. M. (1998). *Ethnography: Step by step* (2nd ed.). Thousand Oaks, CA: Sage.

Foley, D. E. (2002). Critical ethnography: The reflexive turn. *International Journal of Qualitative Studies in Education, 15*, 469–490. http://dx.doi.org/10.1080/09518390210145534

Foley, D. E. (2010). *Learning capitalist culture: Deep in the heart of Tejas* (2nd ed.). Philadelphia: University of Pennsylvania Press.

Fontana, A., & Frey, J. (2005). The interview: From neutral stance to political involvement. In N. K. Denzin & Y. S. Lincoln (Eds.). *Handbook of qualitative research* (3rd ed., pp. 138–158). Thousand Oaks, CA: Sage.

Fordham, S. (1996). *Blacked out: Dilemmas of race, identity, and success at Capital High*. Chicago, IL: University of Chicago Press.

Fordham, S., & Ogbu, J. U. (1986). Black students' school success: Coping with the "burden of acting white." *The Urban Review, 18*, 176–206. http://dx.doi.org/10.1007/BF01112192

Foucault, M. (1979). *Discipline and punish*. New York, NY: Pantheon.

Foucault, M. (1990). *The history of sexuality*. New York, NY: Vintage Books.

Freire, P., & Faúndez, A. (1989). *Learning to question*. New York, NY: Continuum.

Giroux, H., & McLaren, P. (1996). *Counternarratives: Cultural studies and critical pedagogies in postmodern spaces*. New York, NY: Routledge.

Grebe, M. E. (1998). Procesos migratorios, identidad étnica y estrategias adaptivas en las culturas indígenas de Chile: Una perspectiva preliminary [Migration processes, ethnic identity and adaptive strategies in the indigenous cultures of Chile: A preliminary perspective]. *Revista Chilena de Antropología, 14*, 55–68.

Greenwood, D. J., & Levin, M. (2005). Reform of the social sciences and of universities through action research. In N. K. Denzin & Y. S. Lincoln (Eds.), *The Sage handbook of qualitative research* (3rd ed., pp. 43–64). Thousand Oaks, CA: Sage.

Guba, E. G. (1981). Criteria for assessing the trustworthiness of naturalistic inquiries. *Educational Communication and Technology: A Journal of Theory, Research, and Development, 29*(2), 75–91.

Gulati, S. (2011). Reflecting on the methodological aspects of critical ethnographic approach used to inform change for adolescents with disabilities. *Qualitative Report, 16*(2), 523–562.

Hall, G., & Patrinos, A. (Eds.). (2012). *Indigenous peoples, poverty, and development*. Cambridge, England: Cambridge University Press. http://dx.doi.org/10.1017/CBO9781139105729

Hemmings, A. (2006). Navigating cultural crosscurrents: (Post)anthropological passages through high school. *Anthropology & Education Quarterly, 37*, 128–143. http://dx.doi.org/10.1525/aeq.2006.37.2.128

Hernández, I. (2003). *Autonomía o ciudadanía incompleta: el pueblo mapuche en Chile y Argentina* [Autonomy or incomplete citizenship: The Mapuche people in Chile and Argentina]. Serie Población y Desarrollo No. 41. Santiago, Chile: Cepal/UN.

Hoffman, D. M. (1998). A therapeutic moment? Identity, self and culture in the anthropology of education. *Anthropology & Education Quarterly, 29*, 324–346. http://dx.doi.org/10.1525/aeq.1998.29.3.324

Holland, D., Lachicotte, W., Jr., Skinner, D., & Cain, C. (2001). *Identity and agency in cultural worlds*. Cambridge, MA: Harvard University Press.

Hornberger, N. H. (1996). *Indigenous literacies in the Americas: Language planning from the bottom up*. Berlin, Germany: Mouton de Gruyter.

Instituto Nacional de Estadística de Chile (INE). (2002). *Resultados Oficiales del Censo de Población del 2002* [Official results of the population census of 2002]. Santiago, Chile: Imprenta INE.

Jameson, F. (1990). *Postmodernism, or, the cultural logic of late capitalism*. Durham, NC: Duke University Press.

Krefting, L. (1991). Rigor in qualitative research: The assessment of trustworthiness. *The American Journal of Occupational Therapy, 45*, 214–222. http://dx.doi.org/10.5014/ajot.45.3.214

Larraín, J. (2004). *Identidad Chilena* [Chilean identity]. Santiago, Chile: LOM Ediciones.

LeCompte, M. D., & Schensul, J. J. (1999a). Analyzing and interpreting ethnographic data. In M. D. LeCompte & J. J. Schensul (Eds.), *Ethnographer's toolkit* (Vol. 5, pp. 1–247). Walnut Creek, CA: AltaMira Press.

LeCompte, M. D., & Schensul, J. J. (1999b). Designing and conducting ethnographic research. In M. D. LeCompte & J. J. Schensul (Eds.), *Ethnographer's toolkit* (Vol. 5, pp. 1–221). Walnut Creek, CA: AltaMira Press.

Levinson, B. A., Foley, D. E., & Holland, D. C. (1996). *The cultural production of the educated person: Critical ethnographies of schooling and local practice.* Albany: State University of New York Press.

Levinson, B. A., & Holland, D. C. (1996). The cultural production of the educated person: An introduction. In B. A. Levinson, D. E. Foley, & D. C. Holland (Eds.), *The cultural production of the educated person: Critical ethnographies of schooling and local practice* (pp. 1–54). Albany: State University of New York Press.

López, L. E. (2008). Top-down and bottom-up: Counterpoised visions of bilingual intercultural education in Latin America. In N. Hornberger (Ed.), *Can schools save indigenous languages? Policy and practice on four continents* (pp. 42–65). New York, NY: Palgrave Macmillan.

Macedo, D. (1999). Decolonizing indigenous knowledge. In L. M. Semali & J. L. Kincheloe (Eds.), *What is indigenous knowledge? Voices from the academy* (pp. xi–xvi). New York, NY: Falmer Press.

McCarty, T. L., Borgoialkova, T., Gilmore, P., Lomawaima, K. T., & Romero, M. E. (2005). Indigenous epistemologies and education—self-determination, anthropology, and human rights. *Anthropology & Education Quarterly, 36,* 1–7. http://dx.doi.org/10.1525/aeq.2005.36.1.001

McDermott, R. P. (1974). Achieving school failure: An anthropological approach to illiteracy and social stratification. In G. D. Spindler (Ed.), *Education and cultural process: Toward an anthropology of education* (pp. 82–118). New York, NY: Holt, Rinehart and Winston.

McLaren, P. (2006). *Life in schools: An introduction to critical pedagogy in the foundations of education* (5th ed.). Boston, MA: Pearson.

Ministerio de Planificación de Chile (MIDEPLAN). (1999). *Línea de base del área de desarrollo indígena Lago Budi* [Baseline of the indigenous development area of Lake Budi]. Santiago, Chile: MIDEPLAN.

Munoz, V. I. (1995). *"Where something catches:" Work, love, and identity in youth.* New York, NY: State University of New York Press.

Ogbu, J. U. (1978). *Minority education and caste: The American system in cross-cultural perspective.* New York, NY: Academic Press.

Ogbu, J. U. (1987). Variability in minority school performance: A problem in search of a solution. *Anthropology & Education Quarterly, 18,* 312–334. http://dx.doi.org/10.1525/aeq.1987.18.4.04x0022v

Ogbu, J. U., & Simons, H. D. (1998). Voluntary and involuntary minorities: A cultural-ecological theory of school performance with some implications for education. *Anthropology & Education Quarterly, 29,* 155–188. http://dx.doi. org/10.1525/aeq.1998.29.2.155

Ortiz, P. (2009a). *Indigenous knowledge, education and ethnic identity: An ethnography of an intercultural bilingual education program in a Mapuche schools in Chile.* Saarbruken, Germany: VDM-Verlag.

Ortiz, P. (2009b). Indigenous knowledge and language: Decolonizing culturally relevant pedagogy in a Mapuche intercultural bilingual education program in Chile. *Canadian Journal of Native Education, 32,* 93–114.

Pignatelli, F. (1998). Critical ethnography/poststructuralist concerns: Foucault and the play of memory. *Interchange, 29,* 403–423. http://dx.doi.org/ 10.1023/A:1026417203110

Quantz, R. A. (1992). On critical ethnography (with some postmodern considerations). In M. D. LeCompte, W. L. Millroy, & J. Preissle (Eds.), *The handbook of qualitative research in education* (pp. 447–506). San Diego, CA: Academic Press.

Rabinow, P. (1984). *The Foucault reader.* New York, NY: Pantheon.

Relmuán, M. A. (2001). *El contexto de uso de seis tipos de discurso Mapuche y su posible inserción en el aula y la formación docente* [The context of use of six types of Mapuche discourse and their possible inclusion in the classroom and educational training]. Thesis. Universidad Mayor de San Simón (PROEIB Andes), Cochabamba, Bolivia.

Saavedra, A. (2002). *Los Mapuches en la sociedad Chilena actual* [The Mapuches in the current Chilean society]. Santiago, Chile: LOM.

Schensul, S., Schensul, J. J., & LeCompte, M. D. (1999). Essential ethnographic methods: Observations, interviews and questionnaires. In M. D. LeCompte & J. J. Schensul (Eds.), *Ethnographer's toolkit* (Vol. 2, pp. 1–321). Walnut Creek, CA: AltaMira Press.

Scott, J. C. (1992). *Domination and the arts of resistance: Hidden transcripts.* New Haven, CT: Yale University Press.

Semali, L. M., & Kincheloe, J. L. (1999). *What is indigenous knowledge? Voices from the academy.* New York, NY: Falmer Press.

Shenton, A. K. (2004). Strategies for ensuring trustworthiness in qualitative research projects. *Education for Information, 22,* 63–75.

Singleton, J. (1974). Implications of cultural transmission. In G. Spindler (Ed.), *Education and cultural process: Toward an anthropology of education* (pp. 26–38). New York, NY: Holt, Rinehart & Winston.

Spindler, G. (2006). *Innovations in educational ethnography: Theories, methods, and results.* Hoboken, NJ: Erlbaum.

Spindler, G., & Spindler, L. (1992). The enduring, situated, and endangered self in fieldwork: A personal account. In B. Boyer (Ed.), *The psychoanalytical study of society* (pp. 23–28). Hillsdale, NJ: Analytic Press.

Spradley, J. P. (1979). *The ethnographic interview.* New York, NY: Harcourt Brace Jovanovich.

Spradley, J. P. (1980). *Participant observation*. New York, NY: Holt, Rhinehart, and Winston.

Stavenhagen, R. (1997). Las organizaciones indígenas: Actores emergentes en América Latina [Indigenous organizations: Emerging actors in Latin America]. *Documentos Cepal/ONU, 62*, 61–73. Santiago, Chile.

Trueba, H., & Zou, Y. (1998). *Ethnic identity and power: Cultural contexts of political action in school and society*. Albany, NY: State University of New York Press.

Vanciana, J. (1985). *Oral tradition as history*. Madison: University of Wisconsin Press.

Williamson, G. (2012). Institucionalización de la educación intercultural bilingue en Chile: Notas y observaciones críticas [Institutionalization of intercultural bilingual education in Chile: Critical notes and observations]. *Perfiles Educativos, 34*(138), 126–147. Ciudad de México: IISUE-UNAM.

Williamson, G., Pinkney-Pastrana, J., & Gomez, P. (2005). Reflexiones a partir de un estudio sobre educación intercultural y participación en comunidades Mapuche en la Novena Región de La Araucanía, Chile [Reflections from a study of intercultural education and participation in Mapuche communities of the Ninth Region of La Araucanía, Chile]. *Archivos Analíticos de Políticas Educativas, 13*(4), 1–17.

Willis, P. (1981). *Learning to labor: How working class kids get working class jobs*. New York, NY: Columbia University Press.

Woods, P. (1986). *Inside school: Ethnography in educational research*. London, England: Routledge.

Zou, Y., & Trueba, H. (Eds.). (2002). *Ethnography and schools: Qualitative approaches to the study of education*. Lanham, MD: Rowman and Littlefield.

4

STUDYING ETHNIC SCHEMAS: INTEGRATING COGNITIVE SCHEMAS INTO ETHNICITY RESEARCH THROUGH PHOTO ELICITATION

WENDY D. ROTH

Ethnic identity is a complex construct that is shaped by both individual and social factors. Yet, much of ethnic identity research has focused on the self—how a person asserts and experiences his or her own ethnic identity. This is the case in both considerations of process, such as how ethnic identity develops and changes over an individual's life, and of content, such as how strongly a person identifies with an ethnicity and what that identification signifies. This focus on the self can overlook the important role of intergroup relations, particularly as they shape categorization processes and shared cultural meanings about ethnic groupings.

Some scholars have criticized the overreliance on the concept of identity. The term *identity* is used so frequently and broadly that its meaning is often ambiguous, and it loses a sense of who is doing the identifying (Brubaker, 2004; Brubaker & Cooper, 2000). The tendency to treat identity as an embodied characteristic held by an individual can also draw attention away from

http://dx.doi.org/10.1037/14618-005
Studying Ethnic Identity: Methodological and Conceptual Approaches Across Disciplines, C. E. Santos and A. J. Umaña-Taylor (Editors)

collective processes or actions of constructing ethnicity by creating and rein-forcing boundaries between ethnic groups (Brubaker, Loveman, & Stamatov, 2004; Wimmer, 2008, 2009). Anthropologist Frederik Barth (1969) power-fully argued that ethnicity is not a matter of shared traits or culture but of practices of categorization. How a person classifies himself or herself and oth-ers, and the distinctions made between categories of people, shapes ethnic boundaries and defines what ethnic groupings exist. Ethnic identity, then, develops from the interplay between self-classification and categorization by others (Jenkins, 1997; Okamura, 1981). But ultimately self-identification is only one part of this cognitive process of sorting people into distinct catego-ries (Brubaker et al., 2004).

I conceptualize ethnicity as a cognitive structure that divides people into groups that are perceived as having common ancestry, memories of a shared history, and a cultural focus involving symbolic elements that define their peoplehood (Cornell & Hartmann, 1998; Roth, 2012). Often these groups are hierarchically ranked, drawing on sociohistorical processes that have reserved higher status and greater resources for certain ethnic groups within most societies. Borrowing from cognitive science, we can think of this structure as a form of schema—a mental structure that represents knowledge and processes information. Schemas involve groups of categories and a com-plex of information about the relationship between them, including rankings that cause some to be treated as subordinate to others. Schemas also guide perception and recall that allow us to process and categorize new experiences. Like a set of mental rules to help us recognize new people, events, or stimuli, schemas allow us to treat such information as new instances of an already familiar category (Casson, 1983; D'Andrade, 1995; Fiske, 1986).

We can think of an ethnic schema, then, as the bundle of ethnic cat-egories a person perceives and the set of rules for what they mean, how they are ordered, and how to apply them to oneself and others. The categories within an ethnic schema inhere in their relationship to one another, in who is defined as inside or outside the group and what that means for how people are treated within a society. Like all cognitive schemas, ethnic schemas are culturally shared representations, which is why they overlap across individu-als in a community (Brubaker et al., 2004; DiMaggio, 1997). They also differ across societies, so that people in different nations have different schemas of what ethnicities exist and how they relate to one another. Similarly, as people move between societies and as subcultures develop, multiple and diverse ethnic schemas can be held by different subgroups in a single society (Roth, 2012).

Studying individuals' ethnic schemas provides an understanding of both how people identify themselves and where those identities fit within a broader cognitive map of the ethnic categories and classifications they perceive in their society. This is particularly useful in research considering how ethnic classifications change over time, within and across societies, and as people immigrate to new lands.

Photo elicitation can provide a valuable technique for uncovering the ethnic categories people perceive and exploring how ethnic classifications are made and understood. In my own work, I have used photo elicitation to study racial schemas—the collection and organization of racial categories—perceived by Puerto Ricans and Dominicans, both those who had migrated to the mainland United States and those who remained in Puerto Rico and the Dominican Republic. I conceptualize race as a cognitive structure, like ethnicity, but one that divides people into hierarchically ordered categories on the basis of certain physical or biological characteristics, commonly revealed in appearance, that are believed to be inherent. These biological characteristics are referred to in delimiting a racial group or category, but deciding which characteristics define the race—whether it is skin color, hair texture, eye shape, or any other features—is a social process, which people in different societies do differently (Cornell & Hartmann, 1998; Roth, 2012).

As a method, photo elicitation is more common in research studying racial classification than ethnic classification. It may lend itself more naturally to the study of race because of its visual component. However, it can be valuable for studying ethnicity as well. Perceiving ethnicity is also partly visual (see also López et al., Chapter 5, this volume). Perceptions of other people's ethnicity are based on numerous visual cues, including dress, hair style, background location or context, and social status, which may lead observers to change their assessments—and treatment—of a given person as more information becomes available (Freeman & Ambady, 2011; Freeman, Penner, Saperstein, Scheutz, & Ambady, 2011; Gold, 1991; Penner & Saperstein, 2008; Roth, 2010). Ethnicity and race sometimes overlap. Social closure among people with a common ancestry typically leads to marriage within the community, which can produce physical resemblances among people of that ethnic origin. In the United States, for instance, many people have an image of what an Italian American or a Jewish American "looks like," even if not all members of the group conform to that image. This can involve developing a "somatic norm image" of an ethnic or nationality group, in spite of recognizing the physical variation within it (Candelario, 2007; Hoetink, 1967). Groups that were initially distinguished racially may also develop a sense of shared culture and history—as Cornell and Hartmann (1998) argued has occurred for African Americans—leading them to become both ethnicity and race at the same time. Some scholars have maintained that race and nationhood should be subsumed within the concept of ethnicity, as the processes for constructing them are theoretically similar (American Anthropological Association, 1997; Brubaker et al., 2004; Fullilove, 1998; Loveman, 1999; Wimmer, 2008, 2009).

Certainly the conceptual distinction between race and ethnicity is highly dependent on culture and local context. In the United States, race remains a salient concept (American Sociological Association, 2003; Omi & Winant, 1994). But in many countries, the term is rarely used or is folded into the concept of ethnicity. In Italy, for example, population diversity is understood largely in terms of ethnicity, and even when physical characteristics are referenced—say, to distinguish a North African immigrant from a native Italian—the difference is understood as ethnic rather than racial (Maneri & Morning, 2013).

Photo elicitation is therefore a useful technique for understanding the shared cultural meanings and cognitive schemas of all ethnicities or races that individuals perceive in their society. Combining this technique with qualitative interviewing to explore what the categories mean, how they are distinguished and the relations between them, and where the respondent places himself or herself within the ethnic schema can help us achieve greater clarity about ethnic identity and the broader structures that shape it.

OVERVIEW OF PHOTO ELICITATION FOR STUDYING ETHNIC SCHEMAS

Photo elicitation can refer to a variety of techniques involving photographs in research interviews. Typically respondents are shown specific photos and asked questions about them, although some photo elicitation research has asked the respondents to take photographs themselves or share existing family photographs and discuss their meaning with the researcher (e.g., Clark-Ibáñez, 2004; Winddance Twine, 2006). According to Harper (2002), the parts of the brain that process visual information are evolutionarily older than those that process verbal information, causing images to evoke deeper elements of human consciousness than words. Photographs can therefore trigger latent memories, associations, emotions, or other information that may not be evoked through words alone (Collier, 1957). Photographs can also provide a focus for discussing difficult or abstract concepts and may help generate information about processes that respondents experience only semiconsciously.

The form of photo elicitation that lends itself most directly to understanding ethnic or racial classifications is to show respondents a series of images of different individuals and ask them to classify the ethnicity or race of each one or sort them into categories. The format for this exercise can vary considerably, depending on the goals of the research. Classification questions may be open-ended or closed-ended. They may be done as part of an in-person interview with physical photographs and qualitative probing about the classification process or through computer-based, self-completion interviews with images appearing on a screen. Images may be carefully orchestrated or electronically morphed to produce desired looks, backgrounds, and points of comparison, or they may capture "real" scenarios and contexts in the lives of focal individuals or communities. Although most elicitation studies use photographs, drawings, cartoons, computer-generated graphics, or other visual images can be used as well (Harper, 2002).

To elicit individuals' cognitive ethnic schemas specifically, researchers would show photographs or images of people of different ethnicities to respondents and ask them, ideally in open-ended terms, to identify the ethnicity of each one or sort them into piles representing different ethnic groups. This exercise would lead to in-depth discussion of the classifications respondents made, the basis for those classifications, relations between the groups, where the respondent places himself or herself within those groupings, and related questions probing the respondents' understanding of ethnic groups and boundaries in their society.

RESEARCH USING PHOTO ELICITATION TO STUDY ETHNIC AND RACIAL CLASSIFICATION

Although there is substantial and diverse research using photo elicitation to study ethnic and racial classification, studies using photographs or images to elicit a cognitive map of the relevant ethnic or racial groups perceived by respondents are still quite rare. Most of the research, rather, is quantitative, uses closed-ended classification items, and often uses facial images that are devoid of context.

An exception to this dominant trend is Gold's (1991) study of the ethnic boundaries between Vietnamese and Chinese Vietnamese refugees in California. His work illustrated how photo elicitation can be profitably used to study ethnic classifications, especially the boundaries that separate subdivisions within them. In the Vietnamese enclaves Gold studied, a specific refugee subpopulation of ethnic Chinese families who had lived in Vietnam owned a disproportionate number of the Vietnamese businesses. Gold was interested in the ethnic boundaries and relations between these refugee populations and whether adaptation to life in the United States affected those boundaries—particularly whether the groups were increasingly adopting a common identity in the United States or were establishing separate identities and distinct communities. Gold took photographs depicting small groups of either Vietnamese or Chinese Vietnamese individuals in the contexts in which he encountered them in the community. The photos are rich with information about the social context, showing clothing and hairstyles, social groupings, and settings such as ethnically owned businesses or homes.

In qualitative interviews, Gold showed the photographs to two groups of refugee respondents: older refugees with "Vietnam-based" world views and younger refugees with "American-based" world views. He asked respondents if the people the photos depicted were Vietnamese or Chinese Vietnamese, how they could tell, and how they felt about them. Gold discovered that his respondents had high levels of knowledge about the ethnic boundary between the Vietnamese and Chinese Vietnamese and were generally able to identify the ethnicity of the people shown. However, the older generation could discuss ethnic differences with little conscious reflection, whereas younger refugees had to recall information they had been told and paid less attention to cultural cues. The discussions also revealed which traits respondents saw as identifying and distinguishing each of the two communities. This photo elicitation study illustrated how refugees identify and categorize each other and revealed the existence of an ethnic boundary between these populations, yet one that was becoming less salient for younger generations. Thus, immigrant generation played a role in the cognitive process of identifying ethnic distinctions.

In contrast, the predominant trend in photo elicitation studies of ethnic or racial classifications is quantitative research on how individuals perceive and classify multiracial individuals or ambiguous faces.[1] Images are typically computer generated or electronically morphed to control facial appearance, particularly the amount of ambiguity or extent of visual influence from each of two monoracial groups. A few studies use yearbook photos of real multiracial and monoracial individuals whose self-identifications are known (e.g., Herman, 2010; Pauker & Ambady, 2009). Respondents are typically shown different images and asked to classify each one from a set of closed-ended response options. The central questions are usually what factors influence the classifications and how does the classification process occur. Peery and Bodenhausen (2008), for example, created racially ambiguous images by morphing Black and White faces, with even contributions from each of the two source photos, and compiled them with untreated Black and White faces.[2] When they asked respondents to judge whether the faces were Black/not Black and White/not White as quickly and accurately as possible, the respondents most frequently classified the ambiguous faces as Black, suggesting the tendency to reflexively follow the principle of hypodescent, where individuals with any Black ancestry are classified as Black. But with more

---

[1]Additional work uses researchers' coding of information in photographs. Although not photo elicitation in the sense that the respondents are not the ones classifying the photos, such research uses visual information as part of its data on social processes. See, for example, Feliciano and Robnett's (2013) study of how observed race, coded through photographs of Internet daters, shapes Latinos' dating preferences and assimilation trajectories.

[2]The images were taken from a facial perception database (Minear & Park, 2004).

thoughtful reflection—when respondents were not asked to make quick assessments and were allowed to either type in their own racial description[3] or select "multiracial" as an option—multiracial classifications increased. Freeman et al. (2011) showed that status cues also influence classifications. When racially ambiguous morphs of Black and White individuals were shown in business attire, a White attribution increased, but Black classifications increased when these individuals were shown dressed as janitors.

Research has provided mixed findings on whether characteristics of the observer influence classifications. Herman (2010) found that most characteristics of observers—including their own racial identity, gender, and amount of interracial contact—had no influence on how they classified the race of multiracial individuals in yearbook photos. However, D. R. Harris (2002) found that the probability of a match between an observer's classification and self-identified race varied significantly by the race and gender of the observer. Women and multiracial men were more likely to classify racially ambiguous faces as multiracial than were White or Asian men. The context of how information is presented also influences classifications. According to Halberstadt, Sherman, and Sherman (2011), classifications are influenced by learning strategies—the order in which individuals learn about new groups. Shown faces that were morphs of Chinese and Caucasian photographs, their respondents tended to classify the ambiguous images as members of the second of the two groups presented.

Other studies have used photo elicitation to understand how the process of classifying others works. This may involve what parts of the brain are activated when respondents view and are asked to classify racially ambiguous faces (Willadsen-Jensen & Ito, 2006, 2008), how much time it takes people to make classifications of more ambiguous images (Freeman et al., 2011; D. R. Harris, 2002), or how the amount of time available influences those classifications (Peery & Bodenhausen, 2008). The complexity of how observers arrive at monoracial classifications when viewing ambiguous faces can be found by tracking their movement of the mouse between two single-race response buttons on a computer screen (Freeman, Pauker, Apfelbaum, & Ambady, 2010; Freeman et al., 2011). Photos of racially ambiguous people have also been used to study how the presence of racial labels along with the image influences memory of that image (Pauker & Ambady, 2009) and the perception of that individual as appearing more similar to the indicated racial label than the image actually did (Eberhardt, Dasgupta, & Banaszynski, 2003).

Very few general social surveys include photo elicitation to capture how respondents classify race or ethnicity. Bailey (2008) analyzed one such

---

[3]Peery and Bodenhausen (2008) is one of the only quantitative studies to provide a test condition allowing open-ended racial descriptions; however, those responses are not reported in the article.

example, a unique Brazilian survey created to coincide with the implementation of racial quotas in many public Brazilian universities. Although the Brazilian census had long used a three-category classification system (White, Mulatto, Black) to capture a color continuum that many Brazilians perceive and represent informally with even more categories of their own, the implementation of racial quotas for Blacks required a dichotomous division of the population into those who met the policy criteria and those who did not. To illustrate who would be included under the Black label in a dichotomous classification system (Black, White), the survey asked respondents to classify not only themselves but also a set of photographs using both the three-category and two-category question formats. Although the Afro-Brazilian movement that had successfully mobilized for racial quotas in public universities envisioned those quotas applying to both Blacks and Mulattos, the survey data showed that many of the target individuals who were identified as Mulatto under the census classifications were recategorized as White under the dichotomous system and thus might be denied race-targeted benefits.

For my particular focus in this chapter—studying the ethnic or racial schemas that individuals use—some of the most valuable research relies on the set of drawings developed by anthropologist Marvin Harris (1970) in his seminal work on Brazil. Harris's instrument used a deck of 72 facial drawings constructed out of the combination of three skin tones (light, medium, dark), three hair forms (straight, wavy, kinky), two lip forms (thin, thick), two nose forms (narrow, wide), and two sex types (male, female). All other features were held constant. In his initial study, Harris asked 100 Brazilians to categorize the drawings in their own terms, without indicating what categories were considered to be part of the cultural domain. A general question asked respondents for the "type" or "race" of the person depicted in the drawing— or, as a last resort, the "color"—to generate the lexicon of terms within the cognitive domain of racial identity. The study generated 492 different categorizations, with each drawing identified by more than 20 sets of terms. Harris concluded that Brazilians' cognitive domain of race is characterized by ambiguity, with little apparent agreement over shared categories or how they are applied. However, a year later, Sanjek (1971) reapplied the same (male) drawings to another Brazilian sample and found that although a large number of terms were generated, only a small portion of the terms formed the cognitive map of most of his respondents and organized the bulk of the cultural domain. He argued that Brazilian racial categorization was considerably more organized and consensual than Harris had indicated and identified skin color and hair type as the organizing principles of the domain.

Byrne and Forline (1997) used contemporary statistical and analytical techniques to reanalyze Harris's (1970) data. They identified only four core terms used by more than 50% of respondents. And although they found support for Harris's contention that the entire sample of respondents could not reach consensus on a shared set of cultural categories, they did find consensus within specific geographical regions, suggesting that the cultural domain is partly demarcated by regional differences. They further found support for Sanjek's (1971) claim that skin color and hair type were the primary determinants of classification. Gravlee (2005) applied similar analytical methods to analyze new data using Harris's images collected in southeastern Puerto Rico. His results also indicated a small set of only five categories applied by the majority of respondents and confirmed that category distinctions rely primarily on skin color and hair form, with sex, nose, and lip form having little influence on categorization. High agreement on classifications across respondents indicated strong evidence of a single cultural model of what he called ethnic or "color" classification.

The studies that used Harris's facial drawings represent some of the most valuable research using images to elicit the classifications applied to others. They are particularly useful for analyzing cultural domains because respondents are not restricted in the categories they must apply to the images and can instead generate emic categories—the self-selected terms they consider culturally appropriate (Byrne & Forline, 1997). The drawings are especially appropriate for focusing on how specific facial features contribute to classifications. Because certain features of the drawings (skin color, hair, lips, nose) are clearly varied systematically, and respondents are shown all the images in turn with each combination of features, they are led to focus specifically on those characteristics in making classifications. However, this may not fully approximate the classification processes individuals experience when they encounter a new individual in their daily lives, where they may also draw on visual cues such as dress and background. For this reason, in my own work I use photographs of real individuals in social contexts they actually inhabit. The following section describes this work to provide a detailed example of this research method. Although I focus on racial schemas in my work, the technique can also be profitably used to study ethnic schemas, as I discuss further in the next section.

IN-DEPTH EMPIRICAL ILLUSTRATION

My research on the racial schemas used by Dominicans and Puerto Ricans—both those who migrate to New York and those who remain in Santo Domingo and San Juan, respectively—provides an illustration of how photo elicitation can be used to understand the racial classifications that groups of people perceive, how they understand those categories, and how schemas may change. Further details about the study, as well as the photographs used in this research, may be found in Roth (2012).

One of my central interests in this study was to examine whether migrants experience *racial acculturation*—that is, whether they pick up and use an Americanized way of understanding and classifying race over time. In the United States, race has traditionally been understood as a strict dichotomy between White and Black. When any mixing occurred between those groups, the principle of hypodescent dominated (Davis, 1991; Roth, 2005). The Hispanic Caribbean is often contrasted to the United States for its distinct classification system—a continuum from light to dark with mixes of European, African, and Indigenous ancestries, and a plethora of labels to identify the various types of racial mixes (Duany, 1998; Hoetink, 1985; Howard, 2001). Intermediate labels between *blanco* and *negro*, such as *trigueño*, *jabao*, and *indio*, indicate different combinations of skin color and features, which historically in the United States would all have been classified as Black on the basis of the principle of hypodescent. Furthermore, although racial classification in the United States has traditionally been based on ancestry—a person with any Black ancestry, even if they looked completely White, was still considered to be Black—in the Hispanic Caribbean, according to the literature, it has been based more on appearance. Racial categories there describe how a person looks, such that full siblings may be described as different races (Duany, 1998; Rodriguez, 1974; Torres-Saillant, 1998). A common experience of early migrants from the Hispanic Caribbean was to discover, for the first time on arriving in the United States, that they were Black (Rodriguez, 1974; Shorris, 1992; Thomas, 1967).

Much of the data on how Dominicans and Puerto Ricans in the United States see race focuses on the self-identification labels they assert. Studies often use data from the U.S. Census, which uses racial categories that many migrants may not themselves adopt. Defining Hispanic origin as an aspect of ethnicity, the census has long asked all Latinos to classify themselves using standard U.S. race categories such as White, Black, American Indian, Asian, and Other. For many decades, large proportions of Latinos have classified themselves as "Some Other Race." Some scholars consider those who check White or Black on the census to be accepting U.S. racial categories, whereas those who check Other are rejecting them (Denton & Massey, 1989; Massey & Denton, 1992; Rodríguez, 1989, 1991). The problem, though, is that some people in Latin America do think of themselves as *blanco* or *negro*, although not necessarily the same people Americans would see as White or Black. Are the Latinos who identify as White adopting an Americanized understanding of race or a Latin American one? We cannot tell from their identification labels alone, without considering whether their "White" identification is part of a cognitive schema involving only White and Black or one also involving *mulato*, *jabao*, and *trigueño*, for instance. This is one reason why it is valuable to focus on cognitive schemas and understand where migrants see their place within the racial or ethnic order of their society and where group boundaries lie. Photo elicitation can provide this cognitive map.

Constructing the Instrument

The photographic instrument I used in this research was selected from a set of photographs I took of individuals in public places who appeared to be of Latino ethnicity. My primary goal was to collect images of people who would represent the range of typical appearances found in Puerto Rico and the Dominican Republic. It was not necessary that every image be of someone who was actually Puerto Rican or Dominican, but I did seek out locations to take photographs where I expected to find people from these groups.

I submitted a separate application to my institutional review board for the project of compiling a photographic instrument. This included a consent form that explained the purpose of taking the photos and how they would be used in the interview and in subsequent publications and talks; each person was offered $5.00 in exchange for allowing me to take and possibly use their photograph. I took photographs in two primary locations—a neighborhood in Boston with a large Dominican population and the campus of a community college in New York with a large Latino student population. In the Boston neighborhood, I approached people on the street and in shops. On the college campus, I approached people in a student union building, most of whom were sitting down to study or to eat in the cafeteria. Because my goal was to capture people of a range of skin colors and facial features, it was useful for me to approach individuals I saw and ask them to participate. I supplemented these photographs with a few more of people I knew and a few of employees in a shop that I frequented. I took approximately 45 photos in total.

I used both a digital camera and a film camera and took a few shots of each individual with both cameras. Each photograph was a close-up shot of the person's face and shoulders in the setting where I encountered them. This meant that the backgrounds and the lighting conditions varied in each photograph. Clothing, accessories, and hairstyles also varied, depending on how the person was dressed at the moment I encountered them. These are aspects of an image that some researchers may want to control, as they sometimes did influence the classifications my interview respondents made. For quantitative studies that seek to measure whether different aspects of an image influence outcomes and the extent of the influence, controlling these aspects of the image is usually of central importance. My interest was in capturing images of "real" people—the types of people my respondents might actually encounter and form judgments about in their daily lives. I wanted to allow my respondents to decide for themselves what to focus on in attributing race and to allow that process to unfold as closely as possible to the way it might in an actual social encounter. When comparison across respondents is a goal of the study and small numbers require that they are all shown the same images, systematic variation of particular aspects of the images may be obvious to respondents and may draw their attention. When numbers are large and different respondents can be shown random subsets of images—as in a computerized survey—this is less of a concern. Because my study was qualitative, I could ask questions about what had influenced my respondents' classifications. I was also particularly interested in comparing responses between categories of respondents—migrants and nonmigrants, as well as Dominicans and Puerto Ricans—so I was less concerned with differences in lighting or background across photographs as long as all my respondents viewed the same images.

I did not ask the people I photographed for their ethnic or racial background, or their preferred self-identification label, although some people volunteered this information as I was taking their picture. Because I was interested in the classifications that people make and how they arrive at those decisions, I did not want to be armed with the knowledge of whether their classifications were "right." In fact, this was a central preoccupation of many of my interview respondents. After we finished going through the photographs, the first question many of them asked was, "Did I get it right?" It was some small consolation to be able to tell them that I honestly did not know and that I was not trying to test them. However, when the research goals include understanding observers' abilities to classify target individuals as they identify themselves, or whether the target's ancestry influences this process (D. R. Harris, 2002; Herman, 2010), such information can be easily gathered at the time of collecting the photographs.

I consulted with two people who met the criteria of my target respondent population to whittle my collection of 45 photographs down to 20 that best represented the range of phenotypes common in Puerto Rico and the Dominican Republic and the variety of racial labels that predominate there (see Roth, 2012, Table 3, p. 19). One consultant was a female Puerto Rican migrant and the other was a male Dominican migrant. With each of them, I presented a list of the racial labels that had been referenced in the literature on Puerto Rico and the Dominican Republic, and they selected images that they felt best matched each label. I put the final set of 20 photographs in a random order and labeled each one with a number.

Photo Elicitation in Interviews

During the qualitative interviews, I showed the photographs to all respondents in the same order and asked them to identify the race of the person in each photograph in whatever terms they would normally use. I gave no other instructions about the kind of categories they should use; instead, I allowed the photographs to evoke a set of categories that respondents use in their daily lives. Most respondents went through the photographs one at a time and said aloud its number and then their classification. A few respondents looked through the entire collection first; some sorted them into piles. I told them they could do as they liked, but they should indicate the race of each one. If they sorted them into piles, I asked them to tell me what the piles represented, and then I said aloud what each group was and the numbers of the photographs placed within it to capture this information on the audio recorder. Afterwards, I used respondents' classifications of the photographs to initiate an in-depth discussion of how they decide what labels to apply, what those categories mean, how they relate to one another, and how the respondents understand race more generally. Although I had some sample probe questions written out in my interview guide, much of this discussion was improvised; I often asked follow-up questions about specific classifications they made, such as why one photo was classified one way and a similar one was classified differently.

The following excerpt from my interview with Alicia[4] gives an example of how the photo elicitation and a subsequent discussion unfolded.[5] Alicia has always lived in the Dominican Republic, where she works as a school teacher. She is 44 years old and is a single mother. Her appearance is mostly European, with light skin and predominantly European features, sandy blonde hair, and light brown eyes. With some college education, she has a relatively high level of education for the Dominican Republic. After establishing rapport with a few "easy" topics—her family background, connections to people who have migrated to the United States, and her own attitudes toward immigrating—I introduced the photo elicitation exercise:

> Interviewer: One of the segments of this study . . . is how people classify the race of others. And there is no correct or incorrect answer for this. It is to understand how people make the classifications and what categories are used in each country. I have a group of pictures of different people. Could you tell me how you would classify the race of these people? You can group them on the table or you can tell them to me one by one, but please say out loud the number first and then—

> Respondent: Do you want me to tell you what I believe, or what people believe?

---

[4]This is a pseudonym.
[5]Interviews were conducted in Spanish and were translated by native Spanish speakers. Racial categories are left in the original Spanish.

I: First what you believe.

R: For me they are all *mestizos*. This person is of *blanca* skin tone, Number 1. But he has strong hair, hard hair. He has to have a *negra* grandmother or mother, [someone *negra*] really close[ly related]. / This one also . . . Number 2. His skin is *blanca*, but he has kinky hair. I think that also he could be a *mestizo*. / She is what we call, Number 3, I can't say *negra*. Here I would call her *india* . . . That is a term that I use a lot, to differentiate them from *negra* people that have darker skin—

I: Darker than her [Number 3]?

R: [Yes.] Darker than her. And their hair is curly.

I: And that is the main reason you can't call her *negra*?

R: Exactly.

I: The color?

R: [Yes.] The color. The intensity of her color is from her negritude and the limpness of her hair. I think she has limp hair. She is an *india*. / Number 4, I think is a *blanca* person. He is *blanco*. / Number 5 is *mestiza*. / . . . Number 6, *negro*. Here we say *prieto*, but it is disrespectful.

I: Is it always?

R: Always. Unless it is among people of the same color that call each other *prieto*. But if I, I am a bit more *blanca* . . . I am also *negra*. My father is *negro*. I consider myself *negra*.

I: Yes [you do]?

R: Yes. But if I call him *prieto* he could feel bad. / *Mestizo*, Number 7, also. / Number 8, *blanco*, Caucasian. / Number 9, *mestiza*. / Number 10, *blanca*. She is *blanca*. / Number 11, *blanca*. / Number 12, *mestiza*. / Number 13, *indigena*. / Number 14, *mestiza*. / Number 15, *mestizo*. He is *mestizo*. / Number 16, she is *blanca*. / Number 17—[giggles] I have never done this. It is difficult. Her nose is *neg—afro*, right? I am going to say *mestiza*, for 17. / Number 18, he is *negro*. What we call *negro*. / Number 19, she is *mestiza*. / Number 20, he is an *indio*. He is *indio*. Like her too [Number 3].

From just her classification of the photographs, Alicia provides extremely rich data about her understanding of racial classifications in the Dominican Republic. First, she adopts a racial schema that resembles the model of race as a continuum with multiple categories between Black and White that represent different racial mixes. The categories she uses for the different photos are *blanco, mestizo, indio, indigeno,* and *negro*. She also reveals useful information about the meaning of many of those categories for her. For example, someone who has light (*blanca*) skin but kinky or "hard" hair would be considered *mestizo*. Someone whose skin color shows African ancestry but is not too dark and who has straight or more European hair would be considered *indio*. She has also made several evocative statements or "signposts" that point to complex systems of meaning that can be explored in depth (Weiss, 1994). She has hinted that the way she sees people's races differs from how they think of themselves. And she has provided an initial glimpse of how she thinks about racial classification and her own identity. Alicia claims that everyone is *mestizo*, but that she considers herself *negra*, despite her primarily European appearance, because her father was *negro*. This sounds closer to the American principle of hypodescent than the continuum model associated with the Hispanic Caribbean. The subsequent conversation and follow-up questions allowed me to explore all of these statements.

Although each conversation exploring the photo classifications differed, I usually began by exploring why certain photos had been classified as they had been, to understand the meaning and boundaries of the categories that were used. While going through the photographs, Alicia put some of the photos into a separate pile from the others. I began our conversation by asking about how she had sorted them:

I: So this group over there, are these people *indios?*

R: [Yes.] They are *indios*, what they call *indio* here.

I: Ok, so the *indio* group are 3, 12, and 20 . . . Ok. And Number 20, why is he *indio* and not *negro?*

R: Because of the texture of his hair. It doesn't seem curly. It seems, like more, not wavy. That's why. It's a criterion. If he had hair like *he* has—

I: —Number 2.

R: [Yes.] If he [20] had his hair like Number 2 or like Number 18, I could tell you that he is *negro* . . . But he looks like his hair isn't wavy, right?

I: So to be *negro*, one has to have not only dark skin but also *negro* features?

R: [Yes.] Features, mouth, and kinky hair . . .

The people depicted in Photos 18 and 20 have a similar skin color. Pulling out these two photos for comparison helps Alicia articulate why she classifies them differently and specify what separates an *indio* classification from *negro*. I typically picked out several photographs in this way—either two images that resembled one another but differed on certain features that were classified differently, or classifications that surprised me or that had taken the respondent more time to decide. Exploring the classifications the respondent made in this way allowed me to understand what differentiated each of the categories from one another.

After probing the meaning of the different categories, I typically followed up on the respondent's "signposts," the evocative statements that needed more unpacking. With Alicia, I began by asking about her initial question to me, and this eventually led into an exploration of the other intriguing issues she raised about everyone being *mestizo* and her identity as *negra*.

I: This is very interesting. And before doing the experiment you asked me if I wanted to know what you thought or what people here thought. Are they different?

R: Yes, because I believe that we are all *mestizos* here. For example, I'm going to give you the case of my sister, which is more illustrative. She is very *blanca*, has blue eyes and blond hair . . . because my mother has Spanish and European relatives so it seems like a gene got in through there. But I consider her a *mestiza*. She is mixed. My father is dark, *negro-negro* [very *negro*]. With hair—my father is like that . . . like Number 20. Exactly like that. The color of the skin is the same. The type of hair that is wavy but not kinky. Here we call it *indio lavado* [washed Indian]. . . .

I: So for you race doesn't have to do only with appearance? If a person like your sister seems very *blanca*, she is not necessarily *blanca* if she is has a *negro* parent?

R: Yes. I think that race does not have to do with the appearance . . . because there are people who are mixed and come out a different color . . . I think that the race does not have to do with the color of skin . . .

I: And do you believe that there are White Dominicans or no, all Dominicans are *mestizos*?

R: There are very *blanca* people, with heritage of, here there were many Italians, Chinese, immigrants. But definitely they have mixed with the Dominicans. That is, we cannot point out anyone pure from here.

I: Very interesting. And you said that you believe that you are *negra*.

R: I believe that I am *negra* because I identify a lot—it's not that I identify a lot, I think that what I am has more to do with the *negro* than with the *blanco*.

I: And why?

R: Well, because of the music, the type of music I like to listen to. A lot of drums, a lot of African rhythms . . . Religion, belief factors could also be, it could be something of that.

I: Do you think that you have more interaction with your father's family than with your mother's family?

R: Yes because my mother's family was very proud of being *blanca*. Then the children didn't come out that *blancos*, and it always seemed to be a bit shocking, right? That they were so conceited . . . They brag about being Spanish.

I: But you have people in the family that are darker?

R: Yes, but one thing—those darker people there are, like my aunt Juanita that already died, are people that are "children of the street" . . . meaning children not of a marriage, illegitimate children. One of those *blancos* of Santiago decided he liked a *negra* and nothing, they had a child. And there are like three or four cases in my mother's family that is like that. Children of the street that didn't come out *blancos*, they came out like Number 20, Number 3. My aunt Juanita was a person like Number 3. . . .

I: And these members of the family that are not from a marriage, does the family consider them part of the family?

R: Yes, yes, yes. They have integrated them to the family. They integrated them. Yes, yes, yes. Even in terms of what was inheritance they got an equal part. . . .

I: Is your mother's family upper class?

R: Upper middle class. They were, now not as much anymore, right?

I: And was it a bit strange when she married your father?

R: Uff [response to signal a lot]. Very strange. Horrible. What happens is that my father also came from a family, from San Francisco de Macoris . . . There is Santiago, really close to San Francisco de Macoris and they met at a party. He was already a civil engineer. He had graduated with very good grades, and that seems like it had a weight. And my great grandfather—that was military, was *blanco*, light eyes, straight hair—at the beginning pouted a lot. But finally it was imposed.

I: And how are the relations between the family of your mother and your father now?

R: Very few of my mother's family members are left. And they are ancient, and with respect to my father's family, they treated each other well. They were cordial relationships. They would get together, could even sometimes eat together at the same table, have a conversation. . . .

I: And what you told me how you made a decision to identify yourself more with your father's family and not with your mother's because of their ideas about race and the importance that they give being *blancos*, that is not very common right? I imagine that you are very unique, being like that.

R: Well I think that the fact of admiring my father a lot. I admire him a lot. The person I most admire in the world. He made me take sides. And additionally it's what I tell him, why think that I am *blanca*, if I live in a country where we all are *mestizos*, and where Africa had such a strong presence in this country.

I: But more or less at what age did you decide all that?

R: Well, [giggles], what happens is I am talking to you, now, in the present time, of things in the past. That I am now reflecting on. It's not something that I can tell you, on such a date, I made that decision. It's difficult, but I can tell you that at 15, I more or less had like my, my concept on the issue.

We learn a number of valuable things from this excerpt. Alicia reveals that she believes all Dominicans are *mestizos* because they are all racially mixed to some extent. This is apparent in the case of her and her sister, who have one White and one Black parent. But she also applies it to all other Dominicans, none of whom, she says, is "pure." Even those with very White appearance and largely European ancestry have some racial mixture in their family background. For her, *mestizo* means racially mixed. In further probes, I asked her what types of mixtures are included under the *mestizo* label and she clarifies that she understands it as the mixture, in any degree, of White and Black.[6] Alicia understands race not as a continuum based on appearance, as the literature suggests, but in a way that more closely resembles the American system based on ancestry—except in her racial schema, a person who is a mix of White and Black even in trace amounts is *mestizo*, and only someone without any mixture would be considered Black.

Alicia also reveals that she identifies with more than one racial label. She considers herself *mestiza* because of her racial ancestry, but she also identifies as *negra*. As she explains, *negra* is more of a symbolic identification. She prefers aspects of African culture and has a strong connection to her father and his family. She embraces a *negra* label, even as she realizes that others will not identify her as *negra*. She reveals, in describing her own family dynamics, the social hierarchy in her society that treats *negros* as subordinate, yet still ultimately as part of the family. Her identification with them is partly a political statement, to show that she spurns the ideology held by her maternal relatives of rejecting the people and cultures of African origins. Rich data such as these helped me realize how people use multiple racial schemas at

---

[6]See Roth (2012, p. 44) for a discussion of why Alicia chooses the term *mestizo* rather than the more common term *mulato* to represent the mix of White and Black.

the same time (see Roth, 2012). Identifying in one moment as *mestiza* and in another as *negra* is not a contradiction but represents different ways that people understand and use race in particular social contexts.

Because I gave respondents no guidance on what categories to use in identifying the race of the people in the photographs, some of the responses I received surprised me. There were certainly some unusual categories unique to particular respondents (for instance, one person identified most people as "Caribbean"). Borgatti (1998) suggested that unique responses such as these can be disregarded when the goal is to determine the shared content of a cultural domain, and analysis can focus on the categories that are used by most people. In cases in which unexpected categories are used by many respondents, however, some reconsideration of assumptions is required. For example, I was surprised to find that many respondents used nationality labels—like Puerto Rican, Dominican, or Mexican—to classify the race of the people in the photographs. At first, I was concerned that the technique was not capturing their understanding of race as I had intended. With considerable probing, rereading of the literature, and reflexivity about the context of the interview and the influence of my presence, I came to a clearer understanding of what it meant when respondents used these types of labels. In fact, it meant different things to different respondents. With in-depth probing about what these categories meant, I discovered that respondents with high education levels—among both migrants and nonmigrants— *were* using racial labels in the way I had envisioned. They simply racialized these nationality labels and thought of "Puerto Rican" as a mixed-race category that could be distinguished from "Dominican," "Mexican," and other nationality groups. Respondents with lower education levels were not necessarily making this connection, however. They were tapping into a different understanding of race that was common in Latin America. This concept associated "race" more closely with social groupings of people rather than biological groupings (Pitt-Rivers, 1973). In the Dominican Republic, for instance, the word *raza* has been used synonymously with "a people" or "nation" since the late 19th century (Howard, 2001; Sagás, 2000; Torres-Saillant, 1998). North American scholars associate this concept with ethnicity, but this was the cultural meaning that was salient for respondents. Furthermore, this was the schema that made sense to them in the context of a formal interview for an American scholar that highlighted national distinctions. Although this was not the only racial schema they used—and I used the interviews to probe the other schemas they used in different contexts—the photo elicitation allowed me to compare across respondents in a similar context and understand how factors such as their education level influenced which racial schema they used in this particular setting.

To examine respondents' knowledge of and use of additional racial schemas, I asked more directed questions during the interviews about their understanding of different racial terminology and how race is understood in the

United States and their society of origin. At one point in the interview, I asked them to classify the race of the friends they had listed in their social network, again with no guidance as to the racial categories they should use. This exercise again allowed them to apply their own labels, but with more context for who these people are and how they have thought of them in the past. Later in the interview, I asked specifically whether they had heard terms like *trigueño* or *indio* and asked them to list all the terms like this that they could recall. Then I showed them a list of such terms that are described in the literature on race in Latin America—specifically *negro, azulito, prieto, pardo,*[7] *grifo, moreno, de color, cenizo, mulato, trigueño, mestizo, indio, piel canela, café con leche, blanco con raja, jabao, colorao, rosadito, rubio, cano, jincho, blancusino, blanquito,* and *blanco.* I asked them to define those terms that are used in their home country. If they had not already used these terms to identify the photographs, I asked them to go through the photographs a second time, using terms from the list or other similar terms used in their country to classify the people in the photographs. I also asked respondents how they would identify themselves using such terms and several follow-up questions about what these categories mean, when they are used, and how they relate to one another. Combining opportunities for open-ended and closed-ended classifications, as well as different contexts for those classifications, provides a rich exploration of the range of schemas that respondents maintain; it captures not just the schemas they use, but also the bits of cultural knowledge that they have internalized but may not use (Vaisey, 2008).

By comparing how Dominican and Puerto Rican migrants to New York classified the photographs, compared with those who remained in Santo Domingo and San Juan, I was able to see that *racial acculturation* did occur, but in a different way than I had expected. Migrants who had been in the mainland United States longer were not more likely to group all types of mixtures between White and Black into one of those two categories. To the extent that racial acculturation did occur, it was primarily a phenomenon of upwardly mobile migrants—those who had attended college in the United States or worked in mainstream American workplaces. But the American racial schema they adopted was not just composed of Black and White. They added a third category—Latino—because they had learned from these interactions with non-Latino Americans that they were not really seen as White or Black. They perceived Americans as categorizing people racially as White, Black, or Latino. Although professional migrants recognized and even used other schemas at different points in the interviews, they used this racial schema on the photographs, revealing how they understood race in the United States and their place within it.

---

[7]The term *pardo,* which is used in Brazil but is not common in Puerto Rico or the Dominican Republic, was included to see if respondents would admit not recognizing a term.

STRENGTHS OF USING PHOTO ELICITATION

The previous example was focused primarily on measuring racial schemas, but one advantage of this methodological approach is in revealing the intersections of race and ethnicity. Ethnic and racial distinctions are made through similar processes of boundary construction. Although lines may be drawn on the basis of physical or cultural characteristics, the cognitive processes of distinguishing groups and identifying individuals within them are largely the same. Furthermore, individuals' identities are comprised of both ethnic and racial elements, informed by the sociohistorical context, and the study of each one is enhanced by the other. It is also valuable not to focus too narrowly on racial or ethnic distinctions because these are concepts that may overlap for many individuals. Some people—including many of my respondents—racialize ethnic or nationality categories like Puerto Rican and Dominican; others do not understand the academic distinction and simply use the terms interchangeably. Although a photo elicitation method can just as easily ask people to identify the ethnicity of depicted individuals, while focusing on the boundaries that distinguish one group from another, the approach is most effective when researchers are open to the intersecting lines of meaning that participants attribute to concepts of ethnicity and race.

Yet whether used for studying racial classifications or ethnic ones, photo elicitation combined with open-ended categorization and in-depth discussion can provide valuable insight into individuals' cognitive schemas. The discussions about how respondents decide on their classifications reveal their perception of what distinguishes different racial or ethnic groups and can open the door to rich information about ethnic or racial group relations and dynamics. Such topics can be awkward and difficult to evoke in an interview setting. The photographs can facilitate a discussion of ethnic or racial difference and differentiation by providing a concrete focal point for the conversation. The visual nature of the images can also trigger memories and semiconscious processes that just asking them to list ethnic or racial categories may not induce.

Photo elicitation is particularly useful for comparative research on ethnic or racial classification. It provides the same stimuli, or target individuals, to all respondents in a standardized context. Surveys asking for ethnic or racial self-identification effectively have different target individuals for each subject (the respondent), making comparisons of the classification process considerably more difficult, particularly when information about appearance or other characteristics that shape classification are missing. For studies of cultural change, such as immigrant acculturation, using photo elicitation to reveal individuals' cognitive schemas is especially valuable. These aspects of shared cultural understanding represent the knowledge about how to behave and interact that people use to guide and interpret their social experience (Borgatti, 1998; Gravlee, 2005). To the extent that immigrants have internalized such knowledge in a new society, it represents a stronger measure of cultural acquisition than their preference for particular ethnic or racial labels on a survey.

Using photographs in research can also help researchers gain orientation to the communities they are studying and develop rapport with respondents (Gold, 2007). The work of taking the photographs can help researchers develop familiarity with the community's physical sites and bring them into contact with its members. When the photographs shown during the elicitation exercise are of the respondent's own community or group, it can break the ice as respondents discuss the images or want to know more about them. My respondents frequently asked me where the pictures were taken and, oddly, told me they thought they knew one of the individuals shown. This never turned out to be the case, but the fact that the individuals depicted seemed familiar suggested that the photographs did represent on some level the types of individuals they might interact with in their daily lives. Many respondents saw the photo elicitation as a game or remarked that it was fun or interesting, even if some people found it challenging. As the types of questions academics ask are often not meaningful to nonacademics, using photographs of people "like them" can help bridge the gap between these worlds (Harper, 2002).

BEST PRACTICES/AVOIDING COMMON PITFALLS

For those interested in using photo elicitation to study ethnic schemas, the photographic instrument itself will likely present the first challenge. Few standardized visual instruments have been developed to provide a basis for comparison in different studies of ethnic or racial schemas. A notable exception is the collection of facial drawings developed by anthropologist Marvin Harris (1970) for his research on what "race–color" categories are used in Brazil. Not only have these drawings been used in other studies to provide a body of comparative work (Byrne & Forline, 1997; Gravlee, 2005; Sanjek, 1971), but they also have been made available for future research.[8] As discussed previously, however, these drawings are most valuable when researchers want to analyze how the specific aspects of the drawings that are systematically varied (skin tone, hair type, nose type, lip type, and sex) affect respondents' classifications.

Other scholars have drawn sets of images from yearbook photos, workplace employment photos, candid photographs taken during ethnographic

---

[8]Anthropologist Clarence Gravlee has restored and provided these images on his website (http://www.gravlee.org/research/harris/).

fieldwork, or computer-generated images. There are several databases for the study of facial recognition, memory, and emotion. These typically involve numerous images of a small number of individuals under different conditions—lighting, expressions, angle, and so on.[9] But few databases are constructed to provide racial or ethnic diversity of the type that might be useful for eliciting a respondent's ethnic or racial schemas.

If these resources do not provide the level of ethnic variation researchers are looking for, researchers can take their own photographs. Best practice involves submitting this activity for review by an institutional ethics review board to ensure that the individuals being photographed give informed consent to have their images used in the variety of contexts that researchers can foresee using the instrument. To gather the photographs, some scholars have set up a booth in a shopping center or busy public area and invited anyone interested to be photographed (Minear & Park, 2004). However, this gives the researcher less control over the appearance of the people who are photographed. Particularly when less common appearances are needed, the ability to select who to approach is desirable.

In constructing the photo instrument, researchers face a trade-off between greater control over the elements within the composition and greater authenticity. The photographs I compiled veered toward the latter end of this continuum, trying to capture real individuals as they appear in actual social contexts. But contextual information can influence classifications. If it matters to the goals of the research that respondents focus only on the individuals and not on their clothing, hairstyles, or background, researchers will need to standardize these elements of the image. In cases where this consistency is desirable, or when people with very specific appearances are needed, researchers might want to consider organizing a photo shoot or involving a modeling agency. Pilot interviews or consultations with members of target study population will be valuable to assembling the photographs into an instrument that captures the desired types of ethnic distinctions.

When trying to capture the cognitive set of categories that respondents use, allowing them to use open-ended classifications is crucial, as respondents may use categories that are quite different from those researchers have imagined. Providing examples may bias respondents toward answering with a particular type of schema. If researchers want to provide a particular context for respondents to think about the photographs—for example, "How would you classify these people if you saw them on the street in your neighborhood?"—the same context must be provided to all respondents in the same way. Of course, open-ended responses necessitate more complex

---

[9]A valuable resource listing many of these databases can be found at http://www.face-rec.org/databases/ (see also Gross, 2005; Minear & Park, 2004).

techniques for qualitative analysis.[10] Cognitive schemas are not always coherent. People sometimes combine different schemas or adopt variants of their own. Although this type of hybridization is another form of cultural change, it can make it difficult to provide analytical coherence to the resulting data. Connecting the results to theoretical frameworks of expected categories can be particularly helpful here.

My discussions with respondents relied on their beliefs about what influenced their classification decisions, but they may not be conscious of everything that influences their decisions. Although it is possible to look for discrepancies in what respondents say and what they do in qualitative interviews, quantitative studies do a better job of testing what factors influence respondents' classifications, including subconscious influences.

When asking people to classify the race or ethnicity of others, providing an explanation for the exercise is also important. Although some of my respondents found the task interesting, others exhibited some concern about whether they were "doing it right." People may worry that they are being asked to objectify or racialize others (see Roth, 2012, pp. 215–216). I found that providing a brief explanation for why the exercise was being done and what it hoped to achieve can offset these concerns. Reminding respondents that everyone makes judgments about the identities of others, whether they realize it or not, also helps to normalize the activity and make respondents more comfortable—as does reminding them of their contributions to research about a social process that is still not well understood.

CONCLUSION AND FUTURE DIRECTIONS

Focusing on self-assertions of one's own ethnicity is an important part of understanding ethnic identity, but we can put these self-assertions into context when we understand the individual's cognitive map of the ethnic categories that exist and the boundaries that distinguish them. Focusing on culturally shared ethnic or racial schemas will not be appropriate for all studies of ethnicity. Yet all scholars can benefit from thinking of the ways that ethnic identities represent cognitive knowledge and fit within larger classification systems.

Social science research on ethnic categories as cultural domains has much to gain from the photo elicitation technique. But several data resources would facilitate the contributions it can offer. At present, there are few standard photographic instruments that can be used across studies for comparative

---

[10]Valuable resources for analyzing qualitative data of the type that would be generated by this photo elicitation technique include Lofland, Snow, Anderson, and Lofland (2006), Miles and Huberman (1994), and Strauss and Corbin (1998).

research on ethnic or racial classifications. Developing a collection of images of real people of different ethnicities and races would be a major asset for this field. Showing the same individuals in different compositional arrangements—for instance, in their own clothing and settings, in standardized clothing and settings indicating high status (business attire and offices), low status (casual attire and urban streetscapes), and neutral clothing and settings like the photographs in Bailey's (2008) data—would help researchers build a body of work that allows comparisons and does not involve reinventing the wheel each time.

Ideally such a collection of images would involve people of ethnicities and races from all over the world. My own instrument included people who appeared to be of Latino ethnicity, making it less useful for comparison studies in other populations. There are numerous possibilities for comparative research using such photographs to map out the cognitive ethnic schemas of people in different nations, different ethnic groups within a community, different schemas used by immigrants and the native born, or how people perceive ethnic categories to be changing over time.

Although qualitative research is extremely valuable for exploring ethnic classifications and boundaries, survey data allowing open-ended classification of photographs also offers enormous possibilities. The tools exist to conduct powerful quantitative analyses of emic ethnic classifications evoked by photographic images (Byrne & Forline, 1997; Gravlee, 2005). Combining these tools with representative samples of different ethnic and racial populations or regional, national, and international populations can open up our understanding of ethnic identity as never before. As more scholarship considers the multiple dimensions of ethnicity and race (Brubaker & Cooper, 2000; Campbell & Troyer, 2007; Feliciano & Robnett, 2013; Okamura, 1981; Roth, 2010; Telles & Lim, 1998), such new and creative approaches to measuring those aspects will become increasingly important to advancing the field.

REFERENCES

American Anthropological Association. (1997). *Response to OMB Directive 15: Race and ethnic standards for federal statistics and administrative reporting.* Arlington, VA: Author.

American Sociological Association. (2003). *The importance of collecting data and doing social scientific research on race.* Washington, DC: Author.

Bailey, S. R. (2008). Unmixing for race making in Brazil. *American Journal of Sociology, 114,* 577–614. http://dx.doi.org/10.1086/592859

Barth, F. (1969). Introduction. In F. Barth (Ed.), *Ethnic groups and boundaries: The social organization of culture difference* (pp. 9–38). Boston, MA: Little, Brown and Company.

Borgatti, S. P. (1998). Elicitation techniques for cultural domain analysis. In J. Schensul & M. LeCompte (Eds.), *The ethnographer's toolkit* (pp. 1–26). Walnut Creek, CA: AltaMira Press.

Brubaker, R. (2004). *Ethnicity without groups.* Cambridge, MA: Harvard University Press.

Brubaker, R., & Cooper, F. (2000). Beyond "identity." *Theory and Society, 29*, 1–47. http://dx.doi.org/10.1023/A:1007068714468

Brubaker, R., Loveman, M., & Stamatov, P. (2004). Ethnicity as cognition. *Theory and Society, 33*, 31–64.

Byrne, B., & Forline, L. (1997). The use of emic racial categories as a tool for enumerating Brazilian demographic profiles: A re-analysis of Harris' 1970 study. *Boletim do Museu Paraense de História Natural e Ethnographia (Antropologia), 13*, 3–25.

Campbell, M. E., & Troyer, L. (2007). The implications of racial misclassification by observers. *American Sociological Review, 72*, 750–765. http://dx.doi.org/10.1177/000312240707200505

Candelario, G. E. B. (2007). *Black behind the ears: Dominican racial identity from museums to beauty shops.* Durham, NC: Duke University Press. http://dx.doi.org/10.1215/9780822390282

Casson, R. W. (1983). Schemata in cognitive anthropology. *Annual Review of Anthropology, 12*, 429–462. http://dx.doi.org/10.1146/annurev.an.12.100183.002241

Clark-Ibáñez, M. (2004). Framing the social world with photo-elicitation interviews. *American Behavioral Scientist, 47*, 1507–1527. http://dx.doi.org/10.1177/0002764204266236

Collier, J., Jr. (1957). Photography in anthropology: A report on two experiments. *American Anthropologist, 59*, 843–859. http://dx.doi.org/10.1525/aa.1957.59.5.02a00100

Cornell, S., & Hartmann, D. (1998). *Ethnicity and race: Making identities in a changing world.* Thousand Oaks, CA: Pine Forge Press.

D'Andrade, R. (1995). *The development of cognitive anthropology.* New York, NY: Cambridge University Press. http://dx.doi.org/10.1017/CBO9781139166645

Davis, F. J. (1991). *Who is Black? One nation's definition.* University Park, PA: Pennsylvania State University Press.

Denton, N. A., & Massey, D. S. (1989). Racial identity among Caribbean Hispanics: The effect of double minority status on residential segregation. *American Sociological Review, 54*, 790–808. http://dx.doi.org/10.2307/2117754

DiMaggio, P. (1997). Culture and cognition. *Annual Review of Sociology, 23*, 263–287. http://dx.doi.org/10.1146/annurev.soc.23.1.263

Duany, J. (1998). Reconstructing racial identity: Ethnicity, color, and class among Dominicans in the United States and Puerto Rico. *Latin American Perspectives, 25*, 147–172. http://dx.doi.org/10.1177/0094582X9802500308

Eberhardt, J. L., Dasgupta, N., & Banaszynski, T. L. (2003). Believing is seeing: The effects of racial labels and implicit beliefs on face perception. *Personality and Social Psychology Bulletin, 29*, 360–370. http://dx.doi.org/10.1177/0146167202250215

Feliciano, C., & Robnett, B. (2013, August). *Latinos' online dating choices: How racial classification by others shapes racial acceptance of others.* Paper presented at the American Sociological Association annual meeting, New York, NY.

Fiske, R. R. (1986). Schema-based versus piecemeal politics: A patchwork quilt, but not a blanket of evidence. In R. R. Lau & D. O. Sears (Eds.), *Political cognition: The 19th annual Carnegie symposium on cognition* (pp. 41–53). Hillsdale, NJ: Erlbaum.

Freeman, J. B., & Ambady, N. (2011). A dynamic interactive theory of person construal. *Psychological Review, 118,* 247–279. http://dx.doi.org/10.1037/a0022327

Freeman, J. B., Pauker, K., Apfelbaum, E. P., & Ambady, N. (2010). Continuous dynamics in the real-time perception of race. *Journal of Experimental Social Psychology, 46,* 179–185. http://dx.doi.org/10.1016/j.jesp.2009.10.002

Freeman, J. B., Penner, A. M., Saperstein, A., Scheutz, M., & Ambady, N. (2011). Looking the part: Social status cues shape race perception. *PLoS ONE, 6*(9), e25107. http://dx.doi.org/10.1371/journal.pone.0025107

Fullilove, M. T. (1998). Comment: Abandoning "race" as a variable in public health research—an idea whose time has come. *American Journal of Public Health, 88,* 1297–1298. http://dx.doi.org/10.2105/AJPH.88.9.1297

Gold, S. J. (1991). Ethnic boundaries and ethnic entrepreneurship: A photo-elicitation study. *Visual Sociology, 6*(2), 9–22. http://dx.doi.org/10.1080/14725869108583688

Gold, S. J. (2007). Using photography in studies of immigrant communities: Reflecting across projects and populations. In G. C. Stanczak (Ed.), *Visual research methods: Image, society, and representation* (pp. 141–166). Los Angeles, CA: Sage.

Gravlee, C. C. (2005). Ethnic classification in southeastern Puerto Rico: The cultural model of "color." *Social Forces, 83,* 949–970. http://dx.doi.org/10.1353/sof.2005.0033

Gross, R. (2005). Face databases. In S. Z. Li & A. J. Jain (Eds.), *Handbook of face recognition* (pp. 301–327). New York, NY: Springer. http://dx.doi.org/10.1007/0-387-27257-7_14

Halberstadt, J., Sherman, S. J., & Sherman, J. W. (2011). Why Barack Obama is Black: A cognitive account of hypodescent. *Psychological Science, 22,* 29–33. http://dx.doi.org/10.1177/0956797610390383

Harper, D. (2002). Talking about pictures: A case for photo elicitation. *Visual Studies, 17,* 13–26. http://dx.doi.org/10.1080/14725860220137345

Harris, D. R. (2002). *In the eye of the beholder: Observed race and observer characteristics* (Population Studies Center Research Report No. 02-522). Ann Arbor, MI: Population Studies Center, University of Michigan.

Harris, M. (1970). Referential ambiguity in the calculus of Brazilian racial identity. *Southwestern Journal of Anthropology, 26,* 1–14.

Herman, M. R. (2010). Do you see what I am? How observers' backgrounds affect their perceptions of multiracial faces. *Social Psychology Quarterly, 73,* 58–78.

Hoetink, H. (1967). *The two variants of Caribbean race relations: A contribution to the sociology of segmented societies.* London, England: Oxford University Press.

Hoetink, H. (1985). "Race" and color in the Caribbean. In S. W. Mintz & S. Price (Eds.), *Caribbean contours* (pp. 55–84). Baltimore, MD: Johns Hopkins University Press.

Howard, D. (2001). *Coloring the nation: Race and ethnicity in the Dominican Republic.* Oxford, England: Signal Books.

Jenkins, R. (1997). *Rethinking ethnicity: Arguments and explorations.* Thousand Oaks, CA: Sage.

Lofland, J., Snow, D., Anderson, L., & Lofland, L. H. (2006). *Analyzing social settings: A guide to qualitative observation and analysis* (4th ed.). Belmont, CA: Wadsworth Thomson.

Loveman, M. (1999). Is "race" essential? *American Sociological Review, 64,* 891–898. http://dx.doi.org/10.2307/2657409

Maneri, M., & Morning, A. (2013, March). Cultural translation of groups and their boundaries: How to compare Italian "Razza" to U.S. "race"? Paper presented at the Eastern Sociological Society Mini-Conference on Comparative Cultural Sociology, Boston, MA.

Massey, D. S., & Denton, N. A. (1992). Racial identity and the spatial assimilation of Mexicans in the United States. *Social Science Research, 21,* 235–260. http://dx.doi.org/10.1016/0049-089X(92)90007-4

Miles, M. B., & Huberman, M. A. (1994). *Qualitative data analysis: An expanded sourcebook.* Thousand Oaks, CA: Sage.

Minear, M., & Park, D. C. (2004). A lifespan database of adult facial stimuli. *Behavior Research Methods, Instruments, & Computers, 36,* 630–633. http://dx.doi.org/10.3758/BF03206543

Okamura, J. (1981). Situational ethnicity. *Ethnic and Racial Studies, 4,* 452–465. http://dx.doi.org/10.1080/01419870.1981.9993351

Omi, M., & Winant, H. (1994). *Racial formation in the United States from the 1960s to the 1990s.* New York, NY: Routledge.

Pauker, K., & Ambady, N. (2009). Multiracial faces: How categorization affects memory at the boundaries of race. *Journal of Social Issues, 65,* 69–86. http://dx.doi.org/10.1111/j.1540-4560.2008.01588.x

Peery, D., & Bodenhausen, G. V. (2008). Black + White = Black: Hypodescent in reflexive categorization of racially ambiguous faces. *Psychological Science, 19,* 973–977. http://dx.doi.org/10.1111/j.1467-9280.2008.02185.x

Penner, A. M., & Saperstein, A. (2008). How social status shapes race. *Proceedings of the National Academy of Sciences, USA, 105,* 19628–19630. http://dx.doi.org/10.1073/pnas.0805762105

Pitt-Rivers, J. (1973). Race in Latin America: The concept of "Raza." *European Journal of Sociology, 14,* 3–31. http://dx.doi.org/10.1017/S0003975600002630

Rodriguez, C. E. (1974). Puerto Ricans: Between Black and White. *New York Affairs*, *1*, 92–101.

Rodríguez, C. E. (1989). *Puerto Ricans: Born in the U.S.A.* Boston, MA: Unwin Hyman.

Rodríguez, C. E. (1991). The effect of race on Puerto Rican wages. In E. Melendez, C. Rodríguez, & J. B. Figueroa (Eds.), *Hispanics in the labor force: Issues and policies* (pp. 77–98). New York, NY: Plenum Press. http://dx.doi.org/10.1007/978-1-4899-0655-7_4

Roth, W. D. (2005). The end of the one-drop rule? Labeling of multiracial children in Black intermarriages. *Sociological Forum*, *20*, 35–67. http://dx.doi.org/10.1007/s11206-005-1897-0

Roth, W. D. (2010). Racial mismatch: The divergence between form and function in data for monitoring racial discrimination of Hispanics. *Social Science Quarterly*, *91*, 1288–1311. http://dx.doi.org/10.1111/j.1540-6237.2010.00732.x

Roth, W. D. (2012). *Race migrations: Latinos and the cultural transformation of race.* Stanford, CA: Stanford University Press.

Sagás, E. (2000). *Race and politics in the Dominican Republic.* Gainesville, FL: University Press of Florida.

Sanjek, R. (1971). Brazilian racial terms: Some aspects of meaning and learning. *American Anthropologist*, *73*, 1126–1143. http://dx.doi.org/10.1525/aa.1971.73.5.02a00120

Shorris, E. (1992). *Latinos: A biography of the people.* New York, NY: W. W. Norton.

Strauss, A., & Corbin, J. (1998). *Basics of qualitative research: Techniques and procedures for developing grounded theory.* Thousand Oaks, CA: Sage.

Telles, E. E., & Lim, N. (1998). Does it matter who answers the race question? Racial classification and income inequality in Brazil. *Demography*, *35*, 465–474. http://dx.doi.org/10.2307/3004014

Thomas, P. (1967). *Down these mean streets.* New York, NY: Vintage Books.

Torres-Saillant, S. (1998). The tribulations of Blackness: Stages in Dominican racial identity. *Latin American Perspectives*, *25*, 126–146. http://dx.doi.org/10.1177/0094582X9802500307

Vaisey, S. (2008). Socrates, Skinner, and Aristotle: Three ways of thinking about culture in action. *Sociological Forum*, *23*, 603–613. http://dx.doi.org/10.1111/j.1573-7861.2008.00079.x

Weiss, R. S. (1994). *Learning from strangers: The art and method of qualitative interview studies.* New York, NY: Free Press.

Willadsen-Jensen, E. C., & Ito, T. A. (2006). Ambiguity and the timecourse of racial perception. *Social Cognition*, *24*, 580–606. http://dx.doi.org/10.1521/soco.2006.24.5.580

Willadsen-Jensen, E. C., & Ito, T. A. (2008). A foot in both worlds: Asian Americans' perceptions of Asian, White, and racially ambiguous faces. *Group Processes & Intergroup Relations*, *11*, 182–200. http://dx.doi.org/10.1177/1368430207088037

Wimmer, A. (2008). The making and unmaking of ethnic boundaries: A multi-level process theory. *American Journal of Sociology, 113,* 970–1022. http://dx.doi.org/10.1086/522803

Wimmer, A. (2009). Herder's heritage and the boundary-making approach: Studying ethnicity in immigrant societies. *Sociological Theory, 27,* 244–270. http://dx.doi.org/10.1111/j.1467-9558.2009.01347.x

Winddance Twine, F. (2006). Visual ethnography and racial theory: Family photographs as archives of interracial intimacies. *Ethnic and Racial Studies, 29,* 487–511. http://dx.doi.org/10.1080/01419870600597909

5

UNDERSTANDING THE ASSOCIATION BETWEEN PHENOTYPE AND ETHNIC IDENTITY

IRENE LÓPEZ, LOVEY H. M. WALKER, AND MELEK YILDIZ SPINEL

Does it matter how you look? Is there a connection between your physical appearance and your feelings toward your ethnic group? Or can your phenotype, defined as your skin color and racial features, affect how members of your ethnic group feel toward you? In this chapter we review the literature on the complex relations between phenotype and ethnic identity and discuss how the associations between these two variables are not always direct, linear, or stable. We begin by defining ethnic identity and phenotype and then discuss how the ways in which these variables have been conceptualized and measured have necessitated more complicated assessments, designs, and analyses. We then present the results of our own work on phenotype and ethnic identity to illustrate how results can differ depending on the group studied and the methods and assessments used. We conclude with a reflection of the challenges faced in conducting such research and suggest future directions for those who may be interested in pursuing research in this area.

http://dx.doi.org/10.1037/14618-006
Studying Ethnic Identity: Methodological and Conceptual Approaches Across Disciplines, C. E. Santos and A. J. Umaña-Taylor (Editors)

CONCEPTUALIZATIONS AND MEASUREMENT
OF ETHNIC IDENTITY

Ethnic identity can broadly be defined as the degree to which individuals feel that they belong to a group that shares a common nationality or culture (Betancourt & López, 1993; Smith & Silva, 2011). Yet, although self-identification as a group member would appear to be a crucial component of ethnic identity, self-identification per se has not typically been considered a sufficient indicator of identity because the saliency, or centrality, among other dimensions of identity, can still vary even among self-identified group members (Sellers, Chavous, & Cooke, 1998; Umaña-Taylor, Diversi, & Fine, 2002). Thus, the study of ethnic identity is not simply about the identification with a specific group, but rather concerns the deeper affiliative bonds that individuals feel toward their group. As such, ethnic identity research, which is typically grounded in either social identity or ego identity theory, has emphasized and explored the emotional significance that individuals hold toward their own ethnic group (Phinney & Ong, 2007; Tajfel & Turner, 1986), with particular focus on experiences or components that detail cultural exploration, resolution/commitment, and affirmation (Umaña-Taylor et al., 2002).

Related to this, a growing body of research has also highlighted the social affiliative aspects of language use and has argued that rather than being a behavioral indicator of acculturation, language use can simultaneously shape and reflect various social identities, including ethnic identity (Jaspal & Coyle, 2009; Khatib & Ghamari, 2011). Hence, using the language of one's ethnic group can create and strengthen group boundaries and affiliation. This is when one's group identity is sometimes perceived to be conditional on language fluency or under conditions in which groups feel marginalized or threatened (Jaspal, 2009). Language use, fluency, and self-perceived competency can, therefore, be intimately tied to a person's subjective sense of group belonging and should consequently be assessed when studying ethnic identity (Acevedo, 2000; López, Dent, Ecosto, & Prado-Steiman, 2011; Niño-Murcia & Rothman, 2008). Thus, in our own work, we have specifically looked at the role that language fluency played in the association between ethnic identity and physical appearance.

Apart from such definitional issues, studies have also differed on the ways to assess ethnic identity. For example, some contend that ethnic identity can be measured by an overall score on a continuous scale if the focus of a study is on the assessment of how a specific dimension within ethnic identity is related to an outcome of interest (Cokley, 2007). However, others believe that ethnic identity should be measured by the separate mean tabulation of different subscores, or specific questions, that assess various statuses (Phinney,

1989; Umaña-Taylor, Yazedjian, & Bámaca-Gómez, 2004). Additionally, researchers have disagreed on whether measures of identity are best assessed by group-specific or global measures. That is, some studies have used measures that assess endorsement of specific cultural values or experiences of particular ethnic groups (e.g., Cortés, Rogler, & Malgady, 1994; Sibley & Houkamau, 2013), whereas other studies have used more global measures that have assessed identity development across various ethnic groups (e.g., Phinney, 1992; Umaña-Taylor et al., 2004). However, despite these differences in conceptualizations and measurement, many of the crucial components of ethnic identity, such as group commitment and affirmation, have, in some way or another, been assessed in relation to phenotype.

MEASUREMENT AND CATEGORIZATION OF PHENOTYPE

Briefly defined, *phenotype* refers to a set of physical characteristics that are typically found in high prevalence among groups that share a historically common gene pool (Brunsma & Rockquemore, 2001; Codina, 1990; López, Gonzalez, & Ho, 2012). These characteristics typically refer to features such as hair texture and color, eye color and shape, and the size of the nose and mouth (Blair, Judd, & Fallman, 2004; Montalvo, 1991; Robinson, 2011), although less frequently body size and frame may also be used to judge group racial/ethnic appearance (López & Walker, n.d.-b).

Of all of these characteristics, skin color is the most studied variable, although there is ongoing debate over whether people use primarily skin color or physical features when making racial categorizations (Hagiwara, Kashy, & Cesario, 2012). In all likelihood, people use both color and features when categorizing others, with the allowance that these categorizations may differ depending on the time spent making these assessments, as well as on the skin color of the participant being evaluated (Stepanova & Strube, 2012). In addition to categorization, the measurement of phenotype itself has had a long and problematic history (Jablonski, 2012). For example, early forays into the assessment of skin color involved comparing a participant's skin to various objects, such as glass-colored tiles, wheels, or swatches, which not only figuratively reduced participants to objects, but also yielded highly unreliable and unstable results. Only later, when light reflectance meters, or spectrophotometers, were devised could more precise and reliable quantification of light intensity and skin color pigment be obtained; although, as we later explain in our work, participants can still experience this type of measurement as intrusive and objectifying. More to the point, although the reliable assessment of skin color is helpful, more is still needed to help us understand the social significance of skin color and race.

Similarly, early attempts to quantify race by measuring various physical features were also problematic and resulted in measurements, such as a series of single scores or combined indices, which were inconsistent and had very little validity. For example, whereas some studies measured specific facial features such as noses, lips, and jaws according to their thickness or protrusion, others used more complex ratios that bore little association to the lived experience of race or of racial differences (Jackson, 2010). These ratios, such as the cephalic index, which was the ratio of the length and breadth of the skull, and the facial angle, which was determined by a horizontal line drawn through the jaw followed into the ear (e.g., Guthrie, 2003; Stratton, 1934), only served to reify the pseudo-biological construction of race (Gould, 1996; Guthrie, 2003; Jablonski, 2012; Smedley & Smedley, 2005). Furthermore, by attempting to illustrate the gradation of races, researchers produced scientifically questionable assessments that were ultimately objectifying and degrading.

Researchers have also relied on interviewer evaluations of participant phenotype, although these have been problematic because the assessments have typically used simplistic binary categories of light/White versus dark/non-White, or light, medium, and dark skin (Codina & Montalvo, 1994; Maldonado & Cross, 1977), which may not have accurately reflected how minorities describe their own skin color. In particular, Latinos, depending on the context or motive, may use either North or Latin American racial categories to describe themselves or others (López, 2008a), and these terms are not always interchangeable. For example, although the term *trigueño* can be used to indicate a person of a darker complexion, it cannot easily be subsumed under the North American category of Black because *trigueño* can strategically be used to distance a person from the Black Latino community ("*Yo no soy negra, soy trigueña*"/"*I'm not Black, I'm trigueña*").

Additionally, how does one judge whether someone has a "medium" phenotype? Should it be a combination of skin color and physical features, or should these aspects be evaluated separately? More specifically, what reference group should evaluators use when rating others—especially if it is someone who is different from his or her own cultural and reference group? That is, should skin color be assessed according to ranges found within a particular ethnic or racial group (i.e., emic perspective), or should individuals be categorized independent of reference group norms (i.e., etic perspective)? These questions are particularly pertinent when we consider that the assessment of phenotype, and racial classifications, varies not only across interviewers and participants, but also across time and context (Brunsma & Rockquemore, 2001; Rodriguez, 1974, 2000). Additionally, perceptions of reflected appraisals, or how participants believe others view them, can further affect how participants may classify or view themselves (Khanna, 2004). In short, the measurement and categorization of phenotype has been plagued with a number of methodological problems, which have limited our understanding of the role of phenotype in the lives of ethnic and racial minorities.

THE RELATION BETWEEN PHENOTYPE AND ETHNIC IDENTITY

Despite these issues in measurement, the body of research on the effect of within-group differences on objective and subjective life indices has been growing (Hersch, 2011). Briefly, *objective life indices* refer to such quantifiable variables as years of employment or education, whereas *subjective life experiences* refer to interpersonal experiences, such as ethnic identity.

With regard to objective life indices, a growing body of research on within-group differences has indicated that darker skinned individuals typically fare worse than their lighter skinned peers. Specifically, darker skinned individuals generally earn less money, have less education, and are more likely to be employed in jobs with lower occupation prestige and to live in more segregated communities than their lighter skinned peers (Frank, Akresh, & Lu, 2010; Hersch, 2011; Morales, 2008). Darker skin color is, therefore, associated with less access to resources and consequently, according to sociological theory, with fewer chances to improve one's future opportunities. However, it is important to note that these associations have varied by the specific ethnic group studied (Espino & Franz, 2002) and by the way skin color has been categorized (see Flores & Telles, 2012, for an extensive discussion of this topic). Thus, especially among Latinos, context and measurement must be attended to when evaluating the effects of phenotype.

Furthermore, these issues become increasingly important when we consider the association between phenotype and more interpersonal or subjective life experiences, such as ethnic identity. For example, early research indicated that among Mexican-origin children, a greater preference for lighter skinned dolls and friends over darker skinned dolls and friends, along with their tendency to incorrectly racially identify themselves when asked about their own skin color, was indicative of a lowered, or confused, ethnic identity (Cota-Robles de Suárez, 1971; Teplin, 1976). Yet, skin color preference or self-identification among children may not necessarily be indicative of a child's ethnic identity (Banks, 1976) but may instead reflect the child's understanding of racial bias (Corenblum & Annis, 1993).

Hence, studies such as these have confounded racial classification with ethnic identity, and most studies on phenotype have not considered the measurement and significance of race for Latinos. Because Latinos are at once an ethnic group and a multiracial group, race may take precedence over ethnicity for some Latinos, whereas for others ethnicity may take precedence over race (Araújo & Borrell, 2006). Additionally, for some, race and ethnicity may be used interchangeably or not at all. Thus, even though Latinos are often more likely to identify as White (Golash-Boza & Darity, 2008), the meaning of such designations is not always clear and is not always indicative of ethnic identity. In other words, identification as White or Black does not necessarily mean that a participant identifies as more or less Latino. Instead, racial classifications may be more indicative of racial attitudes and discrimination than an indicator of ethnic identity or affiliation. Finally, as is often the case with skin color among Latinos, the propensity to racially identify with one group over another is often contingent on place, ethnic group, or even the way a question is asked (Landale & Oropesa, 2002).

Yet, even if for some Latinos racial identification may be independent of ethnic identity, it is possible that variations in appearance may still be associated with the aforementioned components of ethnic identity, such as a sense of belonging or strength of affiliative bonds. A review of the extant literature indicates that although a handful of studies have not found a direct association between phenotype and ethnic identity (Alarcón, Szalacha, Erkut, Fields, & García Coll, 2000; Ayers, Kulis, & Marsiglia, 2013), for some, phenotype may be directly related to ethnic identity. For example, in early research with Mexican-origin individuals, darker skinned participants used more ethnically defined self-descriptors, expressed more interest in the Latino community (Vazquez, Garcia-Vazquez, Bauman, & Sierra, 1997), and had a greater preference for speaking Spanish than their lighter skinned counterparts (Arce, Murguía, & Frisbie, 1987). More recent research has found that ethnic identity affirmation was positively associated with familial ethnic socialization, particularly for darker skinned and more Latino-appearing adolescents (Gonzales-Backen & Umaña-Taylor, 2011). Thus, at least on the basis of this research, having darker skin appears to be related to various components of ethnic identity, such as greater ethnic affirmation, belonging, and commitment, perhaps because others more readily identify or expect darker skinned individuals to be "more ethnic or Spanish" or perhaps because their lighter skinned peers may more easily pass as non-Hispanic White (e.g., Lewin, 2005).

These findings are particularly important when we consider that darker skinned Latinos have reported more negative self-perceptions, more depressive affect and symptomatology, and lower self-esteem than their lighter skinned peers (Maldonado & Cross, 1977; Ramos, Jaccard, & Guilamo-Ramos, 2003; Telzer & Vazquez Garcia, 2009). Furthermore, a growing body of research has indicated that negative racial stereotypes are activated more quickly, especially among those with negative racial attitudes, when evaluating faces of individuals with more Afrocentric features (Blair, Chapleau, & Judd, 2005; Stepanova & Strube, 2012). For example, those with more Afrocentric features, regardless of race, are typically judged to be more violent and often receive harsher sentences than those with less Afrocentric features (Blair,

Judd, & Chapleau, 2004). It may, therefore, be hypothesized that ethnic identity may be particularly important for darker skinned individuals because it can protect against feelings of discrimination and distress. In fact, a growing number of studies have found that ethnic identity does serve as a moderator in the relation between phenotype and psychological distress (Kiang & Takeuchi, 2009; Perry, Stevens-Watkins, & Oser, 2013).

Still, the protective effects of ethnic identity may not be exclusive to darker skinned participants. That is, despite the economic advantages and social capital of having lighter skin, lighter skin has also been associated with feelings of estrangement and perceived rejection from one's community (Cunningham, 1997; Hunter, 2007). Thus, the relation between ethnic identity and phenotype, as well as the benefits incurred from ethnic identity, may differ depending on one's appearance and may be contextually dependent. For example, Codina and Montalvo (1994) found that although darker skin was related to poorer mental health for Mexican men born in the United States, a darker skin color was conversely related to better mental health among women born in Mexico.

In sum, the relation between phenotype and ethnic identity is complex and not always direct, linear, or stable. Although group belonging is important for psychological health for ethnic minorities (Smith & Silva, 2011), the associations between ethnic identity and phenotype may vary according to how each variable is measured. Moreover, the meaning and function of ethnic identity may vary according to one's phenotype and how that appearance is evaluated within a given context. With this in mind, we now turn to our studies that assessed the associations between phenotype and ethnic identity in a group of English- and Spanish-speaking Puerto Rican women.

OVERVIEW OF SELECTED WORK

Puerto Rican women are a convergence of Indian, African, and Spanish ancestry (López, 2008b). As a result, they have a broad range of characteristics, such as variations in skin color and physical features, which makes them an ideal group in which to study the associations between phenotype and ethnic identity. Within this group, one sample of 75 English- and Spanish-speaking women were interviewed to (a) assess the relations among ethnic identity, phenotype, and self-esteem among the English-dominant women (Study 1); (b) assess the relations between ethnic identity, phenotype, and appearance anxiety among the Spanish-dominant women (Study 2); and (c) qualitatively and quantitatively assess the experiences of ethnic misidentification among both groups of women (Study 3). This body of work is noteworthy because we not only used multiple measures of phenotype within each study, but we also strived to illuminate the more complex associations between the study variables among different language groups.

DESCRIPTION OF SAMPLE

Across all three studies, participants were Puerto Rican women between the ages of 19 and 50 who resided in a major metropolitan city. Participants were recruited from a major northeastern metropolitan city historically known to have a large number of Puerto Ricans. Within this city, predetermined areas with high concentrations of Puerto Ricans were selected on the basis of U.S. Census blocks. Recruitment was done through a variety of methods, including word of mouth, although the primary method of contact was through snowball sampling. With this technique, various gatekeepers of the community, ranging from local neighborhood contacts to professional members of the community, were first contacted and asked to refer eligible participants, and then the recruited participants were asked to nominate others for the study. This technique was effective in recruiting a large number of participants in a relatively short amount of time (6 weeks). However, in practice, it meant that participants ended up recruiting other members who were most like themselves, economically and phenotypically, which yielded a relatively homogenous sample. Once participants were recruited, informed consent was obtained and most interviews were conducted in participants' homes.

MEASURES

All of the studies assessed the relation between phenotype and ethnic identity, although they varied as to whether they assessed self-esteem or appearance anxiety in either English- or Spanish-speaking women. All measures were back translated prior to the beginning of the study, and the order in which the scales were administered was counterbalanced throughout the study. Descriptive statistics for the measures are given in Table 5.1.

Ethnic Identity

Ethnic identity was measured using an abbreviated 8-item version of Phinney's (1992) Multigroup Ethnic Identity Measure (MEIM). Items (e.g., "I have a strong sense of belonging to my ethnic group") assessed ethnic affirmation and belonging (five items) and commitment (three items) following Martinez and Dukes's (1997) abbreviation of the MEIM. Responses ranged from 1 (*strongly disagree*) to 4 (*strongly agree*), and a composite score was created, with higher scores indicating a higher level of ethnic identity.

TABLE 5.1
Descriptive Statistics and Intercorrelations Among Main Study Variables Among English-Dominant Participants ($N = 53$)

Measures	M	SD	95% CI	α	1	2	3	4	5	6	7	8	9
1. Self-esteem	3.42	.50	1.67–4.00	.86	—	.31*	.09	.38**	-.04	.03	-.12	.06	-.03
2. Ethnic identity	3.45	.52	1.88–4.00	.84		—	.23	.41**	.36**	-.26	.17	.26	.32
3. English proficiency	3.86[a]	.25	3.00–4.00	.82			—	.18	.06	.08	.05	.12	.06
4. Spanish proficiency	3.03[a]	.62	1.00–4.00	.89				—	.10	-.07	-.01	-.03	.04
5. Lightness	59.32	3.72	50.44–65.59	—					—	-.76***	.73***	.82***	.95***
6. Yellow pigment	20.50	2.28	15.67–24.94	—						—	-.70***	-.73***	-.87***
7. Participant rating	5.89	1.71	3.00–9.00	.86							—	.80***	.84***
8. Interviewer rating	5.96	2.23	1.00–9.00	.92								—	.92***
9. All color ratings	12.71	2.29	7.63–16.64	—									—

Note. CI = confidence interval. Adapted from "'But You Don't Look Puerto Rican': The Moderating Effect of Ethnic Identity on the Relation Between Skin Color and Self-Esteem Among Puerto Rican Women," by I. López, 2008, *Cultural Diversity and Ethnic Minority Psychology, 14,* p. 104. Copyright 2008 by the American Psychological Association.
[a]Participants had greater English than Spanish proficiency, paired $t(52) = 9.72$, $p < .001$. [b]$N = 52$.
*$p < .05$. **$p < .01$. ***$p < .001$.

Language Proficiency

Language proficiency was assessed using a subscale of Marín and Gamba's (1996) Bidimensional Acculturation Rating Scale for Hispanics. This measure is a 12-item scale that assesses proficiency in either English or Spanish (e.g., "How well do you speak English/Spanish?"). Items were scored on a 4-point Likert scale, ranging from 1 (*almost never/very poorly*) to 4 (*almost always/very well*), and were summed to create separate mean composite scores of linguistic fluency in either English or Spanish, with a higher score indicating greater self-reported fluency. Although language use is typically a proxy for acculturation, as we show, we believe language proficiency was used as a way to affirm group identity.

Phenotype

Phenotype was assessed by measuring skin color and facial features. Skin color was assessed using the Color Guide hand-held spectrophotometer (Version 45/0, UMM Electronics, Indianapolis, Indiana). This was a small, portable, battery-operated reflectance meter that generated two reflectance scores. The first was a measurement of light intensity, and the other was a pigment-related score that assessed yellow melanin. To ensure reliability, two spectrophotometer readings were taken from each participant, and a composite score was computed for each index. In accordance with standard procedures (Weiner & Lourie, 1969), the medial surface of a participant's upper left arm was cleaned with an alcohol swab before any readings were taken.

Phenotype was measured using similarly worded participant and masked interviewer ratings that were specifically developed for this study. The phenotype scales were composed of 10 items that assessed various physical features (e.g., hair, mouth, nose, eyes) and skin color. However, the items that assessed hair and eye color were subsequently dropped because they were difficult to consistently assess, and their inclusion resulted in negative interitem correlations. The majority of response options ranged from 1 (*very light/thin*) to 9 (*very dark/broad*). Unlike previous studies, the skin color measures were not dichotomized into light and dark (Codina & Montalvo, 1994). Instead, participants had to separately describe their skin color using Puerto Rican and American skin color classifications, as previous research has noted that Latin American color classifications may differ from North American racial classifications (e.g., Telles, 2004). These items were rated on a 9-point scale in which all participants were first asked to mark, on a continuous scale, whether they considered themselves *Blanca* (1–3), *Trigueña* (4–6), or *Negra* (7–9), and later if they were *White* (anchored at 1) or *Black* (anchored at 9). Items were reverse coded and summed to create a composite score so that, similar to the lightness score obtained on the spectrophotometer, a higher score was indicative of more White features.

Self-Esteem

In Study 1, self-esteem was assessed using the Rosenberg Self-Esteem Scale (Rosenberg, 1965). Responses were rated on a 4-point scale ranging from 1 (*strongly disagree*) to 4 (*strongly agree*) and coded so that a higher score was indicative of greater self-esteem. One item, "*I wish I could have more respect for myself*," was dropped because of its low item–total correlation, which is in keeping with other studies that have also noted problems with this particular item (Farruggia, Chen, Greenberger, Dmitrieva, & Macek, 2004). A composite score of the remaining nine items was obtained by summing the total of all responses and obtaining the mean, with a higher score indicative of greater self-esteem.

Appearance Anxiety

In Study 2, we assessed appearance anxiety using an abbreviated version of the Appearance Anxiety Scale (Dion, Dion, & Keelan, 1990). This scale asked participants to rate how characteristic they felt an item described their feelings toward their physical appearance (e.g., "I feel nervous about aspects of my physical appearance"). Items were rated on a 4-point scale, ranging from 0 (*never*) to 4 (*almost always*), and a composite scale score was created, with higher scores indicative of greater appearance anxiety (i.e., discomfort with one's appearance).

STUDY 1: PHENOTYPE, ETHNIC IDENTITY, AND SELF-ESTEEM AMONG ENGLISH-DOMINANT WOMEN

In Study 1, we assessed whether ethnic identity would serve as moderator in the relation between phenotype and self-esteem in a sample of 53 English-dominant Puerto Rican women (see López, 2008b). As a first step, we examined the validity of the measures of skin color (see Table 5.1). As expected, spectrophotometer readings were highly correlated with one another, with lightness inversely related to yellow pigment. The two objective spectrophotometer scores were also highly correlated with the subjective participant and interviewer ratings of skin color and features. These subjective ratings were, in turn, associated with one another. Given the strong correlations between the phenotype ratings, a composite index of the four measures was created. With regard to the main study variables, only lightness

TABLE 5.2
Summary of Hierarchical Multiple Regression Predicting
Self-Esteem (N = 53)

Variables	$R^2\Delta$	Ethnic Identity × Skin Color B (SE)	β
Step 1: Control variables	.30***		
Age		.01 (.01)	.16
Spanish proficiency		.25 (.10)*	.31
Ever visited Puerto Rico		.46 (.17)***	.33
Step 2: Composite phenotype ratings	.00	−.02 (.06)	−.03
Ethnic identity	.00	−.08 (.07)	.15
Interaction term	.12**		
Ethnic Identity × Phenotype		.16 (.05)**	—

Note. R^2 .42/Adjusted R^2 .35. Only final order statistics presented. Adapted from "'But You Don't Look Puerto Rican': The Moderating Effect of Ethnic Identity on the Relation Between Skin Color and Self-Esteem Among Puerto Rican Women," by I. López, 2008, *Cultural Diversity and Ethnic Minority Psychology, 14,* p. 106. Copyright 2008 by the American Psychological Association.
*$p < .05$. **$p < .01$. ***$p < .001$.

was associated with ethnic identity, and only greater Spanish fluency was associated with higher self-esteem and ethnic identity.

A hierarchical multiple regression was run in which Step 1 included three control variables (i.e., age, Spanish fluency, and visits to Puerto Rico), Step 2 included the standardized composite of phenotype ratings, Step 3 was the standardized variable of ethnic identity, and Step 4 was the interaction between the cross-products of phenotype and ethnic identity (see Table 5.2 for final order statistics). As shown, 30% of the variance in self-esteem was explained by Spanish fluency and visits to Puerto Rico, which aligns with previous research noting that greater Spanish fluency can help U.S. Latinos affirm their ethnic membership (Jimenez, 2004). However, neither phenotype nor ethnic identity was related to self-esteem. Instead, a significant interaction emerged between ethnic identity and phenotype in predicting self-esteem, which explained an additional 12% of the variance in self-esteem, above and beyond the aforementioned variables, $F(1, 46) = 9.35, p < .01$.

To assess this interaction, we initially ran a separate regression for both high and low values of the standardized predictors, as indexed by the median split, and then plotted and visually inspected the interaction (López, 2008b). However, the median splits are not an optimal choice for continuous predictors (Aiken & West, 1991), and visual inspection does not quantify under what conditions a predictor is significantly related to an outcome (Holmbeck, 2002). Thus, we probed this interaction by conducting a test of the simple slopes for phenotype and self-esteem, at high and low levels of ethnic identity, as indexed by one standard deviation above and below the mean. As shown in Figure 5.1,

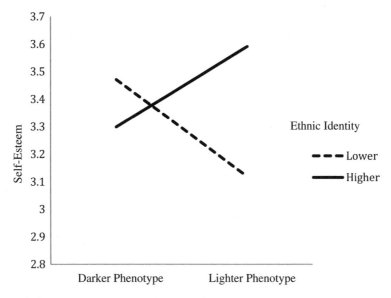

Figure 5.1. Interaction between ethnic identity and phenotype. Adapted from "'But You Don't Look Puerto Rican': The Moderating Effect of Ethnic Identity on the Relation Between Skin Color and Self-Esteem Among Puerto Rican Women," by I. López, 2008, *Cultural Diversity and Ethnic Minority Psychology, 14*, pp. 102–108. Copyright 2008 by the American Psychological Association.

a lower ethnic identity was associated with significantly worse self-esteem for those with lighter skin and more Europeanized features, as opposed to their darker skinned peers, $b = -.175$, $SE = .081$, $t = -2.159$, $p < .05$. Additionally, there was a trend for a higher ethnic identity to be associated with better self-esteem for lighter women, $b = -.146$, $SE = .08$, $t = 1.815$, $p = .08$.

In keeping with previous research, our study indicated that ethnic identity functioned as a moderator or buffer between skin color and self-esteem. Yet, why wasn't a high level of ethnic identity equally (or more) beneficial for darker skinned women? One reason may be that as a group, lighter skinned women may not routinely be ascribed an ethnic or minority affiliation, and thus having a higher ethnic identity allows them to claim affiliation to their group. Hence, having a strong sense of ethnic belonging can protect against being misidentified as White and non-Latino. In contrast, among darker skinned women, the addition of ethnic identity did not substantially alter the relation between phenotype and self-esteem, perhaps because they may already be readily identified as minorities (although not necessarily Latinos). Additionally, for darker skinned Latinos, it may be that more than ethnic identity is needed to substantially modulate their self-esteem given their well-documented experiences with overt discrimination and economic hardship.

Given these findings, in our next study we wished to assess the effects of phenotype and ethnic identity with an outcome variable that was more closely linked to appearance and skin color. Thus, we assessed the associations between phenotype, ethnic identity, and appearance anxiety, as no studies to our knowledge have assessed appearance anxiety with phenotype. Additionally, given previous research noting that for Latinos the associations and meaning of phenotype may differ by context (Rodriguez, 2000), we wished to extend our analysis to assess the relations between phenotype, identity, and appearance in a group of Spanish-dominant women. Thus, in contrast to our first study, we wanted to assess the association of these variables in a group that was linguistic secure and dominant in Spanish and presumably more culturally immersed within traditional Puerto Rican culture.

STUDY 2: PHENOTYPE, ETHNIC IDENTITY, AND APPEARANCE ANXIETY AMONG SPANISH-DOMINANT WOMEN

In our second study, we assessed appearance anxiety in a sample of 22 Spanish-dominant mainland Puerto Rican women (Lopez & Walker, n.d.-a). *Appearance anxiety* refers to the discomfort or apprehension related to aspects of one's physical appearance and concerns over how the self is evaluated by others (Dion et al., 1990). To date, most of the research on appearance anxiety with women has focused on issues related to body dissatisfaction or eating disorders (e.g., Koskina, Van den Eynde, Meisel, Campbell, & Schmidt, 2011; Monro & Huon, 2005). As a result, other aspects of physical appearance, such as evaluative comments concerning facial features, hair, and skin color, have not been sufficiently explored even though these are issues of concern for a number of minority women (Buchanan & Acevedo, 2004; Comas-Díaz, 1994; De Casanova, 2004; Robinson, 2011; Stephens & Fernández, 2012).

As in Study 1, we first validated the measures of phenotype and the spectrophotometer ratings (see Table 5.3). As expected, lightness and yellow pigment were similarly and inversely related. Participant and interviewer ratings of skin color were also highly associated with one another. However, despite the strong association between the interviewer and participant ratings, only the interviewer ratings were, in turn, associated with the two spectrophotometer readings. Closer inspection of the ratings indicated that the interviewer ratings had more variability and spread in comparison to the participant ratings. For example, the 95% CI for interviewer ratings was 4.70–6.09, whereas for the participant ratings it was 5.46–6.41. In practice, this meant that when skin color was assessed according to Puerto Rican color standards, only one participant rated her own skin color as darker than *trigueña*, whereas the interviewer rated eight participants as darker than *trigueña*. Thus, participants

TABLE 5.3

Descriptive Statistics and Intercorrelations Among Phenotype Variables
For Spanish-Dominant Women ($N = 22$)

Measures	M	SD	95% CI	α	1	2	3	4
1. Lightness	58.89	5.02	56.66–61.11	—	—	−.76**	.27	.61*
2. Yellow pigment	20.16	2.10	19.23–21.09		—	—	−.42	−.60*
3. Participant ratings	5.93	1.07	5.46–6.41	.73			—	.67**
4. Interviewer ratings	5.39	1.57	4.70–6.09	.90				—

Note. CI = confidence interval.
$p < .06.$ *$p < .01.$ **$p < .001.$

rated themselves as lighter than the interviewer ratings, $t(21) = -2.18, p < .05$. Consequently, a composite measure of skin color ratings could not be created as had been done for the English-dominant sample.

Additional analyses revealed that neither the spectrophotometer nor the interviewer ratings were linearly associated with any of the main study variables (i.e., appearance anxiety, ethnic identity, or language fluency). Instead, it was the participants' ratings of their own appearance, which combined skin color and facial features, that were related to appearance anxiety, $r = .47, p < .05$. In particular, appearance anxiety was greatest among women who rated their phenotype as more fair. Also, ethnic identity was inversely related to appearance anxiety, $r = -.43, p < .05$. Finally, contrary to our hypothesis, among this small group of Spanish speakers, neither English nor Spanish fluency was related to either appearance anxiety or ethnic identity. However, English proficiency was negatively associated with a darker self-rated phenotype, $r = -.54, p < .05$. In sum, the rating of skin color differed according to the language of the participant. Additionally, the pattern of associations between phenotype and ethnic identity varied between English- and Spanish-speaking women. And finally, the effects of language proficiency differed according to the language group studied.

STUDY 3: MISIDENTIFICATION AMONG
PUERTO RICAN WOMEN

Our final study surveyed both English and Spanish-speaking women ($N = 75$) and centered on understanding the experience of ethnic misidentification. As we have detailed among traditionally marginalized groups, a sense of belonging, or group attachment, is important because it serves to unify and rally members in the face of various threats and provides a shared sense of community

(López, 2008b). However, as a mixed-race group, Latinos differ along a number of physical dimensions and are, therefore, often subject to inquiries regarding their ancestry. Hence, we wished to understand what occurs when group members are misidentified and told that they do not look like their group.

Study Design

For this study we used a mixed methods design in which we concurrently collected quantitative assessments of the association of the various skin color measures with appearance anxiety, as well as qualitative data on the experience of misidentification (Creswell & Plano Clark, 2007). As such, this convergent designed study simultaneously assessed the quantitative patterns between our variables and also allowed for the textual analysis of polyvocal narratives among those who have been misidentified, but not sufficiently represented in the literature (Bartholomew & Brown, 2012; López, 2005).

Measures

In addition to the aforementioned phenotype and ethnic identity scales, the primary investigator asked the following three open-ended questions: "Has anyone ever told you that you don't look Puerto Rican?" (which allowed for the assessment of prevalence); "Why do you think that happened?" (which allowed us to explore and tabulate the proposed mechanisms or risk factors for cultural misidentification); and "How did that make you feel?" (which allowed us to list and describe any psychological outcomes). Questions were asked in either English or Spanish depending on the preference of the participant.

Collection and Analyses of Data

Once the participants completed the surveys, the aforementioned questions were asked by the interviewer, who then wrote down the responses of the participant verbatim. These responses were then read back to the participants to either correct for any errors and, whenever needed, to follow up with clarifications. At the completion of the study, the interviewer then gave the sheet of responses to a separate rater who typed up each of the participants' responses. Responses for each of the questions were typed onto index cards that were color coded according to participant language. Hence, there was a card for every participant, and raters took turns in using the cards to sort and code themes. Raters first went through each of the three questions on the card and coded the themes according to each of the questions. To prevent bias, the coding of responses was never written on the card but was carried out on separate data sheets.

Using grounded theory, the principal investigator, a Puerto Rican woman, and the secondary rater, a mixed-race woman, individually reviewed the data and open coded the cards into broad themes (Ryan & Bernard, 2003; Strauss & Corbin, 1998). Following this, we coded more minutely into sub-themes or axial codes and then discussed until consensus was reached (Hill, Thompson, & Nutt Williams, 1997; Ryan & Bernard, 2003). Throughout the process, themes were coded using an inductive approach. However, during the final confirmative stage of our qualitative analysis, we applied a deductive approach to identify individual cases that did not fit neatly into our afore-mentioned categories (Patton, 2002). This further scrutiny of the data, along with the analysis of the quantitative data, helped us get a richer picture of the process of misidentification. Finally, by using two independent raters, we tried to address issues of reliability and triangulation.

RESULTS

The results of our quantitative analysis found that, similar to our earlier smaller study with Spanish-dominant women, appearance anxiety was negatively related with ethnic identity, $r = -.40$, $p < .01$. However, there were no significant associations between any of the skin color variables and appearance anxiety. Additionally, our qualitative research indicated that approximately 80% of the participants had been told that they did not look Puerto Rican ($n = 42$), with close to half ($n = 20$) also volunteering that it happened frequently, especially when they were younger. Hence, in this sample, although skin color per se was not associated with appearance anxiety, misidentification was a highly prevalent and frequent experience.

Reasons for Misidentification

In response to the second question, "Why do you think that you were told that you did not look Puerto Rican?" participants indicated that they were most likely misidentified because of their physical appearance ($n = 36$), language ($n = 10$), and/or behaviors ($n = 8$).

Skin Color

In particular, women were most commonly told that they did not look Puerto Rican because of their skin color—either because they were too light or too dark ($n = 20$). As a result, one participant even noted that she would preemptively announce her ethnicity when meeting with others to prevent this misidentification from occurring ("Sometimes I'll say I'm Puerto Rican, so it's out in the open").

Physical Features

Following skin color, women also said that they were misidentified because of specific features, such as texture of their hair ("Because they don't think Puerto Ricans can have good hair"), color, and even hairstyle. Others were told that they did not look Puerto Rican because of other features, such as their jaw ("I have a weird broad jawline"); their noses; or because other specific characteristics, such as green eyes, freckles, or birthmarks. Furthermore, at least two women were told that they did not look Puerto Rican because of their body size or, as one participant bluntly stated, because others believed that "Latinas were typically meatier." Most commonly, however, participants stated that they were misidentified on the basis of a host of combined features. In short, women reported being regularly subjected to the scrutinization of others and at times also reported evaluating themselves ("Maybe it's because of my nose, it's too pointy").

Language

Women were also told that they did not look Puerto Rican if they spoke English or if they spoke English without a Spanish accent. Consequently, some women reported using language as a way to mark or authenticate their identity to others ("Sometimes I'll speak Spanish early on in a conversation"). Thus, they consciously code switched into Spanish or at times even changed the way they spoke English to be identified as part of the group. For example, one participant noted, "Sometimes they think I'm Black or Dominican, but once I start speaking they know. I speak really *jibara*, perhaps that gets me identified easier." Thus, in speaking in the language and tone of the *jibaro*, or as a stereotypical Puerto Rican peasant, this participant hopes to get quickly identified, and presumably accepted, as a member of her ethnic group by alluding to this symbol of Puerto Rican national identity. Although such efforts underscored the importance of being identified as a group member, they also highlighted the extent to which some participants performed, and perhaps endorsed, stereotyped views of their own ethnicity. Conversely, for Spanish-dominant participants, language often served as a buffer against misidentification, as one participant noted that "as soon as I open my mouth, believe me they know."

Behavior

In addition to the assumptions regarding how Puerto Ricans looked and talked, participants were sometimes told that they did not look Puerto Rican on the basis of how they acted. In particular, some were told that they did not seem to be Puerto Rican because Puerto Ricans only wore "street clothes" or were "loud and rude." Hence, ethnic group membership was evaluated on the basis of racist, sexist, and classist stereotypes.

RESPONSES TO MISIDENTIFICATION

Women had a variety of responses to misidentification. That is, some were highly offended and angry ("When they say you don't look Puerto Rican, I say what the hell does that mean?") because they felt it was a denial of their identity and a form of discrimination ("Gets me upset because I know who I am [and] they are questioning me based on stereotypes, and judging me"). Still, others were offended because they were misidentified for either another self-perceived lower status group, such as Blacks, or another group with which they have had a long history of rivalry, such as Dominicans ("Truthfully, when they say I'm Dominican, I don't like that [because] the majority that I know have nasty attitudes" or "It's an insult when they say that to me"). Conversely, some participants were not bothered when they were misidentified because of a strong sense of ethnic identity (e.g., "It doesn't bother me because I know my ethnicity and culture"). Thus, for some, ethnic misidentification was perceived as a threat, and for others, a secure sense of ethnic identity appeared to buffer them from distress.

Yet, a few reported feeling flattered, as one participant noted, "In a way I felt complimented because they were identifying me with their culture and so I was flattered." In particular, some also reported feeling proud when they were identified with being White. Notably, one participant reported that she didn't care about being misidentified because she was not proud of her heritage. She endorsed the view of Puerto Ricans as lazy and poor and so, as she explained, "I don't like the welfare thing because I think that's typical 'Rican'—not motivated—so sometimes it's a compliment (to get misidentified)."

Additionally, for some, feeling exceptional made them feel valued and "exotic." For example, one woman stated, "I like it in a way because they want to discover me, I am a curiosity, something of a mystery to others, it's not frustrating or exhausting, I enjoy it." Yet, feeling exceptional did not always make participants feel good; instead, it could make them feel objectified and foreign. For example, one participant remarked, "Once I was at a restaurant and I was asked what I was and then the person says 'you're a light one!'"

Responses to misidentification were often linked to intragroup experiences with racism. Participants noted being especially frustrated when other Latinos misidentified them because they believed that other Latinos, especially other Puerto Ricans, should be better informed. As one lighter skinned participant aptly noted, "It's a sensitive subject with me because I am proud of who I am. I feel especially offended by other Latinos because they should know better—they are trying to say I'm less Puerto Rican because I'm White." Additionally, participants felt excluded when they were misidentified ("It bothers me when I'm around other Puerto Ricans because I want to be part of the community but I don't look like them"), as well as rejected ("I feel bad because it's a rejection, especially if other Puerto Ricans say that, no one wants to feel different, everyone wants a sense of belonging"). As a result, some participants felt the immediate need to try and educate the person ("I try to educate people that Puerto Ricans come in all shapes and colors") after they were misidentified, although they also noted the fatigue of often having to "represent."

In sum, our qualitative research indicated that our participants thought a great deal about their physical appearance, perhaps because others were so frequently asking "what" they were. They informed us of just how prevalent the phenomenon of misidentification was and demonstrated the wide range of feelings that this experience can incur. Many of these experiences, from feeling exotic and attractive to feeling angry, discriminated against, and marginalized have also been found in past research with racially ambiguous and mixed-race women (Edwards & Pedrotti, 2008; Iijima Hall, 2004). Furthermore, our research revealed that the effects of misidentification appear to be more toxic when it was someone within a person's own group who misidentified them. Thus, ethnic identity can be particularly difficult to sustain during intergroup discrimination. Finally, the data described the various ways that participants attempted to prevent, neutralize, or even accentuate the experience of misidentification.

These ranges of responses may explain why we did not find significant linear associations between our quantitative variables. Additionally, it may also be that we did not find a relation between the phenotype variables and appearance anxiety because the Appearance Anxiety Scale did not adequately or sufficiently assess feelings surrounding race-based assessments. Furthermore, although the phenotype variables provided subjective and objective measurements of skin color and features, it did not measure how participants themselves felt about these characteristics. We believe it would have been difficult to understand the associations that emerged in these interviews had we only used quantitative measures.

CHALLENGES ENCOUNTERED

Using multiple measures and mixed methods has allowed us to explore the complex relation between phenotype and ethnic identity. In particular, the use of multiple measures, among both English- and Spanish-speaking groups, was key to establishing content and convergent validity. To assess ethnic identity, we tried to use multiple measures that assessed group belonging, such as the Phinney scale on Multigroup Ethnic Identity (Roberts et al.,

1999), although we also tried to supplement this with measures that have been known to shape group identity, such as language fluency. To this end, our quantitative research did indicate that fluency was associated with a greater sense of group belonging, and this general finding was further echoed in our qualitative research, which showed that language use was sometimes used to accentuate group membership.

Phenotype was assessed using multiple measures, such as the two indices of the spectrophotometer, as well as by subjective measures, such as the separate, but parallel, participant and interviewing ratings. Thus, our quantitative results showed that the generally high correlations between the spectrophotometer ratings and the subjective ratings indicated that we were assessing the same variable. Additionally, the consistency of the spectrophotometer helped with our reliability in the assessment of skin tone, which has historically been quite problematic. Still, the use of the spectrophotometer was at times problematic. That is, despite being small, it was not unobtrusive. Although participants were not afraid of it, some of them were very anxious to find out their "number" and would often ask the principal investigator what her number was to form a comparison. This, however, only highlights how assessment of skin tone is also contextual and relational. Indeed, future studies should assess how participant responses to skin color measures, and ethnic identity are in part influenced and mutually constituted by what they believe a researcher believes and wants to hear (Khanna, 2004).

Finally, although mixed methods can certainly provide rich data, investigators interested in understanding the relation between ethnic identity and phenotype need to be creative in how to integrate the quantitative and qualitative data. For example, in our third study we used a convergent design, where we simultaneously collected the quantitative and qualitative data, but investigators can use other designs that place either the quantitative or qualitative component at the forefront, depending on the scope and question(s) of the study.

FUTURE DIRECTIONS AND CONCLUSIONS

As we have hopefully shown, the study of phenotype and ethnic identity is complex. For the budding researcher, or even senior scholar, who is interested in pursuing this topic, we offer the following guidelines on the basis of our review of the research, as well as on our own challenges in completing our work.

Use of Valid Measures

Often in the study of phenotype, scales are created without sufficient explanation to the process involved. More to the point, there is rarely any mention of how the ratings were anchored or whether pilot data were obtained. In our own research, we tried to take into account that our participants could be using multiple reference points when assessing themselves, and so to this end we included parallel measures that assessed skin color using North and Latin American terms.

Additionally, whenever possible, we believe that participants should rate themselves independent of the rating of multiple interviewers, as prior research has noted that these assessments may differ (Rodriguez, 2000). Further, ratings of phenotype should include the indigenous systems of classification used by the participants under study, as these systems may convey different conceptualizations of group identity (Gravlee, 2005; Itzigsohn, Giorguli, & Vazquez, 2005). Raters should be trained and be knowledgeable about phenotypic issues in the communities studied because this knowledge will ensure a more careful and reliable assessment of phenotype. This will also help when trying to understand the associations between phenotype and group membership in particular communities. Given the importance of context, a recommendation for future research is to assess participants' self-ratings of phenotype in different contexts (e.g., when they are in the company of culturally similar individuals vs. in an ethnically dissonant environment).

Use of More Varied Samples and Variables

Most of the research on phenotype and ethnic identity has focused on understanding these issues in either adolescents or emerging adults (see Alarcón, Szalacha, Erkut, Fields, & García Coll, 2000, for an exception). However, if ethnic identity is fluid, then we must begin to understand the development of this process across different age groups. This is especially important as issues surrounding skin color and overall physical appearance begin to take shape during childhood.

Related to this, different ethnic groups should also be surveyed because the relation between appearance and ethnic identity may also change depending on the groups studied. For example, do certain groups have a greater African or European ancestry than others? If so, would this change the importance given to appearance and group belonging? More specifically, do the relations between ethnic identity and phenotype vary within families? If, as Gonzales-Backen and Umaña-Taylor (2011) noted, the family is the central resource for socialization and messages about ethnic identity, then does it also transmit messages with regards to phenotype and how it relates to ethnic identity? Related to this, it is also crucial that discrimination measures are incorporated into studies trying to understand phenotype and ethnic identity. As previous research has indicated, it is not so much one's skin color or features that matter in and of themselves, but rather how these characteristics are valued in a given context.

More Sophisticated Modeling

Given the fluidity and contextual nature of ethnic identity and phenotype, more studies are needed that look at the shifting relationship between these variables over time. Although daily diary studies have noted the daily fluctuations in the feelings and importance attributed to ethnic identity (Torres & Ong, 2010), to our knowledge, there are no current psychological studies that look at the same phenomena with regard to phenotype. This is particularly unfortunate because sociological research has shown that both ethnic and racial identifiers are subject to change over time (Golash-Boza & Darity, 2008), sometimes from survey to survey over the course of a day (Eschbach & Gomez, 1998). In other words, even though our skin color cannot in fact change from day to day without external manipulation, there is reason to believe that the way we label or describe our skin color can change, depending on the day, the context, and over time (Rodriguez, 2000). By extension, it is also reasonable to assume that our feelings toward our appearance can also change accordingly. Longitudinal designs will also enable a clearer understanding of how these variables relate to one another over time.

We began this chapter by asking, "Does it matter how you look?" Our work suggests that there does appear to be a connection between our physical appearance and our feelings toward our ethnic group and that, likewise, the way we look affects how members of our own ethnic group feel toward us. The relation between these two variables, phenotype and ethnic identity, are in turn influenced by a host of contextual variables. Additionally, measurement issues, such as issues related to validity, reliability, and study design, have restricted our understanding of these issues. As we have delineated, one way that researchers can get closer to understanding the relation between phenotype and ethnic identity is through the use of multiple measures and mixed methods. Additionally, we would hope that in the future researchers move away from static models of associations and look more closely at how phenotype and ethnic identity are mutually constitutive, because how you look does affect how accepted and embedded you feel in your group. Conversely, your ethnic group can also influence how you label and see yourself.

REFERENCES

Acevedo, G. (2000). A look at how mainland Puerto Ricans believe themselves to be perceived by their Island counterparts and its impact on their ethnic self-identity and group belongingness. *Dissertation Abstracts International: Section B. Sciences and Engineering, 61*(2-B), 1068.

Aiken, L. S., & West, S. G. (1991). *Multiple regression: Testing and interpreting interactions.* Thousand Oaks, CA: Sage.

Alarcón, O., Szalacha, L. A., Erkut, S., Fields, J. P., & García Coll, C. (2000). The color of my skin: A measure to assess children's perceptions of their skin color. *Applied Developmental Science, 4*, 208–221. http://dx.doi.org/10.1207/S1532480XADS0404_3

Araújo, B. Y., & Borrell, L. N. (2006). Understanding the link between discrimination, mental health outcomes, and life chances among Latinos. *Hispanic Journal of Behavioral Sciences, 28*, 245–266. http://dx.doi.org/10.1177/0739986305285825

Arce, C. H., Murguía, E., & Frisbie, W. P. (1987). Phenotype and life chances among Chicanos. *Hispanic Journal of Behavioral Sciences, 9*, 19–32.

Ayers, S. L., Kulis, S., & Marsiglia, F. F. (2013). The impact of ethnoracial appearance on substance use in Mexican heritage adolescents in the Southwest United States. *Hispanic Journal of Behavioral Sciences, 35*, 227–240. http://dx.doi.org/10.1177/0739986312467940

Banks, W. C. (1976). White preference in Blacks: A paradigm in search of a phenomenon. *Psychological Bulletin, 83*, 1179–1186.

Bartholomew, T. T., & Brown, J. R. (2012). Mixed methods, culture, and psychology: A review of mixed methods in culture-specific psychological research. *International Perspectives on Psychology: Research, Practice, Consultation, 1*, 177–190.

Betancourt, H., & López, S. R. (1993). The study of culture, ethnicity, and race in American psychology. *American Psychologist, 48*, 629–637. http://dx.doi.org/10.1037/0003-066X.48.6.629

Blair, I. V., Chapleau, K. M., & Judd, C. M. (2005). The use of Afrocentric features as clues for judgment in the presence of diagnostic information. *European Journal of Social Psychology, 35*, 59–68. http://dx.doi.org/10.1002/ejsp.232

Blair, I. V., Judd, C. M., & Chapleau, K. M. (2004). The influence of Afrocentric facial features in criminal sentencing. *Psychological Science, 15*, 674–679. http://dx.doi.org/10.1111/j.0956-7976.2004.00739.x

Blair, I. V., Judd, C. M., & Fallman, J. L. (2004). The automaticity of race and Afrocentric facial features in social judgments. *Journal of Personality and Social Psychology, 87*, 763–778. http://dx.doi.org/10.1037/0022-3514.87.6.763

Brunsma, D. L., & Rockquemore, K. A. (2001). The new color complex: Appearances and biracial identity. *Identity: An International Journal of Theory and Research, 1*, 225–246. http://dx.doi.org/10.1207/S1532706XID0103_03

Buchanan, N. T., & Acevedo, C. A. (2004). When face and soul collide: Therapeutic concerns with racially ambiguous and nonvisible minority women. *Women & Therapy, 27*(1-2), 119–131. http://dx.doi.org/10.1300/J015v27n01_08

Codina, G. E. (1990). Race, class, ethnicity, and Chicano mental health: A psychosocial-economical model. *Dissertation Abstracts International, 51*, 1162.

Codina, G. E., & Montalvo, F. F. (1994). Chicano phenotype and depression. *Hispanic Journal of Behavioral Sciences, 16*, 296–306. http://dx.doi.org/10.1177/07399863940163007

Cokley, K. (2007). Critical issues in the measurement of ethnic and racial identity: A referendum on the state of the field. *Journal of Counseling Psychology, 54,* 224–234. http://dx.doi.org/10.1037/0022-0167.54.3.224

Comas-Díaz, L. (1994). LatiNegra: Mental health issues of African Latinas. In R. V. Almeida (Ed.), *Expansions of feminist family theory through diversity* (pp. 35–74). New York, NY: Haworth Press. http://dx.doi.org/10.1300/J086v05n03_03

Corenblum, B., & Annis, R. C. (1993). Development of racial identity in minority and majority children: An affect discrepancy model. *Canadian Journal of Behavioural Science/Revue Canadienne des Sciences du Comportement, 25,* 499–521. http://dx.doi.org/10.1037/h0078858

Cortés, D. E., Rogler, L. H., & Malgady, R. G. (1994). Biculturality among Puerto Rican adults in the United States. *American Journal of Community Psychology, 22,* 707–721. http://dx.doi.org/10.1007/BF02506900

Cota-Robles de Suárez, C. (1971). Skin color as a factor of racial identification and preferences of young Chicano children. *Aztlán: A Journal of Chicano Studies, 2,* 107–150.

Creswell, J. W., & Plano Clark, V. L. (2007). *Designing and conducting mixed method research.* Thousand Oaks, CA: Sage.

Cunningham, J. L. (1997). Colored existence: Racial identity formation in light-skin Blacks. *Smith College Studies in Social Work, 67,* 375–400. http://dx.doi.org/10.1080/00377319709517498

De Casanova, E. M. (2004). "No ugly women": Concepts of race and beauty among adolescent women in Ecuador. *Gender & Society, 18,* 287–308. http://dx.doi.org/10.1177/0891243204263351

Dion, K. L., Dion, K. K., & Keelan, P. J. (1990). Appearance anxiety as a dimension of social-evaluative anxiety: Exploring the ugly duckling syndrome. *Contemporary Social Psychology, 14,* 220–224.

Edwards, L. M., & Pedrotti, J. T. (2008). A content and methodological review of articles concerning multiracial issues in six major counseling journals. *Journal of Counseling Psychology, 55,* 411–418. http://dx.doi.org/10.1037/0022-0167.55.3.411

Eschbach, K., & Gomez, C. (1998). Choosing Hispanic identity: Ethnic identity switching among respondents to high school and beyond. *Social Science Quarterly, 79,* 74–90.

Espino, R., & Franz, M. M. (2002). Latino phenotypic discrimination revisited: The impact of skin color on occupational status. *Social Science Quarterly, 83,* 612–623. http://dx.doi.org/10.1111/1540-6237.00104

Farruggia, S. P., Chen, C., Greenberger, E., Dmitrieva, J., & Macek, P. (2004). Adolescent self-esteem in cross-cultural perspective: Testing measurement equivalence and a mediation model. *Journal of Cross-Cultural Psychology, 35,* 719–733. http://dx.doi.org/10.1177/0022022104270114

Flores, R., & Telles, E. (2012). Social stratification in Mexico: Disentangling color, ethnicity, and class. *American Sociological Review, 77,* 486–494. http://dx.doi.org/10.1177/0003122412444720

Frank, R., Akresh, I. R., & Lu, B. (2010). Latino immigrants and the U.S. racial order: How and where do they fit in? *American Sociological Review, 75,* 378–401. http://dx.doi.org/10.1177/0003122410372216

Golash-Boza, T., & Darity, W., Jr. (2008). Latino racial choices: The effects of skin colour and discrimination on Latinos' and Latinas' racial self-identifications. *Ethnic and Racial Studies, 31,* 899–934.

Gonzales-Backen, M. A., & Umaña-Taylor, A. J. (2011). Examining the role of physical appearance in Latino adolescents' ethnic identity. *Journal of Adolescence, 34,* 151–162. http://dx.doi.org/10.1016/j.adolescence.2010.01.002

Gould, S. J. (1996). *The mismeasure of man.* New York, NY: Norton.

Gravlee, C. (2005). Ethnic classification in southeastern Puerto Rico: The cultural model of "color." *Social Forces, 83,* 949–970. http://dx.doi.org/10.1353/sof.2005.0033

Guthrie, R. V. (2003). *Even the rat was white: A historical view of psychology* (2nd ed.). Boston, MA: Allyn & Bacon.

Hagiwara, N., Kashy, D. A., & Cesario, J. (2012). The independent effects of skin tone and facial features on Whites' affective reactions to Blacks. *Journal of Experimental Social Psychology, 48,* 892–898. http://dx.doi.org/10.1016/j.jesp.2012.02.001

Hersch, J. (2011). The persistence of skin color discrimination for immigrants. *Social Science Research, 40,* 1337–1349. http://dx.doi.org/10.1016/j.ssresearch.2010.12.006

Hill, C. E., Thompson, B. J., & Nutt Williams, E. (1997). A guide to conducting consensual qualitative research. *The Counseling Psychologist, 25,* 517–572. http://dx.doi.org/10.1177/0011000097254001

Holmbeck, G. N. (2002). Post-hoc probing of significant moderational and mediational effects in studies of pediatric populations. *Journal of Pediatric Psychology, 27,* 87–96. http://dx.doi.org/10.1093/jpepsy/27.1.87

Hunter, M. (2007). The persistent problem of colorism: Skin tone, status, and inequality. *Social Compass, 1,* 237–254. http://dx.doi.org/10.1111/j.1751-9020.2007.00006.x

Iijima Hall, C. C. (2004). Mixed-race women: One more mountain to climb. *Women & Therapy, 27*(1-2), 237–246. http://dx.doi.org/10.1300/J015v27n01_16

Itzigsohn, J., Giorguli, S., & Vazquez, O. (2005). Immigrant incorporation and racial identity: Racial self-identification among Dominican immigrants. *Ethnic and Racial Studies, 28,* 50–78. http://dx.doi.org/10.1080/0141984042000280012

Jablonski, N. (2012). *Living color: The biological and social significance of skin color.* Berkeley: University of California Press.

Jackson, J. P., Jr. (2010). What ever happened to the cephalic index? The reality of race and the burden of proof. *Rhetoric Society Quarterly, 40,* 438–458. http://dx.doi.org/10.1080/02773945.2010.517233

Jaspal, R. (2009). Language and social identity: A psychosocial approach. *Psych-Talk*, *64*, 17–20.

Jaspal, R., & Coyle, A. (2009). Reconciling social psychology and sociolinguistics can have some benefits: Language and identity among second generation British Asians. *Social Psychological Review*, *11*(2), 3–14.

Jimenez, T. R. (2004). Negotiating ethnic boundaries: Multiethnic Mexican Americans and ethnic identity in the United States. *Ethnicities*, *4*, 75–97. http://dx.doi.org/10.1177/1468796804040329

Khanna, N. (2004). The role of reflected appraisals in racial identity: The case of multiracial Asians. *Social Psychology Quarterly*, *67*, 115–131. http://dx.doi.org/10.1177/019027250406700201

Khatib, M., & Ghamari, M. R. (2011). Mutual relations of identity and foreign language learning: An overview of linguistic and sociolinguistic approaches to identity. *Theory and Practice in Language Studies*, *1*, 1701–1708. http://dx.doi.org/10.4304/tpls.1.12.1701-1708

Kiang, L., & Takeuchi, D. T. (2009). Phenotypic bias and ethnic identity in Filipino Americans. *Social Science Quarterly*, *90*, 428–445. http://dx.doi.org/10.1111/j.1540-6237.2009.00625.x

Koskina, A., Van den Eynde, F., Meisel, S., Campbell, I. C., & Schmidt, U. (2011). Social appearance anxiety and bulimia nervosa. *Eating and Weight Disorders*, *16*(2), e142–e145. http://dx.doi.org/10.1007/BF03325321

Landale, N. S., & Oropesa, R. S. (2002). White, Black, or Puerto Rican? Racial self-identification among Mainland and Island Puerto Ricans. *Social Forces*, *81*, 231–254. http://dx.doi.org/10.1353/sof.2002.0052

Lewin, E. (2005). Perceptions about skin color and heritage: The experience of Anglo-Indian women in Western Australia. *Social Identities*, *11*, 631–651.

López, I. R. (2005, April). *Mixed methods for a mixed race: Integrating qualitative and quantitative methods in the study of race among Puerto Ricans.* Poster presented at the annual meeting of the Society of Psychological Anthropology, San Diego, California.

López, I. (2008a). "But you don't look Puerto Rican": The moderating effect of ethnic identity on the relation between skin color and self-esteem among Puerto Rican women. *Cultural Diversity and Ethnic Minority Psychology*, *14*, 102–108. http://dx.doi.org/10.1037/1099-9809.14.2.102

López, I. R. (2008b). Puerto Rican phenotype: Understanding its historical underpinnings and psychological associations. *Hispanic Journal of Behavioral Sciences*, *30*, 161–180. http://dx.doi.org/10.1177/0739986307313116

López, I., Dent, T., Ecosto, E., & Prado-Steiman, M. (2011). Theories of acculturation and cultural identity. In A. Zagelbaum & J. Carlson (Eds.), *Working with immigrant families: A practical guide for counselors* (pp. 21–37). New York, NY: Routledge.

López, I., Gonzalez, A. N., & Ho, A. (2012). Skin color. In T. F. Cash (Ed.), *Encyclopedia of body image and human appearance* (Vol. 2, pp. 730–737). San Diego, CA: Academic Press. http://dx.doi.org/10.1016/B978-0-12-384925-0.00116-4

López, I., & Walker, L. (n.d.-a). *Appearance anxiety among Spanish speaking women: Clinical implications from an exploratory study.* Unpublished manuscript.

López, I., & Walker, L. (n.d.-b). *"Bewitched, bothered and bewildered": A mixed method exploration of the psychological costs of misidentification among Puerto Rican women.* Unpublished manuscript.

Maldonado, M., & Cross, W. (1977). Today's Chicano refutes the stereotype. *College Student Journal, 11,* 146–152.

Marín, G., & Gamba, R. J. (1996). A new measurement of acculturation for Hispanics: The bidimensional acculturation scale for Hispanics. *Hispanic Journal of Behavioral Sciences, 18,* 297–316. http://dx.doi.org/10.1177/07399863960183002

Martinez, R., & Dukes, R. L. (1997). The effects of ethnic identity, ethnicity, and gender in adolescent well-being. *Journal of Youth and Adolescence, 26,* 503–516. http://dx.doi.org/10.1023/A:1024525821078

Monro, F., & Huon, G. (2005). Media-portrayed idealized images, body shame, and appearance anxiety. *International Journal of Eating Disorders, 38,* 85–90. http://dx.doi.org/10.1002/eat.20153

Montalvo, F. (1991). Phenotyping, acculturation, and biracial assimilation of Mexican Americans. In M. Sotomayor (Ed.), *Empowering Hispanic families: A critical issue for the 90s* (pp. 97–119). Milwaukee, WI: Family Service America.

Morales, C. M. (2008). The ethnic niche as an economic pathway for the dark skinned: Labor market incorporation of Latina/o workers. *Hispanic Journal of Behavioral Sciences, 30,* 280–298. http://dx.doi.org/10.1177/0739986308320475

Niño-Murcia, M., & Rothman, J. (Eds.). (2008). *Bilingualism and identity: Spanish at the crossroads with other languages.* Amsterdam, The Netherlands: John Benjamins. http://dx.doi.org/10.1075/sibil.37

Patton, M. O. (2002). Designing qualitative studies. *Qualitative Research and Evaluation Methods, 3,* 230–246.

Perry, B. L., Stevens-Watkins, D., & Oser, C. B. (2013). The moderating effects of skin color and ethnic identity affirmation on suicide risk among low-SES African American women. *Race and Social Problems, 5,* 1–14. http://dx.doi.org/10.1007/s12552-012-9080-8

Phinney, J. S. (1989). Stages of ethnic development in minority group adolescents. *The Journal of Early Adolescence, 9,* 34–49. http://dx.doi.org/10.1177/0272431689091004

Phinney, J. S. (1992). The Multigroup Ethnic Identity Measure: A new scale for use with diverse groups. *Journal of Adolescent Research, 7,* 156–176. http://dx.doi.org/10.1177/074355489272003

Phinney, J. S., & Ong, A. D. (2007). Conceptualization and measurement of ethnic identity: Current status and future directions. *Journal of Counseling Psychology, 54,* 271–281. http://dx.doi.org/10.1037/0022-0167.54.3.271

Ramos, B., Jaccard, J., & Guilamo-Ramos, V. (2003). Dual ethnicity and depressive symptoms: Implications of being Black and Latino in the United States.

Hispanic Journal of Behavioral Sciences, 25, 147–173. http://dx.doi.org/10.1177/0739986303025002002

Roberts, R. E., Phinney, J. S., Masse, L. C., Chen, Y. R., Roberts, C. R., & Romero, A. (1999). The structure of ethnic identity of young adolescents from diverse ethnocultural groups. *The Journal of Early Adolescence, 19,* 301–322. http://dx.doi.org/10.1177/0272431699019003001

Robinson, C. L. (2011). Hair as race: Why "good hair" may be bad for Black females. *Howard Journal of Communications, 22,* 358–376. http://dx.doi.org/10.1080/10646175.2011.617212

Rodriguez, C. (1974). Puerto Ricans: Between Black and White. *New York Affairs, 1*(4), 92–101.

Rodriguez, C. (2000). *Changing race: Latinos, the census, and the history of ethnicity in the United States.* New York, NY: New York University Press.

Rosenberg, M. (1965). *Society and the adolescent child.* Princeton, NJ: Princeton University Press.

Ryan, G. W., & Bernard, H. R. (2003). Techniques to identify themes. *Field Methods, 15,* 85–109. http://dx.doi.org/10.1177/1525822X02239569

Sellers, R. M., Chavous, T. M., & Cooke, D. Y. (1998). Racial ideology and racial centrality as predictors of African American college students' academic performances. *Journal of Black Psychology, 24,* 8–27. http://dx.doi.org/10.1177/00957984980241002

Sibley, C. G., & Houkamau, C. A. (2013). The multi-dimensional model of Maori identity and cultural engagement: Item response theory analysis of scale properties. *Cultural Diversity and Ethnic Minority Psychology, 19,* 97–110. http://dx.doi.org/10.1037/a0031113

Smedley, A., & Smedley, B. D. (2005). Race as biology is fiction, racism as a social problem is real: Anthropological and historical perspectives on the social construction of race. *American Psychologist, 60,* 16–26. http://dx.doi.org/10.1037/0003-066X.60.1.16

Smith, T. B., & Silva, L. (2011). Ethnic identity and personal well-being of people of color: A meta-analysis. *Journal of Counseling Psychology, 58,* 42–60. http://dx.doi.org/10.1037/a0021528

Stepanova, E. V., & Strube, M. J. (2012). The role of skin color and facial physiognomy in racial categorization: Moderation by implicit racial attitudes. *Journal of Experimental Social Psychology, 48,* 867–878. http://dx.doi.org/10.1016/j.jesp.2012.02.019

Stephens, D. P., & Fernández, P. (2012). The role of skin color on Hispanic women's perceptions of attractiveness. *Hispanic Journal of Behavioral Sciences, 34,* 77–94. http://dx.doi.org/10.1177/0739986311427695

Stratton, G. M. (1934). Emotional reactions connected with differences in cephalic index, shade of hair, and color of eyes in Caucasians. *The American Journal of Psychology, 46,* 409–419. http://dx.doi.org/10.2307/1415592

Strauss, A., & Corbin, J. (1998). *Basics of qualitative research techniques and procedures for developing grounded theory* (2nd ed.). Thousand Oaks, CA: Sage.

Tajfel, H., & Turner, J. (1986). The social identity theory of intergroup behavior. In S. Worchel & W. Austin (Eds.), *Psychology of intergroup relations* (pp. 7–24). Chicago, IL: Nelson-Hall.

Telles, E. E. (2004). *Race in another America: The significance of skin color in Brazil.* Princeton, NJ: Princeton University Press.

Telzer, E. H., & Vazquez Garcia, H. A. (2009). Skin color and self-perceptions of immigrant and U.S.-born Latinas. *Hispanic Journal of Behavioral Sciences, 31,* 357–374. http://dx.doi.org/10.1177/0739986309336913

Teplin, L. A. (1976). A comparison of racial/ethnic preferences among Anglo, Black and Latino children. *American Journal of Orthopsychiatry, 46,* 702–709. http://dx.doi.org/10.1111/j.1939-0025.1976.tb00968.x

Torres, L., & Ong, A. D. (2010). A daily diary investigation of Latino ethnic identity, discrimination, and depression. *Cultural Diversity and Ethnic Minority Psychology, 16,* 561–568. http://dx.doi.org/10.1037/a0020652

Umaña-Taylor, A. J., Diversi, M., & Fine, M. A. (2002). Ethnic identity and self-esteem of Latino adolescents: Distinctions among the Latino populations. *Journal of Adolescent Research, 17,* 303–327. http://dx.doi.org/10.1177/0743558402173005

Umaña-Taylor, A. J., Yazedjian, A., & Bámaca-Gómez, M. (2004). Developing the Ethnic Identity Scale using Eriksonian and social identity perspectives. *Identity: An International Journal of Theory and Research, 4,* 9–38. http://dx.doi.org/10.1207/S1532706XID0401_2

Vazquez, L. A., Garcia-Vazquez, E., Bauman, S. A., & Sierra, A. S. (1997). Skin color, acculturation, and a community interest among Mexican American students: A research note. *Hispanic Journal of Behavioral Sciences, 19,* 377–386. http://dx.doi.org/10.1177/07399863970193009

Weiner, J. S., & Lourie, J. A. (1969). Skin colour measurement by spectrophotometry. In J. S. Weiner & J. A. Laurie (Eds.), *Human biology: A guide to field methods* (pp. 154–162). Oxford, England: Blackwell Scientific.

6

USING SEMISTRUCTURED INTERVIEWS TO EXAMINE ADOLESCENT RACIAL–ETHNIC IDENTITY DEVELOPMENT

LEOANDRA ONNIE ROGERS AND NIOBE WAY

Question:	What are some of the good things about being Black?
Response:	What's good about it is basically everything. Like you know I've got a goal to do and to me I feel like I've got to achieve something. There are a lot of stereotypes about Black people and I really don't like it, either they're like drug dealers and gang-bangers or dead or in jail. No, since I'm Black I feel like I've got to achieve something other than that.
	—*Devin, Black male, 14*

Question:	What are some of the good things about being Black?
Response:	Oh, like a lot of people are scared of us; that's great.
Question:	Okay, and why is that a good thing?
Response:	Because sometimes it's kind of funny to see that fear in people. . . . *Oh no, I walked into the wrong neighborhood* <laughter>. They're shaking; it's funny to me. . . .
	—*Omar, Black male, 15*

http://dx.doi.org/10.1037/14618-007
Studying Ethnic Identity: Methodological and Conceptual Approaches Across Disciplines, C. E. Santos and A. J. Umaña-Taylor (Editors)

Most of what we know from the empirical literature about racial–ethnic identity is focused on "how much" one likes, is attached to, or values his or her racial–ethnic group. Rarely have researchers investigated what it means to belong to a particular racial–ethnic group or how social identities may intersect with each other. In response to this gap, we have been using semistructured interviews (SSIs) to explore the experience of racial–ethnic identity among African American, Latino, Asian American, and European American adolescents. Our findings indicate that cultural stereotypes provide the basis from which racial–ethnic identities develop and that race, ethnicity, and gender intersect with each other in the construction and maintenance of identities. In this chapter, we describe SSIs and through an empirical example reveal how our method of data collection and analysis allowed us to uncover patterns in identity development that are invisible when using survey methods.

Research on racial–ethnic identity reveals critical information about the extent to which individuals feel attached to, think about, and reflect on their racial–ethnic group; how these thoughts and feelings about their racial–ethnic group change over time and across contexts; and how they influence adjustment such as self-esteem, intergroup relations, academic performance, and career aspirations (Phinney, 1990; Quintana, 2007; Syed, Azmitia, & Cooper, 2011; Tajfel & Turner, 1986). Such research essentially gathers information about "how much" (or "the extent to which") individuals feel positively about their racial–ethnic groups and have thus relied primarily on survey methods for their studies. Few studies, however, have examined the processes by which individuals construct and maintain their racial–ethnic identities and have thus rarely used qualitative methods of investigation (for exceptions, see Carter, 2006; Ferguson, 2000; Fordham & Ogbu, 1986; Nasir, 2011; Spencer, 1999; Spencer, Dupree, & Hartmann, 1997; Syed & Azmitia, 2008). In response to this gap, we have been using SSIs over the past decade to investigate how adolescents speak about their racial–ethnic groups and the processes by which they construct their racial–ethnic identities (Hughes et al., 2008; Niwa, 2012; Niwa, Way, Qin, & Okazaki, 2011; Rogers, 2012, 2013; Rosenbloom & Way, 2004; Way, Hernandez, Rogers, & Hughes, 2013; Way, Santos, Niwa, & Kim-Gervey, 2008). Our findings indicate that cultural stereotypes about social identities form the foundation from which identities develop, and these stereotypic identities interact with each other in the process of identity development.

THE STUDY OF RACIAL–ETHNIC IDENTITY

Identity has been central to the study of human development since its introduction to the science by intellectuals such as William James, George Herbert Mead, and Charles Horton Cooley at the turn of the century. Though identity is about the individual, it is not an individual-level process but one that is part and parcel of the context (Erikson, 1968). For over a century, identity development has been viewed as a psychosocial phenomenon that emerges from interactions with others or as a reflection of others' expectations (Cooley, 1902). Erik Erikson (1968) located identity *"in the core of the individual* and yet also *in the core of his communal culture"* (p. 22, italics in original). He stated that "identity formation employs a process of simultaneous reflection and observation . . . by which the individual judges himself in the light of what he perceives to be the way in which others judge him" (p. 22). This idea of seeing the self in the eyes of others calls attention to the relational nature of identity and how cultural norms and beliefs structure identity experiences. Steele (2011) termed these cultural structures "identity contingencies" or "the things you have to deal with . . . because you have a given social identity" (p. 3). Racial–ethnic identity, then, concerns how individuals interpret and respond to the culturally constructed norms, stereotypes, and expectations that define their own as well as others' racial–ethnic groups (Nasir, 2011; Spencer et al., 1997; Steele, 2011; Ward, 1996; Way & Rogers, 2014).

The empirical literature on racial–ethnic identity, save for a few exceptions (e.g., Carter, 2006; Nasir, 2011; Spencer, 1999; Spencer & Markstrom-Adams, 1990; Spencer et al., 1997; Steele, 2011; Way et al., 2008, 2013), focuses more on the stages of racial–ethnic identity development (e.g., Cross, 1991; Phinney, 1992) and its content—attitudes, affect, and beliefs (e.g., Sellers, Smith, Shelton, Rowley, & Chavous, 1998; Umaña-Taylor, Yazedjian, & Bámaca-Gómez, 2004)—than on the ways that individuals construct and maintain racial–ethnic identities. Collectively, the existing empirical literature on racial–ethnic identity development has described the extent to which one thinks about and feels positively toward one's racial–ethnic group (Altschul, Oyserman, & Bybee, 2006; Pahl & Way, 2006; Quintana, 2007), the correlates of these thoughts and feelings about one's racial–ethnic group (Chavous et al., 2003; Seaton, Scottham, & Sellers, 2006; Umaña-Taylor et al., 2004; Yip, Seaton, & Sellers, 2006), and the family-level factors (e.g., parental socialization) that influence the course of identity development (e.g., Hughes et al., 2006; Umaña-Taylor, 2004). This knowledge base has been instrumental in establishing racial–ethnic identity as a critical area of empirical study and for understanding how racial–ethnic group attitudes, evaluations, and behaviors develop over time and influence social, psychological, and academic outcomes. Yet, it offers little insight into how racial–ethnic identities are constructed and maintained throughout adolescence.

The importance of looking at the process or the experience of racial–ethnic identity development is underscored by the responses of the two Black boys in the opening of this chapter. Although both boys evaluate their racial–ethnic group positively, their reasons differ substantially. For Devin, his positive evaluation hinges on a desire to stand out from racial stereotypes: "Since I'm Black I feel like I've got to achieve something . . ." whereas Omar attaches a positive evaluation to an explicitly negative racial stereotype: "a lot of people are scared of us; that's great." These differences have important implications for understanding how racial–ethnic identities are formed and the strategies used by youth to establish their selves within culture.

In our own research over the past decade, we rely on SSIs to investigate the processes of racial–ethnic identity development (e.g., Niwa, 2012; Niwa et al., 2011; Rogers, 2012, 2013; Rosenbloom & Way, 2004; Way et al., 2008, 2013). In particular, we examine what adolescents think and feel about their racial–ethnic groups and why they think and feel as they do. Our findings reveal the influence of stereotypes about social groups in the construction of identities and the ways in which these stereotypes intersect. As such, they underscore the fact that interviewing methods are not simply a useful addendum in the study of identity development, but are critical to uncovering important processes that are overlooked entirely when the focus of research remains on "how much" questions.

SSIs AND ANALYSIS

SSIs are a qualitative form of data collection that privileges the knowledge and perspective of the participant (Marecek, Fine, & Kidder, 2001). In contrast to structured interviews, which involve a standardized set of questions on an interview protocol with no room allowed for follow-up probes, and unstructured interviews, in which the participant dictates the direction of the conversation (Mishler, 1986), SSIs involve a standardized set of questions but allow for follow-up questions to capture how each interviewee interprets and navigates the conversation (Marecek et al., 2001; Mishler, 1986). SSIs are also closely tied to the analysis method—how a scientist interprets, or makes sense of, the interview data.

There are a wide variety of methods with which to analyze SSIs, such as open coding, content analysis, grounded theory, constant comparison, and case studies (e.g., Denzin & Lincoln, 2005; Huberman & Miles, 2002; Strauss & Corbin, 1990), with each taking a slightly or more radically different approach to the analysis of narrative. Our analysis approach draws on grounded theory/content analysis (Strauss & Corbin, 1990) and the Listening Guide method (Gilligan, Spencer, Weinberg, & Bertsch, 2003), which embeds the narratives and the interpretation of narratives in culture. Thus, an interview about racial–ethnic identity, for example, is examined within the context of the "shared racial [ethnic] storylines" of our communal culture (Nasir, 2011). The cultural narrative of race is used as a sounding board for the individual's narrative of race because the two are coconstructed. This analytic method is a relational one that assumes that the interview is a conversation between the interviewer and interviewee as well as among the interviewees, the interviewer, and the larger macro culture (e.g., American expectations, values, stereotypes, practices). Thus, analysis cannot focus on the interview as an insular piece of data, but rather on the intersections between what was asked and spoken in the interview and the larger cultural context within which the questions are asked and the responses are given.

The Listening Guide method directs analysis along this path. Each transcript is read in four ways (Gilligan et al., 2003). First, we read the interview to listen to who is speaking—taking on the perspective and social position of the speaker—and to the stories that the interviewee is telling in response to our questions. In the second reading, we listen for the voice of the "I" or how the interviewee places herself or himself into the culturally bound stories she or he is telling the interviewer. For the third and fourth readings, we listen for patterns in the content of the stories, how culture shapes the ways in which these stories are told and heard by the interviewers and analysts, and what it means within the cultural context. The result is an understanding of what story is being told (i.e., who is speaking, to whom, and about what) in relationship to the interviewer and within a web of cultural norms, stereotypes, values, and practices (Gilligan et al., 2003).

RESEARCH USING SSIs

Like most areas of scientific study, early studies of identity in the field of psychology relied on qualitative, open-ended interviews, the contents of which were used to develop many of our existing identity scales (e.g., Cross, 1991; Phinney, 1990, 1992; Sellers et al., 1998). McAdams (1990) is a pioneer in the qualitative study of identity. In his identity narrative interview, McAdams viewed the narrative as identity, arguing that individuals construct their identities through their narratives. Using this approach, McAdams (2013) revealed how the stories that we tell about ourselves are intimately tied to the stories of our culture. Thus, American values, beliefs, and ideals shape what and why people construct the types of identity narratives that they do. Rather than a starting point for survey development or an additional data source, the narrative becomes essential to, even inseparable from, identity. Syed and Azmitia (2008) applied the identity narrative method to ethnic identity and similarly found that youths' personal stories about racial–ethnic identity reflect the American story about race-ethnicity—in which minorities have a race and culture and majority group members do not (Perry, 2001). Rather than a comparison of "how much" race or ethnicity matters to an individual, a qualitative approach draws attention to the experience of racial–ethnic identity as a meaning-making process in the context of relationships with others and the larger cultural environment.

Way and colleagues (2008) used SSI and the Listening Guide as their form of analysis to investigate how Black, Puerto Rican, Dominican, and Chinese adolescents spoke about race and ethnicity in their school. They found that adolescents' identities were not only focused on who they are and wanted to be but also about who they did not want to be. Specifically, adolescents did not want to be seen as a stereotype of their racial group: Black youth did not want to be seen as "lazy" or "dumb," and Chinese youth did not want to be seen as "weak" or "soft." In contrast to a literature that focuses mostly on identity development as a process of "becoming," Way and colleagues were able to tap into an alternative story about "avoidance" and how stereotypes inform identity by creating an image of who not to be (Erikson, 1968). This insight into racial–ethnic identity development is detectable only through methods that underscore the cultural context (Brown & Gilligan, 1992; Gilligan et al., 2003). In a subsequent study with middle school students, Way et al. (2013) again found that avoidance dominated the racial–ethnic identity narratives of Black, Chinese, and Dominican youth as well as the ethnic majority White adolescents in their sample—who did not want to be seen as "racists" or "snobby." They further found evidence that racial–ethnic identities were intertwined with other social categories, including gender, nationality, sexuality, and social class. This story about identity intersectionality, although widely acknowledged at the theoretical level (e.g., Shields, 2008), is rarely captured empirically. Thus, listening to youth speak about their identities—with attention to the "what" and "why" of identity—unravels an important story of cultural stereotypes, avoidance, and intersectionality in racial–ethnic identity development.

Other scholars using SSIs have also illustrated the intersectionality of identities. For example, Shorter-Gooden and Washington (1996) used SSIs and open coding to examine racial identity among college-age Black women. Although the women in their study rated race as the most central or important aspect of their identity, they drew on their other identities—gender, religion, and career—to make sense of what it means to be Black. The variations in these other social group identifications then filtered how the Black women constructed and interpreted their racial identities. Nasir's (2011) use of SSIs and sociocultural content analysis further revealed that youth not only engage the cultural story of their own racial–ethnic group but those of others' racial–ethnic groups as well. For example, the cultural belief that "Asians are good at math" presumes that other racial–ethnic groups, namely Blacks and Latinos, are *not* good at math (Nasir, 2011). This framing sheds light on the relational nature of identity and how the racial–ethnic stereotypes of other groups are relevant to racial–ethnic identity development.

Collectively, research using SSIs and forms of analysis that underscore the cultural context has revealed that racial–ethnic identity is about not only how youth feel about their group or whether they participate in racial group activities but also how they are seen in relationship to others and to a larger cultural narrative in which race–ethnicity, gender, sexuality, and class intersect with each other. The following empirical example draws on SSIs that were analyzed using the listening guide to investigate the racial–ethnic identities of Black adolescent boys. It underscores the usefulness of interview methods for studying racial–ethnic identity.

AN EMPIRICAL EXAMPLE

Data for this analysis were drawn from the first author's dissertation and collected at an all-Black male high school located in a Midwestern urban center. For the dissertation, Rogers (2012) gathered both quantitative and qualitative data longitudinally to examine the development and consequences of boys' racial and gender identities for their psychological well-being and academic adjustment. SSIs were used to explore the meaning and experience of racial identity and gender identity from the narratives of Black adolescent males. Two general research questions guided the interviews: How do boys describe their racial and gender identities, and what are the processes through which these identities are constructed? In what ways do racial and gender identities overlap in their narratives?[1]

Method

The present analysis is based on the first author's interviews with 21 boys. Interviews ranged in length from 39 to 105 minutes (with an average of 65 minutes), were audio recorded and transcribed verbatim. Transcripts were analyzed within an *interpretive community*—a diverse group of scholars that read and coded interview excerpts and provided explanations to ensure the validity of data interpretations (Marecek et al., 2001). The analysis method included open coding and matrices to organize emergent themes within and across cases (Huberman & Miles, 2002) and the Listening Guide method (Gilligan et al., 2003). Analysis focused on the subjective meaning and experience of race and identity. The first phase of analysis was to develop narrative summaries for each transcript (Way, 1998). These summaries represent the first "listening" in the Listening Guide method (Gilligan et al., 2003), where we attune to the voice

---

[1]Research questions and findings from the quantitative portion of the dissertation are reported elsewhere (Rogers, 2012; Rogers, Scott, & Way, in press).

of the participant. The second phase of the analysis involved listening for the content of boys' descriptions of their racial group, focusing specifically on interview questions about racial expectations (e.g., What do you think other people think about Black people? Are there certain things you're supposed to do or ways you're supposed to act just because you're Black?). The final phase of analysis focused on direct questions about racial identity (e.g., How would you describe yourself to someone you've never met? What are some of the good/bad things about being Black?). Here we listened to how boys' constructed themselves—their own identity narratives—in relationship to the larger cultural narrative that uniformly defines Black males as delinquent, aggressive, unintelligent, and lazy (Spencer, Fegley, Harpalani, & Seaton, 2004; Stevenson, 1997).

Results

The first set of findings from our analysis of the SSIs focused on how Black males see themselves through the eyes of culture. Boys recounted three recurring stereotypes: Black males are (a) "unintelligent, bad and violent," (b) "physically tough and athletic," and (c) "hypersexual, not feminine or gay." For example, when asked what other people think of Black people, Brandon, 14 years old, said, "Blacks can't succeed in nothing, they're always stealing, killing, all this violence . . . Just the gangsta in the hood that sells crack." Cameron, 14 years old, explained, "It's always like the stereotype I guess that you've got to act more masculine and stuff like that . . . I guess you could say like straight, you know, like women, tough, play sports." Questions about race and stereotypes invariably elicited responses that included race and gender and sexuality weaving these social stereotypes and identities together. In other words, the boys made it clear that to understand their racial identities, we must attune to gender as well.

The next set of findings from our SSIs were generated from our analysis of how boys positioned themselves in this larger conversation—how they responded to the stereotypes and expectations that framed their social group. We used the framework of resistance and accommodation to interpret boys' responses (Anyon, 1984; Gilligan, 2011; Robinson & Ward, 1991; Way, 2011). *Resistance* refers to the ways in which one challenges the dominant narrative, whereas *accommodation* refers to the ways that one endorses or reinforces it. Listening closely to how boys negotiated their identities, we found that rather than seamlessly endorsing stereotypes, the boys' narratives indicated greater evidence of resistance to racial stereotypes and more accommodation to gender stereotypes. In other words, boys tended to challenge beliefs about the inherent "badness," intellectual inferiority, and incompetence of Black people (e.g., "Society says that we are illiterate and that's not true") but also endorsed the idea that as (Black) boys they ought to be independent, emotionally stoic, and heterosexual, thereby reifying gender norms (Way, 2011). Our analysis classified boys into three distinguishable identity patterns: the "accommodators" ($n = 5$), the "exceptions" ($n = 12$), and the "liberators" ($n = 4$).

The "Accommodators": Omar

The accommodators were a group of boys ($n = 5$) who, on the whole, reinforced racial and gender stereotypes in their identity narratives. The accommodators sound like stereotypes—independent, stoic, hypermasculine; the "tough Black male" who is ready to fight and more concerned with girls than school. In these boys' narratives, we hear how racial stereotypes restrict the identity stories that they tell about themselves.

Omar is the case study for the accommodators. He describes himself as "the hood guy": "I'm just a cool individual. Laid back and down-to-earth, so I like to have fun, crack jokes now and then; that's about it." We discuss his experience of being Black:

Q: What are some of the good things about being Black?

A: Oh, like a lot of people are scared of us; that's great.

Q: Okay, and why is that a good thing?

A: Because sometimes it's kind of funny to see that fear in people. . . . Oh no, I walked into the wrong neighborhood [laughter]. They're shaking; it's funny to me. Almost everything be funny to me. I could be in the craziest situation and still be laughing.

It is striking that this is Omar's response to a question about what he likes about being Black—it is one of the first things he uses to define his racial identity. He explained the "benefits" of being seen as a scary Black male: "Like if you're too soft and you're a Black, man everybody is going to mess with you no matter who it is, White people, Hispanics, I mean *everybody* is going to mess with you." Omar sees toughness as a necessary ingredient of being Black (and male) in this society and as a defining feature of his identity.

The accommodators embraced stereotypes as a protective shield (Majors & Billson, 1992); Omar claims that he "likes" the fear he can evoke in White people. At the same time, they resent this positioning. Omar laughs at the idea that people would be afraid of him, suggesting that he knows he really is not scary or dangerous. In fact, when asked what he doesn't like about being Black, Omar said:

Everybody think[s] you're like the other Black person they seen. They think if one Black person is bad they think *every* Black person is bad, no matter who you are, what you say or what you do. . . . And I'm like, don't judge me; let me at least show you what I'm about before you judge me because you never know.

Despite claiming stereotypes as his identity, Omar does not want to be stereotyped.

Youth tend to rely on stereotypes when they feel vulnerable (e.g., Spencer et al., 2004), such as when Omar comments on the violence in his neighborhood: "Over by my house there's been a lot of killing a lot of people getting killed or shot . . . about 10 [shootings] in the last couple of days." Asked how he feels about this, he said,

> Well, it really don't make me feel any kind of way. Because like it's their fault; to me it's their fault if they don't know how to stay in the house and stop doing all that crazy stuff; if they do like me, they'll be okay.

Omar responds stoically, "I don't feel," blames the victims: "It's their fault." Beneath the shield, his vulnerability is palpable:

Q: When you think about your future, what do you hope for?

A: Man, to be alive. Yeah because this is wild, I'll be like man I hope I don't get shot. Because I already know, I'm the hood guy; a lot of people know me and that's kind of good and kind of bad at the same time. So I just make sure I always be right, so I know okay, I know they ain't goin' to try to kill you when I'm sleeping so I'm all good.

Q: And what do you worry about when you think about your future?

A: Um, man I think I'll worry about me being bad; I don't know. I'll be kind of tempted sometimes, like man I mean you need that money dog; I'm trying to be good now. . . . That would be like the only thing I think that really can mess up my future. I ain't trying to be locked up [laughs]. I can't do that, no, no, no. I'm too little to go to jail.

Beyond documenting whether race is important to youth, or even if they are aware of stereotypes, using SSIs can reveal why race is important and how it matters. Interpreting boys' responses within the cultural context of stereotypes shifts our attention from whether they have "negative identities" to considering why and how they are attempting to navigate hostile expectations to cultivate an identity.

The "Exceptions": Jaire

The majority of boys interviewed were clustered in the exceptions ($n = 12$). These boys challenged negative racial stereotypes but principally for themselves. When they spoke about gender, they typically reinforced gender ideals, with heavy reliance on individuality and stoicism. What distinguishes the exceptions from the accommodators is the way that they explicitly position and define themselves in opposition to negative racial stereotypes.

Jaire is the case study for the exceptions. At 13 years old, Jaire stands over 6 feet tall. He exerts great effort to present himself in a "proper manner" because, as he explains, "appearance and acting right" are essential to his success—and his identity: "I have to hold myself to a higher standard because people don't think that African American males can do this and do that, like go to college, accomplish things." This desire to stand up to the negative stereotypes about his racial group drives Jaire's identity.

Asked to describe himself, Jaire said: "I would say that I'm a very intelligent, articulate young man . . . And someone who is genuinely a well-behaved person, a well-dressed or groomed person . . ." Jaire is articulate. But he also stutters, which signals a physical manifestation of the stress of living to a "higher standard," the pressure he feels to be "exceptional" and "not just a regular Black man." It is particularly noteworthy that in his racial identity narrative he stands apart from other Black people. When asked what he likes the most about himself, he said the following:

> I love the fact that people think of me to be a more complex individual and a more intelligent individual. Because there's no 14 year old—let's be real, no 14-year-old African American male—that can use different words in different situations and give his opinion about Barack Obama or the state the economy is in, the Iraq war, and different situations or the lesbian movement or whatever.

At first glance, Jaire appears to be resisting negative stereotypes, specifically the cultural idea that he, as a Black male, lacks intelligence or ability or an informed political opinion. However, he establishes this counteridentity by viewing himself as an exception to the stereotype. In other words, "other" Black boys might be dumb and uneducated but he is not. This is a resistance for survival strategy (Robinson & Ward, 1991), self-focused and isolating. Although trying to make himself an exception to the stereotype, he inadvertently validates and perpetuates the stereotypes.

The exceptions also reinforced gender stereotypes, with rigid and traditional expectations for men and women. Asked what he likes about being a male, Jaire said,

> Um, the best part about being a young man is that we get to, like we're like the um, trendsetters of the world. You know what I'm saying, like the government, the world is ran by men. Men run the world, you know what I'm saying. . . . And I don't think that a woman is fit to run a world. . . . Because men make hard decisions without emotion. And the women get emotional in certain situations. . . . Like their emotions are too high . . . We, we don't express our feelings as much. We don't talk about how we feel, you know.

Jaire's reliance on masculine power and dominance complements his desire to be exceptional, to stand out. His narrative also illustrates how gender stereotypes and expectations, specifically autonomy and stoicism, shape the way that he responds to racial stereotypes. That is, he grounds his racial identity in individuality to survive the racial stereotypes that press in on him.

Certainly, there are benefits to seeing oneself as more than a stereotype, to conceiving of alternative realities and possibilities, and we certainly would not argue that these young men have "negative" identities. In fact, on a survey instrument it would be easy to assume a positive or advanced racial identity. However, the narrow focus on the self actually reinforces stereotypes and inequalities, and the pressure to be exceptional and "prove the stereotypes wrong" is not a sustainable identity strategy (Steele, 2011). Whereas the accommodators constructed their identities in accordance with stereotypes, the racial–ethnic identity development of the exceptions was characterized by a desire not to be seen as a stereotype or a "regular Black guy."

The "Liberators": Marcus

The final group of boys ($n = 4$) resisted stereotypes for themselves and others. The narratives of the liberators were distinguishable from their peers in terms of the prevalence and depth of their critique of culture and their ability to challenge gender stereotypes alongside race. They were more likely to "see" culture as a system that aims to undermine an entire social group (e.g., Black people) and challenge the system rather than as a specific stereotype or individual. Their narratives also suggested that they viewed identity as a relational process rather than an individual one—that is, one that involved, and depended on, others.

Marcus, the case study for the liberators, is able to stay connected with what he knows and feels is true despite the stereotypes that encourage him to disconnect and not know, not feel, and not care. This ability to stay connected is the bedrock of resistance: the ability to remain connected to what one knows and feels in a culture that dismisses what you know and feel (Brown & Gilligan, 1992; Gilligan, 2011; Robinson & Ward, 1991; Ward, 1996; Way, 2011).

The liberators were both aware and critical of the relevant stereotypes in our culture. Asked about racial stereotypes, Marcus said,

> Well, I guess some people are so used to seeing the gang bangers and the gangsters and stuff like that on the outside, so they think that every Black male is like that. But that's actually a stereotype—and, it's just not, I'm not going to say it's not fair because then again it kind of is because that's all they see all the time, so of course they're going to think that. So um, we just trying to change their minds about Black men in general, about being the best that we can be and getting our educations and proving them wrong.

Marcus does not dismiss the stereotypes or assume they just exist out there. He knows that people see the stereotypes on a regular basis but also knows that seeing it does not justify it or make it true. Moreover, he recognizes that changing the cultural narrative about Black males is a collective effort ("we just trying to change their minds . . . [by] being the best that we can be"). Thus, by resisting individuality and questioning the truth of stereotypes, the liberators were able to challenge to racial stereotypes productively.

Asked how the stereotypes affect him, Marcus said,

> I actually get kind of mad but I try to keep that anger under wraps cause you know, you don't want that anger coming out in the wrong way. So um, I try to focus it in, do my schoolwork, so I can like prove, like break the stereotype. And like, I'd like to get out into the community and like tell people that you know this is not how we act, you know, things like that, so I guess you could say that I'm kind of inspired but then again I'm kind of like pissed off. That's kind of how I feel about it.

Unlike the accommodators and the exceptions who tended to dismiss the stereotypes with stoicism, by saying stereotypes "don't affect them" or "don't matter," Marcus acknowledges their impact, names his emotions ("mad," "anger," "inspired," "pissed off"), and articulates how he uses this emotion to fuel a healthy resistance.

The liberators also stood out for their resistance to gender stereotypes. Marcus explains the expectations he encounters as a Black male:

> Like guys aren't supposed to be feminine or guys aren't supposed to be sensitive or show their feelings, or cry. That's a big one, like guys aren't supposed to cry. . . . It's like but if you get hit or you get a bone broken or your mama or someone close to you dies like, you know, of course you gonna cry cause that's like human nature, you're supposed to cry, that's why you have tear ducts in your body.

Reconstructing emotion as "human nature," Marcus rejects our culture's gender binary, which denies boys' inherent emotionality and sensitivity (Gilligan, 2011; Way, 2011), a stereotype of toughness that is especially enforced for Black men (Majors & Billson, 1992; Spencer et al., 2004; Stevenson, 1997). Asked to explain further, he continues:

> 'cause I guess society thinks that if men or boys act feminine that they're gay or they just assume that they're gay. And I think that's a bad stereotype because guys need to express their feelings too. I'm not going to say that guys are supposed to be tough all the time . . . and they're supposed to like man up and like cover that up with hardness or whatever. It's okay to let yourself cry and be heartbroken. I don't think that's a good stereotype because that's like telling kids not to care about anything that happens.

Engaging the cultural stereotype that limits emotions to girls and gay males, Marcus calls culture for what it is: a "misread" of nature (Gilligan, 2011, p. 82). Knowing the falsehood, Marcus identifies stereotypes as the cause and a careless culture as the consequence. Each of the identity patterns illustrates a unique way that youth construct and maintain a racial–ethnic identity. And, as we discuss next, these different identity strategies may be linked to distinct psychosocial and academic outcomes.

DISCUSSION

Using SSIs as a method in the investigation of racial–ethnic identity development reveals the centrality of stereotypes, the intersectionality of identities, and the within-group variability in pathways of racial–ethnic identity. Although prior work has shown that how an individual evaluates his or her racial–ethnic group (e.g., the extent to which he or she feels attached to his or her racial–ethnic group) is an important aspect of identity development, it reveals, to a large extent, the "outcome" of a process of racial–ethnic identity (i.e., whether one feels attached to their group; e.g., Quintana, 2007; Seaton et al., 2006; Umaña-Taylor, 2004). Data drawn from SSIs reveal the underlying processes of racial–ethnic identity development.

In our studies, the boys' interviews indicate that their attachment to their racial–ethnic group relies on their responses to racial–ethnic stereotypes or the ways in which they challenge or reinforce stereotypes (e.g., Nasir, 2011; Spencer et al., 1997; Ward, 1996). These findings suggest that racial–ethnic identity research should distinguish between youth who construct their racial–ethnic group identities in alignment with negative cultural stereotypes (accommodation) and those who define their identities in contrast to them (resistance). Those who accommodate to such stereotypes may be positively attached to their racial–ethnic group, but they may not thrive to the same degree as those who challenge the stereotypes both individually and broadly (i.e., they don't just claim that they are the exception, they reject the stereotype entirely for their group). Those who resist negative stereotypes of their group on an individual level but not on a more broad level (e.g., they feel that they are the exception within their group) may feel less attached to their group but thrive more than those who accommodate because they are resisting negative stereotypes. Both Omar and Marcus in the data presented previously suggest they are close to other Black people, but the nature of these relationships is quite different—the former is established by negative stereotypes, whereas the latter was cultivated by standing in opposition to the dominant narrative.

The data also suggest that racial–ethnic identity is not purely about race or ethnicity. Rather one's racial–ethnic identity is in response to stereotypes about a range of social identities including gender, sexuality, and social class. Thus research that solely examines racial–ethnic identity is not able to see how these identities are enmeshed. Although scholars have created theories centered on the intersectionality of social identities (e.g., Azmitia, Syed, & Radmacher, 2008; Shields, 2008; Spencer et al., 1997), there remain few empirical investigations of how social identities overlap with each other and why such intersectionalities matter (Carter, 2006; Nasir, 2011; Ward, 1996; Way, 2011). The data presented in this chapter suggest that stereotypes may forge the link between social identities. Because of these stereotypes (Ghavami & Peplau, 2013), what Black boys see in the "social mirror" (Suárez-Orozco, 2004) differs from what Black girls see, and racial–ethnic and gender stereotypes together provide the foundation, or the backdrop, of racial identities for both Black boys and girls. Gender stereotypes, for example, played a key role in the difference between the accommodators and in the liberators. The accommodators were bound to a cultural definition of Blackness that involved a masculine toughness and independence, whereas the liberators were joined to other Black people through rejecting isolation and stoicism. In essence, it was the intersection of cultural stereotypes that provided the thread of racial–ethnic identity development for the accommodators and the liberators.

A third contribution of our method of SSIs in the investigation of racial–ethnic identity development is the within-group variability and pathways of racial–ethnic identity development. As Sellers and colleagues (1998) argued, racial identity is diverse, which we also find in our sample of Black males. Prior studies have used clustering techniques to classify youth into racial identity profiles (e.g., Chavous et al., 2003; Yip et al., 2006). Although such methods can place youth into the "high centrality, low public regard" cluster, for example, they cannot explain the process through which these profiles were constructed or the meaning of them. For example, the accommodators defined their identities in alignment with stereotypes, which then informs their behaviors. This form of racial–ethnic identity may parallel the "acting White" phenomenon (Fordham & Ogbu, 1986) and Ferguson's (2000) "bad boys" who effectively construct a racial identity that depends on their adherence to the mainstream notions of what it means to be Black and male. The consequences of this identity strategy are already documented—delinquency, school failure, and poor well-being (e.g., Ferguson, 2000; Majors & Billson, 1992; Spencer et al., 2004).

The exceptions, on other hand, based their racial–ethnic identities by positioning themselves outside of, or separate from, the stereotypes. Like the accommodators, their racial–ethnic identities reinforce negative stereotypes, but they are less likely to experience the same negative behavioral outcomes, such as academic disengagement or school failure. Instead, because they establish their racial identities by separating the self from others (i.e., "other Black people"), they may actually suffer psychological distress from the forced disconnection. For example, Steele's (2011) stereotype threat research showed that carrying the pressure not to confirm a negative racial stereotype is psychologically weighty, particularly when shouldered alone. Similar research on gender has shown that boys who separate themselves from others in their social group demonstrate greater psychological distress (Cressen, Way, Gupta, & Hughes, 2012; Gupta et al., 2013; Santos, 2010; Way et al., 2014) and decreased academic performance (Santos, Galligan, Pahlke, & Fabes, 2013; Santos, Way, & Hughes, 2011). Thus, constructing a racial–ethnic identity that is based on being different and separate from members of the group not only reinforces stereotypes, but may also increase the risk for negative outcomes.

The liberators represent a path of resistance, formulating a racial–ethnic identity that is grounded in rejecting or counteracting negative stereotypes and thus likely to lead to positive adjustment (Robinson & Ward, 1991; Way, 2011). Spencer (Spencer et al., 1997) referred to this as "proactive coping," whereas Robinson and Ward (1991) asserted that racial–ethnic identities that are established by challenging the system of social inequality and oppression pave the way for "liberation." Studies have shown that youth who resist or reject limiting or overtly negative stereotypes are more likely to report higher levels of psychological and academic adjustment than those who do not (Cressen et al., 2012; Gilligan, 2011; Gupta et al., 2013; Perry, 2004; Santos, 2010; Spencer et al., 1997; Ward, 1996; Way, 2011; Way et al., 2014). In other words, it appears that those youth on a "liberating" path of racial–ethnic identity formation are more likely to thrive than those who do not.

In sum, using interview methods to understand racial–ethnic identity development allows us to see the role that stereotypes play in the development of identities, to see the ways that stereotypes and social identities intersect with each other and are in fact infused with each other, and to understand the different ways that youth engage with these stereotypes. With this understanding, we have a richer and deeper understanding of the process of racial–ethnic identity development and the ways in which they are shaped by the context of culture and its stereotypes and expectations.

SSIs: STRENGTHS, CHALLENGES, AND BEST PRACTICES

As illustrated in the empirical example, applying the interviewing method to one's examination of racial–ethnic identity development allows us the opportunity to investigate the meaning of racial–ethnic identity; the ability to engage in data-driven, bottom-up, theory-building rather than top-down theory testing; and the ability to see the larger context in which the adolescent is embedded, as it is through language that the macro context is often revealed (Way, 2011). Furthermore, it allows us to see the person as an active participant in the process of identity development, rather than as simply a recipient of socialization infused with negative stereotypes. The pathways of racial–ethnic identity revealed in the empirical example underscore the agentic nature of identity development. Some youth chose to reject or resist stereotypes, and others chose to accommodate; these strategies have significant implications for the understanding the health-related outcomes of racial–ethnic identity development.

Although there are a number of strengths to using an interview methodology in the study of racial–ethnic identity development, there are also challenges. A key challenge of this approach is getting high-quality interviews in which the interviewees are able to express their genuine opinions in response to the interviewers' question. Interviewers must be trained to listen carefully and create a safe space so that the interviewees will feel comfortable revealing what they "really" know about themselves, rather than simply stating what they feel they should say about their own racial–ethnic group. In a culture imbued with stereotypes about ethnicity and race, there is great macrolevel pressure on youth to construct their experiences in such a way so that it fits cultural expectations. Interviewers must allow for responses that are not necessarily consistent with their views. Only with the creation of a safe space will interviewees feel comfortable sharing what they "really think" (see Brown & Gilligan, 1992). An interviewer must listen and be able to recognize and value responses that are inconsistent with what the interviewer wants or expects to hear so that the complex process of racial–ethnic identity development is clearly revealed.

Quality interviewer training is also critical to conducting research that relies on SSIs. Such training requires in-depth and ongoing discussions in which interviewers practice conducting, listening to, and critiquing their own and others' interviews. In this process, the interviewer learns how to listen and probe in such a way that the interviewee is able to express genuine stories rather than clichés. Interviewers should have a clear understanding of the interview protocol and intent of each interview questions so that probes from the interviewer will stay relevant and get to the heart of the issue rather than stay on the surface (Gilligan et al., 2003; Mishler, 1986; Way, 1998, 2011).

A related challenge in the application of interview methods is the analysis process. Interview analysis does not merely involve counting how many people reported the same "theme." These are observations of the data. Interpretation of the data means asking "why" these themes exist and what they mean. In this way, interview analysis is an interpretive process that should always involve understanding the context of the data and how the interpreter is responding to the data, asking, for example, "Why is this person telling me this story?" "What does it reveal in the larger context of the person speaking?" and "What is my response to this story, and why?" Answering these questions allows one to achieve a rigorous interpretation that is not simply repeating, verbatim, the quote from the interview (Gilligan et al., 2003; Way, 2011).

An additional challenge of the interview process is the designing of the interview protocol. A well-designed interview protocol is essential for eliciting quality interview data. The protocol must balance consistency with flexibility and authenticity (Mishler, 1986; Warren, 2002; see Appendix 6.1). Probes should ask *why* questions and aim to gather examples from real events and experiences (Clark, 2011; Way, 1998). Furthermore, open questions that give space for youth to question or challenge are also important, as are more focused questions that ask for examples. The question, for example, of "tell me about how you feel about your racial–ethnic group" is likely to elicit an abstract, non-contextualized response and will likely get a survey-like response (e.g., good or not good). In contrast, saying "Tell me about a time when you were aware of being Black and what was that like for you" elicits a story—a time and a place—and allows interviewees to situate themselves in the stories that they tell. To interview youth and to see the world through their eyes, one must develop an interview protocol that reflects a genuine interest in the world of youth and must do it in a language that allows youth to describe events, thoughts, and feelings in their own words and using their own examples from their daily lives.

FUTURE DIRECTIONS

The use of SSIs to study racial–ethnic identity expands the empirical and theoretical literature by offering new ways of thinking about and measuring racial–ethnic identity. For example, SSIs reveal the relational nature of racial–ethnic identity development (e.g., Way et al., 2013), the significance of cultural stereotypes (Nasir, 2011; Rogers, 2013), and the ways in which other social identities (e.g., gender) shape racial–ethnic identity (e.g., Carter, 2006; Nasir, 2011; Rogers, Scott, & Way, in press). On the basis of such findings, new racial–ethnic identity measures can be designed—for example, a survey instrument that measures racial–ethnic identity in the context of peer relationships or a measure that explicitly uses an intersectionality lens, framing questions specific to a racial–ethnic-by-gender group (e.g., Black females). The purpose of such measures would not be to replace SSIs, but to build on them. In this way, SSIs advance both our knowledge of racial–ethnic identity and the quality and specificity of the instruments used to measure it.

CONCLUSION

Racial–ethnic identity is one the most widely researched topics in the social sciences (e.g., Cross, 1991; Oyserman, 2008; Phinney, 1990; Quintana, 2007; Sellers et al., 1998; Syed et al., 2011; Umaña-Taylor et al., 2004). Most of this research has used a survey approach and thus we have a very limited understanding of the processes by which racial–ethnic identities develop. Without an understanding of process, there is little understanding of identity development. Those who have used a qualitative approach to the study of racial–ethnic identity (e.g., Carter, 2006; Nasir, 2011; Niemann, Romero, Arredondo, & Rodriguez, 1999; Perry, 2001; Spencer, 1999; Spencer et al., 1997; Spencer & Markstrom-Adams, 1990; Suárez-Orozco, 2004; Syed & Azmitia, 2008; Way et al., 2008) have underscored the importance of examining the process of development as well as its outcome. It is time that the quantitative versus qualitative divide in the study of racial–ethnic identity development be mended so that we can move forward in the study of identity development with the recognition that methods are not only tools but also provide unique ways of accessing knowledge about both process and outcomes. Thus, the study of racial–ethnic identity development should include an array of methods, including semistructured interviews.

APPENDIX 6.1
Interview Protocol

INTRO

Intro question; salient self-descriptors; info to use throughout interview	Tell me a little bit about yourself.

SCHOOL

Motivations, reasons for attending school; their choice, parents choice, academic, behavioral	Tell me about how you ended up coming to Urban Prep, what was that process like? • How did you hear about the school? • What did your parents think about you coming to an all boys' school?
Perception of school	How would you describe Urban Prep to someone who has never been here? What do you like most about Urban Prep? • Why is that important to you? If you could change anything about Urban Prep, what would you change? • Why is that important to you?
Prove a counterpoint, a contrast for current school environment Knowledge/awareness of "Black boy problem"; interesting in current interviews how boys make sense of purpose and necessity of the school	Besides being all boys, how do you think this school is different from your last school? Do you think it's important to have schools like this one? • Why/why not?
Student–teacher relationships; students' perceptions of teacher perceptions of him	Tell me about your teachers, what are they like? • Who is your favorite teacher? What do you like most about him/her? Why is that important? Sometimes the adults at school have ideas about their students. How do you think the adults at this school see you?

(continues)

PEERS

Student–student relationships

Tell me about the other boys at this school, what are they like?

How do the boys at this school get along with one another?

General friends

Tell me about your friends. Who are they and what are they like?

Do you think it's important to have friends?
- Why/why not?

Closest/best friend

Do you have a closest friend or a best friend?
- Who is he?
- What is he like?
- How did you meet?
- How long have you known him?

Description of friend as a possible reflection of self, or desired self

How would you describe [best friend], what is he like?

Good and bad of friendship

What do you like most about your friendship with [best friend]?

What do you like least?

When was the last time you saw [best friend]? What did you guys do?
- [probe for details]

What kinds of things do you talk about with [best friend]?
- [probe for details]

What kinds of things would you NOT talk about with [best friend]?
- Why not?

SELF

Global self-descriptions

How would you describe yourself?

Family structure; notice if family comes up in self-description

Who do you live with?
- Family structure; siblings

What about you makes you feel really proud?
- Why?

Is there anything about yourself that you're not proud of?

Centrality; core sense of self

What would you say is most important about the person you are?

Understanding of own development; attributions; relational/social support

How do you think you've gotten to be the person you are?

RACIAL IDENTITY

Self-identification; African American vs. Black

What would you say is your ethnicity or race?
• Is being [race] important to you? In what ways?

Good and bad about being [Black]; subjective meaning and experience of racial identity

What do you like about being [race/ethnicity]?
• Why?
• Tell me about a time when you felt this way.
What are some of the things that bother you about being [race/ethnicity]?
• Tell me about the last time you felt this way.

Meaning they attribute/assign to "Black" as a social category

What do you think it means to be Black?
Do you ever feel like there are certain things you're supposed to do or ways you're supposed to be just because you're Black?
What do you think other people think about Black people? (i.e., stereotypes)

Discrimination/unfair treatment based on race

Tell me about a time when you feel you were treated differently because you are Black.

GENDER IDENTITY

Image of a typical boy; behavior, appearance, attitude, dress; own alignment with typical boy; resistance/adherence to typical boy norms

Describe the typical boy. What is he like?
• Do you think that you're like that?
• How so/how not?
Do you ever feel pressure to act like a typical boy?
• How does that make you feel?

Good and bad about being a boy; meaning and experience

What do you like most about being a boy?
What do you like least?
Can you think of a time when wished you weren't a boy?
What do you think other people think about boys? (i.e., stereotypes)

Differential treatment based on gender; experience of being a boy

Can you think of a time when you feel you were treated differently because you were a boy?
• What happened?

Race/gender stereotypes

What are some of the benefits that Black boys have that maybe other boys don't?
• Like what, can you give me an example?
• Why do you think that is?
What are some of the challenges that Black boys face that maybe other boys don't?
• Like what, can you give me an example?
• Why do you think that is?

(continues)

APPENDIX 6.1
Interview Protocol *(Continued)*

Transition to manhood; notions of masculinity; what and how they're moving toward manhood	What do you think it means to become a man? In what ways is Urban Prep helping you become a man? Tell me about a man, either in society or that you know personally, that you consider a role model. • What is he like? • What does he do?
FUTURE	
Academic expectations/aspirations	How far do you expect to go in school? What do you see yourself doing when you are 25 years old? What do you think it's going to take to get there? When you think about your future, what is the thing you worry about the most? What is the thing you hope for the most?

Note. From *Young, Black, and Male: Exploring the Intersections of Racial and Gender Identity in an All-Black Male High School* (Doctoral dissertation), by L. O. Rogers, 2012, pp. 315–320. Copyright 2012 by Leoandra Onnie Rogers. Reprinted with permission.

REFERENCES

Altschul, I., Oyserman, D., & Bybee, D. (2006). Racial–ethnic identity in mid-adolescence: Content and change as predictors of academic achievement. *Child Development, 77*, 1155–1169. http://dx.doi.org/10.1111/j.1467-8624.2006.00926.x

Anyon, J. (1984). Intersections of gender and class: Accommodation and resistance by working-class and affluent females to contradictory sex role ideologies. *Journal of Education, 166*, 25–48.

Azmitia, M., Syed, M., & Radmacher, K. (2008). *The intersections of personal and social identities*. San Francisco, CA: Jossey-Bass.

Brown, L. M., & Gilligan, C. (1992). *Meeting at the crossroads: Women's psychology and girls' development*. New York, NY: Ballantine Books. http://dx.doi.org/10.4159/harvard.9780674731837

Carter, P. L. (2006). Straddling boundaries: Identity, culture, and school. *Sociology of Education, 79*, 304–328. http://dx.doi.org/10.1177/003804070607900402

Chavous, T. M., Bernat, D. H., Schmeelk-Cone, K., Caldwell, C. H., Kohn-Wood, L., & Zimmerman, M. A. (2003). Racial identity and academic attainment among African American adolescents. *Child Development, 74*, 1076–1090. http://dx.doi.org/10.1111/1467-8624.00593

Clark, C. D. (2011). *In a younger voice: Doing child-centered qualitative research*. New York, NY: Oxford University Press.

Cooley, C. H. (1902). *Human nature and the social order.* New York, NY: Scribner.

Cressen, J., Way, N., Gupta, T., & Hughes, D. (2012). *Adherence to norms of masculinity and its link to psychological and social adjustment.* Manuscript in preparation.

Cross, W. (1991). *Shades of Black: Diversity in African American identity.* Philadelphia, PA: Temple University Press.

Denzin, N. K., & Lincoln, Y. S. (Eds.). (2005). *The Sage handbook of qualitative research.* Thousand Oaks, CA: Sage.

Erikson, E. H. (1968). *Identity, youth, and crisis.* New York, NY: Norton.

Ferguson, A. A. (2000). *Bad boys: Public schools in the making of black masculinity.* Ann Arbor, MI: University of Michigan Press.

Fordham, S., & Ogbu, J. U. (1986). Black students' school success: Coping with the "burden of 'acting white'". *The Urban Review, 18,* 176–206. http://dx.doi.org/10.1007/BF01112192

Ghavami, N., & Peplau, L. A. (2013). An intersectional analysis of gender and ethnic stereotypes: Testing three hypotheses. *Psychology of Women Quarterly, 37,* 113–127. http://dx.doi.org/10.1177/0361684312464203

Gilligan, C. (2011). *Joining the resistance.* Cambridge, England: Polity Press.

Gilligan, C., Spencer, R., Weinberg, M. K., & Bertsch, T. (2003). On the listening guide: A voice-centered relational model. In P. M. Camic, J. E. Rhodes, & L. Yardley (Eds.), *Qualitative research in psychology: Expanding perspectives in methodology and design* (pp. 157–172). Washington, DC: American Psychological Association.

Gupta, T., Way, N., McGill, R. K., Hughes, D., Santos, C., Jia, Y., . . . Deng, H. (2013). Gender-typed behaviors in friendships and well-being: A cross-cultural study of Chinese and American boys [Special issue]. *Journal of Research on Adolescence, 23,* 57–68.

Huberman, M., & Miles, M. B. (2002). *The qualitative researcher's companion: Classic and contemporary readings.* Thousand Oaks, CA: Sage.

Hughes, D., Rivas, D., Foust, M., Hagelskamp, C., Gersick, S., & Way, N. (2008). How to catch a moonbeam: A mixed-methods approach to understanding ethnic socialization processes in ethnically diverse families. In S. M. Quintana & C. McKown (Eds.), *Handbook of race, racism, and the developing child* (pp. 226–277). Hoboken, NJ: Wiley.

Hughes, D., Rodriguez, J., Smith, E. P., Johnson, D. J., Stevenson, H. C., & Spicer, P. (2006). Parents' ethnic–racial socialization practices: A review of research and directions for future study. *Developmental Psychology, 42,* 747–770. http://dx.doi.org/10.1037/0012-1649.42.5.747

Majors, R., & Billson, J. M. (1992). *Cool pose: The dilemmas of black manhood in America.* New York, NY: Lexington Books.

Marecek, J., Fine, M., & Kidder, L. (2001). Working between two worlds: Qualitative methods and psychology. In D. L. Tolman & M. Brydon-Miller (Eds.), *From subjects to subjectivities: A handbook of interpretive and participatory methods* (pp. 29–41). New York, NY: New York University Press.

McAdams, D. P. (1990). Unity and purpose in human lives: The emergence of identity as a life story. In A. I. Rabin, R. A. Zucker, R. A. Emmons, & S. Frank (Eds.), *Studying persons and lives* (pp. 148–200). New York, NY: Springer.

McAdams, D. P. (2013). *The redemptive self: Stories Americans live by.* New York, NY: Oxford University Press.

Mishler, E. G. (1986). *Research interviewing: Context and narrative.* Cambridge, MA: Harvard University Press.

Nasir, N. S. (2011). *Racialized identities: Race and achievement among African American youth.* Stanford, CA: Stanford University Press.

Niemann, Y. F., Romero, A. J., Arredondo, J., & Rodriguez, V. (1999). What does it mean to be "Mexican"? Social construction of an ethnic identity. *Hispanic Journal of Behavioral Sciences, 21,* 47–60. http://dx.doi.org/10.1177/0739986399211004

Niwa, E. Y. (2012). The impact of ethnic and racial discrimination on the social and psychological adjustment of early adolescents: A mixed-method, longitudinal study. (Doctoral dissertation). *Dissertation Abstracts International: Section B. Sciences and Engineering, 73*(10-B), 3511454.

Niwa, E. Y., Way, N., Qin, D. B., & Okazaki, S. (2011). Hostile hallways: Asian American adolescents' experiences of peer discrimination in school. In F. T. L. Leong, L. Juang, D. B. Qin, & H. E. Fitzgerald (Eds.), *Asian American and Pacific Islander children and mental health. Vol. I: Development and context* (pp. 193–219). Westport, CT: Praeger.

Oyserman, D. (2008). Racial–ethnic self-schemas: Multi-dimensional identity-based motivation. *Journal of Research in Personality, 42,* 1186–1198. http://dx.doi.org/10.1016/j.jrp.2008.03.003

Pahl, K., & Way, N. (2006). Longitudinal trajectories of ethnic identity among urban Black and Latino adolescents. *Child Development, 77,* 1403–1415. http://dx.doi.org/10.1111/j.1467-8624.2006.00943.x

Perry, P. (2001). White means never having to say you're ethnic/racial: White youth and the construction of "cultureless" identity. *Journal of Contemporary Ethnography, 30,* 56–91. http://dx.doi.org/10.1177/089124101030001002

Perry, T. (2004). *Young, gifted, and Black: Promoting high achievement among African-American students.* Boston, MA: Beacon Press.

Phinney, J. S. (1990). Ethnic identity in adolescents and adults: Review of research. *Psychological Bulletin, 108,* 499–514. http://dx.doi.org/10.1037/0033-2909.108.3.499

Phinney, J. S. (1992). The Multigroup Ethnic Identity Measure: A new scale for use with diverse groups. *Journal of Adolescent Research, 7,* 156–176. http://dx.doi.org/10.1177/074355489272003

Quintana, S. M. (2007). Racial and ethnic identity: Developmental perspectives and research [Special issue]. *Journal of Counseling Psychology, 54,* 259–270.

Robinson, T., & Ward, J. V. (1991). "A belief in self far greater than anyone's disbelief": Cultivating resistance among African American female adolescents [Special issue]. *Women & Therapy, 11*, 87–103.

Rogers, L. O. (2012). *Young, Black, and male: Exploring the intersections of racial and gender identity in an all-Black male high school* (Doctoral dissertation). ProQuest Dissertation Abstracts. (UMI No. 10197)

Rogers, L. O. (2013, April). Black males narrating identities and stereotypes in an all-Black male high school. In S. Sirin (Chair), *Negotiating cultural identities among youth.* Paper presented at biennial meeting for Society for Research on Child Development, Seattle, WA.

Rogers, L. O., Scott, M. A., & Way, N. (in press). Racial and gender identity development among Black adolescent males: An intersectionality perspective. *Child Development.*

Rosenbloom, S. R., & Way, N. (2004). Experiences of discrimination among African American, Asian American, and Latino adolescents in an urban high school. *Youth & Society, 35*, 420–451. http://dx.doi.org/10.1177/0044118X03261479

Santos, C., Way, N., & Hughes, D. (2011, March). *Racially and ethnically diverse boys' trajectories of academic engagement and resistance to norms of masculinity during middle school.* Paper presented at the biennial meeting of the Society for Research in Child Development, Montreal, Quebec, Canada.

Santos, C. E. (2010). *The missing story: Resistance to norms of masculinity in the friendships of adolescent boys.* Available from ProQuest Dissertations and Theses database. (UMI No. 3426967)

Santos, C. E., Galligan, K., Pahlke, E., & Fabes, R. A. (2013). Gender-typed behaviors, achievement, and adjustment among racially and ethnically diverse boys during early adolescence. *American Journal of Orthopsychiatry, 83*, 252–264. http://dx.doi.org/10.1111/ajop.12036

Seaton, E. K., Scottham, K. M., & Sellers, R. M. (2006). The status model of racial identity development in African American adolescents: Evidence of structure, trajectories, and well-being. *Child Development, 77*, 1416–1426. http://dx.doi.org/10.1111/j.1467-8624.2006.00944.x

Sellers, R. M., Smith, M. A., Shelton, J. N., Rowley, S. A. J., & Chavous, T. M. (1998). Multidimensional model of racial identity: A reconceptualization of African American racial identity. *Personality and Social Psychology Review, 2*, 18–39. http://dx.doi.org/10.1207/s15327957pspr0201_2

Shields, S. A. (2008). Gender: An intersectionality perspective. *Sex Roles, 59*, 301–311. http://dx.doi.org/10.1007/s11199-008-9501-8

Shorter-Gooden, K., & Washington, N. C. (1996). Young, Black, and female: The challenge of weaving an identity. *Journal of Adolescence, 19*, 465–475. http://dx.doi.org/10.1006/jado.1996.0044

Spencer, M. B. (1999). Social and cultural influences on school adjustment: The application of an identity-focused cultural ecological perspective. *Educational Psychologist, 34*, 43–57. http://dx.doi.org/10.1207/s15326985ep3401_4

Spencer, M. B., Dupree, D., & Hartmann, T. (1997). A phenomenological variant of ecological systems theory (PVEST): A self-organization perspective in context. *Development and Psychopathology, 9*, 817–833. http://dx.doi.org/10.1017/S0954579497001454

Spencer, M. B., Fegley, S., Harpalani, V., & Seaton, G. (2004). Understanding hypermasculinity in context: A theory-driven analysis of urban adolescent males' coping responses. *Research in Human Development, 1*, 229–257. http://dx.doi.org/10.1207/s15427617rhd0104_2

Spencer, M. B., & Markstrom-Adams, C. (1990). Identity processes among racial and ethnic minority children in America. *Child Development, 61*, 290–310. http://dx.doi.org/10.2307/1131095

Steele, C. M. (2011). *Whistling Vivaldi: How stereotypes affect us and what we can do.* New York, NY: Norton.

Stevenson, H. C., Jr. (1997). "Missed, dissed, and pissed": Making meaning of neighborhood risk, fear and anger management in urban black youth. *Cultural Diversity and Mental Health, 3*, 37–52. http://dx.doi.org/10.1037/1099-9809.3.1.37

Strauss, A., & Corbin, J. (1990). *Basics of qualitative research: Grounded theory procedures and techniques.* Thousand Oaks, CA: Sage.

Suárez-Orozco, C. (2004). Formulating identity in a globalized world. In M. M. Suárez-Orozco & D. B. Qin-Hilliard (Eds.), *Globalization: Culture and education in the new millennium* (pp. 173–202). Berkeley, CA: University of California Press.

Syed, M., & Azmitia, M. (2008). A narrative approach to ethnic identity in emerging adulthood: Bringing life to the identity status model. *Developmental Psychology, 44*, 1012–1027. http://dx.doi.org/10.1037/0012-1649.44.4.1012

Syed, M., Azmitia, M., & Cooper, C. R. (2011). Identity and academic success among underrepresented ethnic minorities: An interdisciplinary review and integration. *Journal of Social Issues, 67*, 442–468. http://dx.doi.org/10.1111/j.1540-4560.2011.01709.x

Tajfel, H., & Turner, J. C. (1986). The social identity theory of intergroup behavior. In S. Worchel & W. Austin (Eds.), *Psychology of inter-group relations* (pp. 7–24). Chicago, IL: Nelson Hall.

Umaña-Taylor, A. J. (2004). Ethnic identity and self-esteem: Examining the role of social context. *Journal of Adolescence, 27*, 139–146. http://dx.doi.org/10.1016/j.adolescence.2003.11.006

Umaña-Taylor, A. J., Yazedjian, A., & Bámaca-Gómez, M. (2004). Developing the ethnic identity scale using Eriksonian and social identity perspectives. *Identity: An International Journal of Theory and Research, 4*, 9–38. http://dx.doi.org/10.1207/S1532706XID0401_2

Ward, J. V. (1996). Raising resisters: The role of truth telling in the psychological development of African American girls. In B. J. Leadbeater & N. Way (Eds.), *Urban girls: Resisting stereotypes, creating identities* (pp. 85–99). New York, NY: New York University Press.

Warren, C. A. B. (2002). Qualitative interviewing. In J. F. Gubrium & J. A. Holstein (Eds.), *Handbook of interview research: Context and method* (pp. 83–102). Thousand Oaks, CA: Sage.

Way, N. (1998). *Everyday courage: The stories and lives of urban teenagers*. New York, NY: New York University Press.

Way, N. (2011). *Deep secrets: Boys' friendships and the crisis for connection*. Cambridge, MA: Harvard University Press. http://dx.doi.org/10.4159/harvard.9780674061361

Way, N., Cressen, J., Bodian, S., Presten, J., Nelson, J., & Hughes, D. (2014). "It might be nice to be a girl . . . then you wouldn't have to be emotionless": Boys' resistance to norms of masculinity during adolescence [Special section]. *Psychology of Men and Masculinity, 15*, 241–252. Advance online publication. http://dx.doi.org/10.1037/a0037262

Way, N., Hernandez, M. G., Rogers, L. O., & Hughes, D. (2013). "I'm not going to become no rapper": Stereotypes as a context of ethnic and racial identity development. *Journal of Adolescent Research, 28*, 407–430. http://dx.doi.org/10.1177/0743558413480836

Way, N., & Rogers, L. O. (2014). "[T]hey say Black men won't make it, but I know I'm gonna make it": Identity development in the context of American culture. In K. McLean & M. Syed (Eds.) *Oxford handbook of identity development* (pp. 269–285). New York, NY: Oxford University Press.

Way, N., Santos, C., Niwa, E. Y., & Kim-Gervey, C. (2008). To be or not to be: An exploration of ethnic/racial identity development in context. *New Directions for Child and Adolescent Development, 2008*(120), 61–79.

Yip, T., Seaton, E. K., & Sellers, R. M. (2006). African American racial identity across the lifespan: Identity status, identity content, and depressive symptoms. *Child Development, 77*, 1504–1517. http://dx.doi.org/10.1111/j.1467-8624.2006.00950.x

7

FRIENDSHIP NETWORKS AND ETHNIC–RACIAL IDENTITY DEVELOPMENT: CONTRIBUTIONS OF SOCIAL NETWORK ANALYSIS

OLGA KORNIENKO, CARLOS E. SANTOS,
AND KIMBERLY A. UPDEGRAFF

One aspect of identity development that has received considerable attention among social scientists for the past 40 to 50 years concerns ethnic–racial identity[1] (ERI) and the role it plays in shaping the socioemotional development of adolescents. This research has linked dimensions of ERI to numerous indicators of mental health (e.g., Fuligni, Witkow, & Garcia, 2005; Phinney, 1990; Roberts et al., 1999). Although ERI has emerged as a critical area of research among social scientists, and recent research has suggested that peers play an important role in shaping ERI processes (e.g., Way, Santos,

This research was supported in part by funds provided by the T. Denny Sanford School of Social Dynamics at Arizona State University as part of the Lives of Girls and Boys Research Enterprise (https://thesanfordschool.asu.edu/lives). The authors thank the graduate and undergraduate students who contributed to this project and the students, teachers, principal, staff, and parents for their participation.

[1]The metaconstruct *ethnic–racial identity* has been proposed to reflect an individual's ethnic background as well as the racialized experiences associated with membership in a particular group in the United States. It is a multidimensional construct that reflects beliefs and attitudes regarding membership in an ethnic–racial group, as well as the processes by which these beliefs and attitudes develop (Umaña-Taylor et al., 2014).

http://dx.doi.org/10.1037/14618-008
Studying Ethnic Identity: Methodological and Conceptual Approaches Across Disciplines, C. E. Santos and A. J. Umaña-Taylor (Editors)

Niwa, & Kim-Gervey, 2008), little is known concerning the role of friend-ship networks and peer influence in ERI development.

In this chapter, we illustrate the conceptual and methodological con-tributions of applying social network analysis (SNA) to the study of ERI. We use data from a longitudinal school-based study of racially and ethnically diverse youths' identity development and friendships. Specifically, we com-bined data on friendship nominations within adolescents' grade with survey data on youths' ERI centrality, an established dimension of ERI that assesses how central youths' ERI is to their sense of self. We analyzed these data using longitudinal SNA methods (Snijders, van de Bunt, & Steglich, 2010). Application of longitudinal SNA methods enables us to examine, for the first time, peer influence on ERI centrality, while controlling for the effects of an individual's ERI centrality and ethnic or racial group membership as impor-tant factors that shape friendship network selection. The purpose of this chapter is to highlight the implications, strengths, and challenges of adopt-ing an SNA approach to the study of ERI to better understand the effects that friendship networks and peer influence can have on ERI processes.

Given the socioemotional prominence of peers during adolescence (for a review, see Parker, Rubin, Erath, Wojslawowicz, & Buskirk, 2006), examining the role of friendship networks for adolescent development is an important goal for research on adolescents' socioemotional development. Our approach is grounded in scholarship that suggests that peers play a critical role in shap-ing how youth experience their ERI (Phinney, 2000; Syed, 2012; Way et al., 2008). Theoretical work has suggested that ERI depends on the social context in which youth are embedded and emerges as a dialectic process of individuals making sense of their ethnic group membership in light of experiences with others (Phinney, 2000). This view underscores that the peer context is likely to have a powerful impact on ERI dynamics, particularly during adolescence, a period marked by greater engagement and time spent with peers compared with earlier stages in development (Larson & Richards, 1991). Indeed, recent research has begun to uncover the potent role of peers in ERI development (e.g., Syed & Juan, 2012).

SNA can contribute to the study of ERI development through the use of conceptual and methodological tools designed to unravel the complex asso-ciation between peer experiences and developmental processes. The SNA approach augments ERI research because SNA examines the reciprocal trans-actions between individuals and their social context (i.e., friendship networks) and thus has the potential to provide insights about the relational nature of how ERI develops, a topic that has received considerable theoretical but little empirical attention. One important contribution of SNA is that it provides sophisticated methods for describing each individual's position in the peer con-text by considering the patterning of ties among friends. Thus, SNA augments the study of ERI through its ability to describe the structure of ties within a peer ecology, which then allows us to quantify various indices of an individual's network position (e.g., friendship network prestige and centrality). It is important to note that an individual's position in a network of friends is likely to have implications for ERI because it emerges as an outcome of an individual's interactions with peers (Crosier, Webster, & Dillon, 2012).

Another important contribution of SNA to the study of ERI comes from a recently developed approach to examine the coevolution of networks and behavior. This approach to longitudinal modeling of networks and behavior is known as stochastic actor-based modeling (SABM; Snijders et al., 2010). Because ERI is, by definition, an evolving aspect of the self, its development needs to be considered over time (Hughes, Way, & Rivas-Drake, 2011); thus, SABM's ability to explore changes in ERI as a part of the coevolution of peer network and behavior is an important methodological contribution to this line of research. SABM also holds the potential to contribute to the study of peer effects on ERI dynamics because it enables researchers to examine peer influence on ERI over time, while controlling for important confounding processes. These confounding processes include the effects of an individual's own ERI and an individual's ethnic and racial group membership on peer network selection. Finally, SABM allows for the examination of peer influence by considering the effects of the broader network of adolescents' social relationships (i.e., multiple friends of the focal individual, friends of friends, etc.). This approach is likely to provide a more nuanced description of the social context and thus further extend emerging research documenting social influences in the formation of ERI (e.g., Syed & Juan, 2012). The use of SABM has gained popularity in developmental research, and this method has been used to unravel complex and reciprocal links between peer networks and various developmental outcomes, including aggressive behavior (Sijtsema et al., 2010), smoking (Schaefer, Haas, & Bishop, 2012), weight and physical activity (de La Haye, Robins, Mohr, & Wilson, 2011), and depressive symptoms (Schaefer, Kornienko, & Fox, 2011; Van Zalk, Kerr, Branje, Stattin, & Meeus, 2010).

In the sections that follow, we review existing research on the role of peers in ERI. Given the lack of empirical work applying SNA methods to the study of ERI (with an exception of studies examining same- and cross-ethnicity/race friendships networks, e.g., Goodreau, Kitts, & Morris, 2009), we draw on previous research focusing on the role of peers and friends more broadly to identify how this research agenda could be advanced by the use of SNA methods and tools. Next, we provide an overview of SNA methods for describing individuals' position in the structure of peer relationships by considering the patterning of ties and identify how network position may be associated with ERI development processes. We then introduce methods for longitudinal SNA (i.e., SABM) that allows for the examination of peer influence on ERI development, and we provide an empirical illustration of the role of peer influence on ERI centrality in a friendship network of eighth-grade students. We conclude with a discussion of the strengths and challenges of applying SNA to the study of ERI development during adolescence.

EXISTING RESEARCH LINKING PEERS TO THE STUDY OF ETHNIC–RACIAL IDENTITY

Modest attention has been paid to the role of peers in shaping youths' ERI. Existing research has linked adolescents' experiences with their peers and their ERI primarily in two ways: (a) by exploring the effects of racial and ethnic composition of schools on youths' ERI and (b) by exploring the effects of ethnic and racial composition of friendship circles on youths' ERI. Even though research exploring racial/ethnic composition of schools as a factor shaping youths' ERI does not typically carry an explicit emphasis on examining the effects of friendships on ERI per se, this work is relevant to the study of how peers influence ERI because it underscores how youth experience their ERI when the peers around them vary in their ethnic/racial composition. Neither of these approaches, however, considers the extent to which peers' own ERI may play a role in friendship formation or peer influence. Rather, these two approaches consider how static racial/ethnic attributes of peers (i.e., categorization as a member of a racial/ethnic group and role as friend or peer in school) affect youths' ERI. Thus, these studies do not examine the inherently reciprocal nature of associations between adolescents' ERI and their friends' ERI such as how ERI affects friendship formation and whether peers influence each others' ERI in friendship networks. As previously noted, this chapter aims to fill this gap by using a novel approach to analyzing friendship network data (i.e., SABM), one that more properly accounts for peer selection and influence. In this section, we review findings from these two existing approaches that explore, implicitly or explicitly, the effects of peers on youths' ERI development.

Considering the first line of prior research that focuses on effects of school racial/ethnic composition on ERI, Yip, Douglass, and Shelton (2013) reported that Asian American adolescents attending schools in which the majority of their peers were White or the school contained no single racial majority, and who reported that their racial identity was not important to their sense of self, reported feeling worse about their racial group on days when they were in greater contact with other Asian peers. In contrast, Asian Americans in the same schools who reported that their racial identity was important to them reported feeling better about their racial group on days when they were around other Asian peers (Douglass & Yip, Chapter 8, this volume). Tatum (2003) highlighted pervasive patterns in peer segregation along racial/ethnic lines in school cafeterias and college dining halls, further illustrating how youth rely on their same-race/ethnic peers to navigate the racialized landscape of friendships throughout schooling.

Using participant observation methods and semistructured interviews, Way and her colleagues (2008) found that peer hierarchies within schools were formed on the basis of ethnic and racial stereotypes that were projected by peers. Youths' narratives regarding whom they were and whom they wanted to be in terms of their ERI was indicative of a process of accommodation and resistance to these stereotypes projected by their peers. Thus, experiences with peers in the context of the school in which this study took place were identified as important markers of how adolescents constructed their ERI.

In terms of the second line of scholarship on the effects of racial/ethnic composition of friends on ERI, Hamm (2000) reported that African American youth were more likely to select friends who were similar to them in terms of their ERI. Kiang, Peterson, and Thompson (2011) found that adolescents with same- and mixed-ethnic friends reported significantly greater ethnic centrality than those with mostly different-ethnic friends. Likewise, in a study that followed a sample of Asian American, Latino, and White youth for 4 years, the ethnic/racial composition of one's friendship group (i.e., proportion of friends who were of the same race/ethnicity) was associated with higher levels of ethnic-racial belonging and exploration (Kiang, Witkow, Baldelomar, & Fuligni, 2010). In a sample of Armenian, Vietnamese, and Mexican American families, Phinney, Romero, Nava, and Huang (2001) documented that, controlling for the effects of parental cultural practices and youths' ethnic language proficiency, within-race/ethnic group peer interaction was positively associated with adolescents' ethnic identity.

Research on youths' experiences with peers (e.g., Syed & Juan, 2012) has also shed light on how peers may influence ERI processes. Using narrative methods, Syed (2012) found that stories of discrimination were most likely to be told to peers, whereas stories about cultural knowledge were most likely to be told to parents, suggesting that peers may be important agents of racial socialization (Syed, this volume). Rivas-Drake, Hughes, and Way (2009) found that ethnic discrimination from peers was associated with more negative perceptions of one's ethnic group (i.e., private and public regard). In a sample of 73 African American children who were followed from third to fifth grade, Rowley, Burchinal, Roberts, and Zeisel (2008) found that having a greater number of same-race friends was positively associated with increases in expectations of discrimination in interactions with students of the other race. Increases in racial centrality were positively associated with increases in discrimination expectations, whereas increases in public regard were negatively linked to discrimination expectations.

Taken together, these studies underscore the potential contribution that peers have in shaping youths' ERI. However, these studies do not consider peers' ERI levels as an important factor influencing friendship network selection and peer influence. Existing studies have primarily focused on the role that ethnic/racial composition of either schools or friendships play in shaping ERI processes among youth. One of the key contributions of longitudinal SNA methods to the ERI scholarship is that SABM accounts for racial and ethnic composition of schools and friendships in addition to exploring the dynamic nature of how ERI develops in the context of friendship networks. Thus, our empirical illustration adds to this growing body of work by adopting a novel method that allows for a more nuanced examination of friendship network selection and peer influence on youths' ERI.

METHODOLOGICAL CONTRIBUTIONS OF SNA TO THE STUDY OF ETHNIC–RACIAL IDENTITY

Examining Effects of Network Position on Ethnic–Racial Identity

The first goal of this chapter is to describe the tools that SNA provides to capture individuals' position in the structure of peer relationships by considering the patterning of friendship ties. To illustrate the implications that network position has for ERI development processes, we briefly note the developmental significance of social networks, introduce key SNA concepts and levels of analysis from which a system of social ties can be considered, and then discuss implications of various indices of network position on ERI development.

Developmental scholars have long viewed social groups to which the developing individual belongs as providing a context for and constraints on development (e.g., Cairns, Xie, & Leung, 1998). Social ties within a group are not formed and dissolved randomly; human behavior in a social system is driven by fundamental motivations to belong and affiliate (Baumeister & Leary, 1995) and to gain and maintain social status (Hawley, 1999). Social network position, thus, can be viewed as an outcome of affiliative and status-attaining processes (for an illustration, see Kornienko, Clemans, Out, & Granger, 2013). Moreover, social networks have important implications for individuals' development because the pattern of network ties provides access to developmentally salient provisions such as social attention and admiration, information, resources, and social support (Borgatti, Mehra, Brass, & Labianca, 2009; Pellegrini, Roseth, Van Ryzin, & Solberg, 2011). The patterning of social ties in a network also provides a structural measure of social status because the patterning of network ties reflects individuals' preferences to affiliate with those of high status (e.g., Kornienko & Santos, 2014). These individual preferences accumulate and lead to popular individuals becoming even more popular (for a review, see Rivera, Soderstrom, & Uzzi, 2010). These preferences produce status differentials that are not easily discernible from the perspective of each individual because they focus on connectivity considered at a systems level.

A network is comprised of (a) a set of actors (i.e., individuals) and (b) a set of relations between these actors (i.e., ties; Wasserman & Faust, 1994). Two levels of analysis are applicable to any network: (a) a local, or an ego-centered, network constructed from a perspective of each individual (referred to as an *ego*) and all other individuals (referred to as *alters*) to whom the ego is connected and (b) a global, or sociocentered, network that is obtained by asking all individuals within a specified ecology (e.g., classroom, grade, or school) to nominate their friends. In other words, a local network is comprised of direct ties among an ego and his or her alters, and a global network involves both direct and indirect (i.e., a friend of a friend) ties within a specified ecology. Considering individuals' position in global networks is an important distinction between SNA methods and sociometric methods that are commonly used in peer relations research that rely solely on direct nominations (e.g., Berndt & McCandless, 2009).

Another level of analysis that is applicable to any network, and is guided by the nature of relations between individuals, concerns the directionality of ties. Specifically, SNA allows considering reciprocated (i.e., Individual A nominates B as a friend, and B nominates A as a friend) and unilateral ties (i.e., A nominates B as a friend but B does not nominate A as a friend). Unilateral ties can also be categorized into two subtypes: incoming ties (i.e., A receives a nomination from B) and outgoing ties (i.e., A sends out a nomination to B). Within the structural tradition of SNA, outgoing ties reflect an individual's activity or gregariousness within a network, whereas incoming ties capture the peer network's perspective on the focal individual and thus provide a more objective view on popularity (Valente, 2010). Whereas reciprocated friendship ties are likely to denote a higher quality friendship tie, unilateral ties likely hold a stronger potential for social influence because Person A who aspires to be friends with B is likely to adopt B's behaviors and attitudes to increase the probability of forming a reciprocated tie, denoting a closer relationship, with B (e.g., Prinstein, 2007). SNA scholars have developed numerous indices to capture aspects of an individual's position in a network, either local or global, by focusing on ties—reciprocated, incoming, or outgoing. The reader is referred to Table 7.1 for a summary of indices of network position that are applicable to each of the noted levels of analysis.

The use of SNA indices of network position to study other developmental processes (e.g., aggressive behavior; Faris & Felmlee, 2011) provides a basis for at least three aspects of social network position that are relevant for understanding the dynamics of ERI development in adolescence. These dimensions of network position include network density, centrality, and prestige. Broadly speaking, *network density* measures the degree of cohesion among friends.

TABLE 7.1
Measures of Individual's Position in a Network

Local network (direct ties)		Global network (direct and indirect ties)
	Unilateral outgoing ties	
Degree centrality		Closeness centrality
Density		Bonacich centrality
		Betweenness centrality
	Unilateral incoming ties	
Degree prestige		Influence domain
Density		Proximity prestige
	Reciprocated ties	
Degree centrality		Closeness centrality
Density		

Specifically, network density describes the degree of interconnectedness among friends of a focal individual and thus is a structural measure of social cohesion among one's friends. *Network centrality* is measured on the basis of outgoing ties and thus has implications for the speed and efficiency of social influence processes that occur through the transfer of attitudes and behaviors from a central individual to others (Borgatti, 2005). An individual's *network prestige* is based on incoming ties, and because it describes how the peer group views an individual, it has implications for social influence processes that occur through the adoption of attitudes and behaviors by the peer group surrounding the individual in a prestigious position.

Network Density

Network density, which can be calculated for local networks and applied to reciprocated and unilateral ties, is computed by dividing the number of ties present in an ego-centered network by a total number of possible ties in this network. Networks with high levels of density have a greater potential for the provision of social support and social influence (Valente, 2010). Thus, it is conceivable that individuals who are embedded in peer networks of high density (i.e., where most of a focal individual's friends are friends with one another) are likely to feel a greater degree of support in general, and perhaps with respect to ERI processes. It may also be likely that such beneficial effects of dense peer networks in terms of ERI processes are going to be pronounced in peer networks that are homogeneous with respect to race and ethnicity because these relational contexts will provide youth with greater opportunities to explore their ethnic identity with peers of the same race/ethnicity. On the other hand, being a part of a dense friendship network among individuals of diverse racial/ethnic backgrounds may limit opportunities for youth to explore ethnic identity with same-race/ethnicity friends.

Network Centrality

Turning to network centrality, *local* or *degree centrality* is a standardized measure of outgoing ties that is calculated by dividing the number of outgoing nominations by a maximum number of possible ties minus one (Wasserman & Faust, 1994). Several measures of global centrality have been introduced. *Closeness centrality* describes how close each particular individual is to all other individuals in a network (Wasserman & Faust, 1994). *Bonacich centrality* is defined as centrality of a focal individual that is weighted by the centrality of his or her friends, capturing the idea that being connected to others who are highly connected increases one's centrality in a network (Wasserman & Faust, 1994). Individuals who occupy a central position in a network have a unique opportunity to transmit information and attitudes to their peers, which may have implications for ERI processes in friendship networks. *Betweenness centrality* measures how often the ego lies on the shortest path between all possible pairs of people in a network (Wasserman & Faust, 1994). Betweenness centrality captures an important property of an individual's position in a network that enables him or her to connect otherwise disconnected individuals in a network. This property has received substantial attention from sociologists, who refer to it as *brokerage* (Burt, Kilduff, & Tasselli, 2013). Sociological research has shown that brokers are integral to connecting and integrating otherwise disconnected parts of the networks (Burt et al., 2013). Given that adolescent friendships tend to be ethnically/racially segregated (e.g., Goodreau et al., 2009), individuals with high betweenness centrality can serve as bridges between ethnically/racially homogenous groups to promote information sharing and positive intergroup relations. It is conceivable that the flow of information and support that is orchestrated by brokers in a network may have implications for ERI processes of the brokers and the otherwise unconnected individuals to whom they are connected. It should be noted that brokerage may have costs for the individual's mental health because of the tension arising from connecting different social groups. Indeed, adolescent girls with high levels of betweenness centrality reported increased social stress and decreased life satisfaction (Carboni & Gilman, 2012).

Network Prestige

Considering network prestige, *local* or *degree prestige* is a standardized measure of incoming ties that is calculated by dividing the number of incoming nominations by a maximum number of possible ties minus one (Wasserman

& Faust, 1994). This measure has been proposed to be a good proxy for perceived peer popularity within peer relations research (Cillessen & Borch, 2008). Several global measures of an individual's position in a network that focus on incoming ties have been developed. *Influence domain* enumerates the number of friends who nominate the focal individuals through direct and indirect ties (Wasserman & Faust, 1994). Another measure is *proximity prestige* that assesses one's friendship network popularity as a function of number of incoming friendship nominations that one receives, the degree of proximity in a network to those friends (i.e., balance between direct and indirect friendship ties), and the degree of the nominators' popularity (i.e., having popular friends send direct nominations boosts one's friendship network popularity relative to having them in two or three degrees of separation; de Nooy, Mrvar, & Batagelj, 2005; Wasserman & Faust, 1994). Because individuals with high levels of proximity prestige are highly visible, their attitudes and behaviors are likely to be more visible to their peers and thus to contribute to establishment of social norms in general and, perhaps, regarding ERI processes.

Examining Peer Influence Effects on Ethnic–Racial Identity

The second goal of this chapter is to describe and illustrate how longitudinal SNA can contribute to the study of ERI development by using SABM to examine peer influence effects over time. To do so, we first consider analytical challenges in the study of peer influence processes, then introduce how SABM can address them, and finally provide an empirical illustration of friendship network selection and influence processes for ERI centrality.

The peer group has been viewed as a prominent source of social influence in childhood and adolescence (for reviews, see Brechwald & Prinstein, 2011; Dishion & Tipsord, 2011). ERI scholars have posited that identity formation processes are context dependent (Phinney, 2000), and given that peers are a key social context for adolescent development (Larson & Verma, 1999), peers likely influence ERI process and content. Peer relationships are complex social systems, and they are reciprocally linked to development (Parker et al., 2006). This interdependence between social networks and development poses methodological challenges in that a trajectory of a developmental outcome is contingent on initial choices of friends who subsequently influence development. In other words, multiple processes such as peer selection and social influence operate in networks. These issues can be tackled with longitudinal SNA methods in the form of SABM (Snijders et al., 2010), which models the coevolution of networks and behaviors. SABM unravels contributions of network selection and influence and controls for structural network effects (e.g., most people want to be friends with popular individuals). Network researchers have identified several fundamental network structural processes

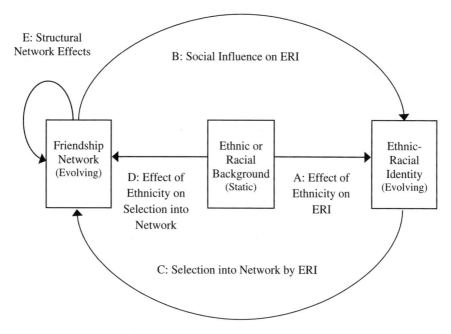

Figure 7.1. Conceptual diagram of network selection and influence on ethnic–racial identity (ERI).

that drive network formation (i.e., reciprocity, popularity, transitivity; for a review, see Rivera et al., 2010) that need to be controlled to obtain unbiased estimates of peer influence.

Although the actor–partner interdependence model (APIM; Kenny, Kashy, & Cook, 2006) has been used for the study of social influence, APIM is limited to a dyad as the unit of analysis (i.e., individuals can only be present in the data one time—either as an actor or a partner). This artificially truncates the number of peers to be considered as sources of influence. Thus, APIM is suitable for examining the influence dynamics occurring within the dyads of best friends, sibling pairs, or romantic partners. However, where youths are embedded in multiple relationships, all of which have a potential to influence them, the SABM is advantageous because it examines peer influence by using information from all of the peers in a network.

We use a conceptual diagram to depict the multiple processes through which the coevolution of network and ERI occurs (see Figure 7.1). These mechanisms include direct selection that occurs when adolescents seek out and form friendships with others who have similar levels of ERI (Path C). Confounding selection mechanisms operate when adolescents choose friends based on other individual-level attributes, such as gender (Mehta & Strough,

2009) or ethnicity or race, which may be correlated with ERI (Path D). Blau (1977) emphasized that homophily on any behavior can emerge as a spurious outcome from selection on other behaviors or attributes that are correlated with the behavior of interest. Thus, it is important to statistically control for individual attributes that are correlated with friendships and ethnic identity, and SABM allows for the inclusion of a number of relevant attributes. Moreover, structural network processes are likely to enhance network selection on ERI processes (Path E), and thus they need to be controlled for. Structural network processes include reciprocity (i.e., if A nominates B to be his or her friend, B is likely to reciprocate that choice compared with another nomination), popularity, or preferential attachment (i.e., individuals want to affiliate with others who are popular), and transitivity (i.e., a friend of my friend is likely to become my friend as well). Specifically, because friendship ties are likely to be transitive, meaning that a friend of my friend is likely to also become my friend, having common friends with an individual, who may have a preference for friends with similar levels of ERI, draws together multiple friends with similar levels of ERI endorsement. Thus, it is important to account for the alternative (i.e., network structural) processes through which similarity on ERI among friends can be generated. ERI development may also vary as a function of ethnic/racial group membership (Path A). Finally, peer influence processes are likely to operate in networks when initially dissimilar individuals become similar over the course of their friendships (Path B), thus inferring that peer influence requires separating the contributions of multiple, simultaneously occurring social processes. SABM enables this type of examination.

EMPIRICAL ILLUSTRATION: PEER INFLUENCE ON ETHNIC–RACIAL IDENTITY CENTRALITY

The goal of this empirical illustration is to apply longitudinal SNA modeling in the form of SABM to examine the role of peer influence on ERI centrality while controlling for the effects of an individual's ERI centrality and ethnic/racial group membership on peer network selection.

Participants

Participants were selected from a larger study being conducted at a middle school located in a southwestern U.S. metropolitan city. Participants in the larger study were recruited from all grades taught at the school (i.e., sixth, seventh, and eighth). Approximately 85% of the youth in the school participated in the study. The analysis presented explored changes that occurred among eighth graders from Time 1 (fall 2011) to Time 2 (spring 2012). Sample size for the present study was 340 adolescents (52.9% females; mean age = 13.5, SD = .52 at Time 1). The school body was composed of racially and ethnically diverse youth, and the sample for the present study consisted of 55.6% Latino/a, 18.5% African American, 11.5% European American, 6.5% Native American, and 7.9% other race/ethnicity. In the analytical sample, 17.6% of students were foreign born. School records indicated that 87% of participants received free and reduced lunch.

Procedure

The study used a passive consent procedure; parents were given the option to opt out of the study. Teachers at the school introduced the study to students and their parents. Student assent was also obtained. Surveys were administered in two waves, 8 months apart. The survey took approximately 90 minutes to complete at each wave. As a way to thank participants for their time, each student received a small gift (i.e., a water bottle or pen). The study was approved by the university's institutional review board.

Measures

Ethnic–Racial Identity

ERI was measured using the centrality subscale of the Multidimensional Inventory of Black Identity–Teen (Scottham, Sellers, & Nguyên, 2008). This subscale has shown to be reliable and valid in prior studies of Latino youth (Hughes et al., 2011) and consists of five items that assess the extent to which participants feel that their ERI is central to their sense of self. A higher score indicates feeling that one's ERI is central to one's sense of self. Response options ranged from (1) *strongly disagree* to (5) *strongly agree*. Mean centrality was 3.47 (SD = .81) at Time 1 and 3.27 (SD = .87) at Time 2. Because SABM requires discrete ordinal behavioral outcome variables, we recoded the continuous ethnic centrality variable into an ordinal variable with six levels, using increments of .75 of the continuous z score (i.e., $z < -1.5, -1.5 \leq z < -0.75, -0.75 \leq z < 0, 0 \leq z < 0.75, 0.75 \leq z < 1.5, z \geq 1.5$).

Friendship Networks

Participants received a roster listing all students from their grade and were asked to nominate up to 10 friends of either gender. These friendship nomination data were used to construct friendship networks of eighth-grade students for Time 1 and Time 2. For Times 1 and 2 of the study, we constructed two network matrices that contained unilateral (i.e., A nominated B) and binary-coded friendship ties such that "1" denoted that a tie existed between A and B, and "0" indicated no tie existed between A and B.

STATISTICAL ANALYSIS

SABM for network and behavior (Snijders, et al., 2010) was estimated to examine peer influence on ethnic identity centrality, controlling for various processes linking friendship networks and ethnic identity (see Figure 7.1 for a graphic depiction). We estimated the SABM using *RSiena* 4.0 package (Simulation Investigation for Empirical Network Analysis; Ripley, Snijders, & Preciado, 2013) in R version 3.0 (R-Project; http://www.r-project.org).

The SABM consists of two submodels that are simultaneously estimated (Snijders et al., 2010). The network dynamics submodel tests the likelihood of friendship ties between adolescents on the basis of various network selection processes. The behavior dynamics submodel captures effects related to change in ERI centrality over time. The SABM estimates changes between the observed network and behavior data using a continuous-time Markov process implying that the current behavior only depends on the preceding state. Continuous time Markov chains are used to identify the likely sequence of unobserved microsteps that are taken by actors when changing their ties or behavior. It is assumed that either one network tie or one behavior can be changed in one microstep. An evaluation function describes the "rules" that guide actors' decisions, which are the model parameters for the hypothesized selection and influence effects. A rate function determines how many opportunities for change (i.e., microsteps) occur between waves. Model parameters are estimated with the method of moments procedure, which uses a series of simulations to adjust the model parameters to improve model fit. Model parameters are tested for significance on the basis of a t ratio (estimate divided by the standard error).

With respect to the SABM specification, for the network submodel, we considered three types of effects of ERI centrality on network selection (Path C). The ERI centrality ego effect estimates the effect of ERI centrality on an adolescent's tendency to nominate others as friends. A negative effect would indicate that adolescents with greater levels of ERI centrality nominated fewer friends over time. The ERI centrality alter effect describes how ERI centrality affects adolescents' likelihood of receiving nominations from peers. A negative effect would indicate that adolescents with greater levels of ERI centrality were less likely to be nominated as friends by their peers. The ERI centrality similarity effect estimates the tendency of adolescents to nominate friends who have similar levels of ERI centrality (measured by their absolute difference). A positive effect of ERI centrality similarity would mean that friendships were more likely among adolescents with similar levels of ERI centrality. Additionally, we estimated the effect of similarity on gender and ethnic/racial background on the likelihood of network selection (Path D). Finally, we included parameters for several network structural processes (Path E). Reciprocity captured whether adolescents were more likely to nominate peers who had nominated them. The transitive triplets effect estimated whether ties were more likely among adolescents as the number of mutual friends increases. The indegree popularity effect estimated whether students who received more nominations were more likely to receive additional nominations over time. Finally, the outdegree popularity effect estimated whether students who sent out more nominations were more likely to receive a greater number of nominations. We used a square-root transformation of indegree and outdegree popularity effects to give greater weight to differences in popularity at low versus high levels. The network function also included effects for outdegree, which controlled for the total number of friendships in the network, and network rate, which represented network change opportunities. These latter two effects were included in all models but were not of substantive interest and are not shown in Figure 7.1.

Turning to the behavior submodel, we tested two effects that represent feedback on ERI centrality. The linear shape effect expresses the basic tendency toward higher or lower values of ERI centrality, whereas the quadratic shape effect allows for the self-reinforcement of ERI centrality that can result in a bimodal distribution of ERI centrality. We then estimated the peer influence effect on ERI centrality (Path B) using total similarity effect. This effect predicts changes in ERI centrality on the basis of how similar an adolescent's ERI centrality is to the level of ERI centrality of his or her friends. A positive effect indicates that changes in ERI centrality bring an adolescent closer to his or her friends' level of ERI centrality. Last, we included ERI centrality rate, which represents behavior change opportunities.

RESULTS

Descriptive Analyses

Figure 7.2 contains a network visualization to represent the associations between ethnic/racial background, ERI centrality, and friendship ties (i.e., reciprocated ties to improve readability of the visualization) among the eighth-grade students at Time 1. Our descriptive analyses of friendship network variables reveal that each individual, on average, had 6.83 and 6.98 outgoing friend nominations at Time 1 and Time 2, respectively. The Jaccard index indicated the stability of network from one wave to the next

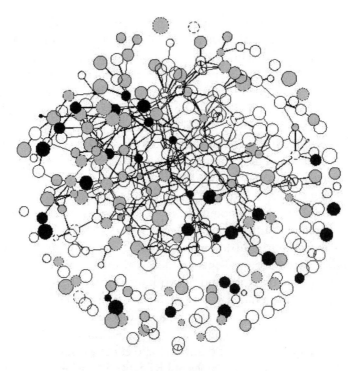

Figure 7.2. Visual representation of the eighth-grade friendship network, ethnic–racial identity (ERI) centrality, and mutual friendships at Wave 1. Node color and type of contour line denote individual's ethnicity or race (White = black color, solid line; African American = gray color, solid line; Native American = gray color, dotted line; Asian American = white color, dashed line; Latino/a = white color, solid line; other race/ethnicity = gray color, dotted line). Node size corresponds to individual's level of ERI centrality, which was divided by a constant of 2 (larger nodes = higher levels of ERI centrality). Links between nodes represent mutual friendship ties.

by documenting that 22% of ties observed at either time were present at both time points. This level of stability is consistent with recommended SABM guidelines (Snijders et al., 2010).

Stochastic Actor-Based Model for Coevolution of Network and Ethnic–Racial Identity Centrality

Before presenting our results regarding the social influence effects on ERI centrality, which was the main focus of our analyses, we discuss results for the structural network effects and potentially confounding dynamics. The results are presented in Table 7.2. We begin with the network function and examine how individual attributes affected friendship selection (Path D). Results indicated significant effects of homophily on sex and race/ethnicity variables, which were

TABLE 7.2
Unstandardized Coefficients and Standard Errors for Coevolution of Friendship Network and Ethnic–Racial Identity Centrality

	Estimate	SE	p value
Network dynamics			
Basic rate	21.15	0.81	***
Outdegree	−1.61	0.17	***
Reciprocity	1.82	0.07	***
Transitive triplets	0.33	0.02	***
Indegree popularity (square root)	0.25	0.03	***
Outdegree popularity (square root)	−0.57	0.06	***
Female similarity	0.38	0.04	***
White similarity	0.07	0.06	
African American similarity	0.17	0.05	***
Native American similarity	−0.04	0.07	
Latino/a similarity	0.14	0.04	***
Other race/ethnicity similarity	−0.16	0.07	*
ERI centrality alter	−0.06	0.02	*
ERI centrality ego	−0.04	0.02	
ERI centrality similarity	0.49	0.21	*
ERI centrality dynamics			
Rate	2.99	0.37	***
Linear shape	0.03	0.05	
Quadratic shape	0.04	0.07	
Total similarity (social influence)	0.44	0.20	*

Note. ERI = Ethnic–Racial Identity.
*** $p < .001$. ** $p < .01$. * $p < .05$.

dummy coded. We observed that friendships were more likely to be formed if the two students were of the same gender, were both African American, or were both Latino/a. In addition to considering these static attributes, we also examined whether ERI centrality affected network selection dynamics (Path C). Our results demonstrated that similarity on ERI centrality was significantly and positively associated with the likelihood of friendship network selection. Our findings show that ERI centrality was negatively associated with the amount of incoming friendship nominations (i.e., alter effects) but not outgoing friendship nominations (i.e., ego effects). This suggests that individuals with greater levels of ERI centrality were less attractive as friends in this network.

Turning to the structural network effects (Path E), we found significant positive effects for reciprocity, transitivity, indegree popularity, and outdegree popularity. The positive reciprocity parameter indicates that adolescents were likely to nominate friends who had nominated them. The positive effect of transitive triplets indicated that adolescents tended to affiliate with friends of their friends. The positive indegree popularity effect showed that adolescents who received a high number of friendship nominations were more attractive for others to send friendship ties to (i.e., high friendship network popularity reinforces itself; Snijders et al., 2010). The negative outdegree popularity effect indicated that adolescents who sent out a high number of friendship ties were less attractive for other students to send ties to. This means that nominating a high number of friends was inversely related to friendship network popularity, because popular students are more selective in whom and how many friends they nominate. Taken together, these effects suggest that adolescents' friendships were structured according to the fundamental processes observed in many other types of networks.

Finally, our primary goal was to examine peer influence on ERI centrality (Path B), while controlling for confounding ERI and network-related processes. We observed a significant positive effect of total similarity on ERI centrality. This suggests that, over time, adolescents changed to be similar in their ERI centrality to the levels of their friends' ERI centrality and that the magnitude of this influence was proportional to the number of friends. Thus, our findings showed that peer influence on ERI centrality operates in friendship networks. In conclusion, controlling for the structural network effects and the effects of static ethnic/racial background on network selection, we documented that ERI centrality was an important dimension that affected network selection and that it was also amenable to peer influence.

DISCUSSION

Both theory and research on ethnic identity suggest that peers play an important role in shaping ERI (Phinney, 2000; Syed, 2012), yet research examining peer influence in ERI is in its infancy. Because ERI development unfolds through the reciprocal transactions between individuals and their social context (Phinney, 2000), SNA provides sophisticated methods to unpack these bidirectional associations between peer experiences and ERI processes. In this chapter, we outlined how SNA can contribute to the study of ERI processes by describing individuals' position in the peer network and using longitudinal network modeling procedures (i.e., SABM) to examine coevolution of networks and ERI. We provided an empirical illustration of SABM and the first examination, to our knowledge, of peer influence on ERI centrality. Our results show that peer selection and peer influence processes on ERI centrality jointly operate in adolescent friendship networks, highlighting the reciprocal nature of associations between social context and development of ERI. Finally, we documented peer selection and influence effects on ERI, while controlling for several important confounding processes such as network selection on static ethnicity/race attributes as well as structural network processes.

Use of SABM to examine the coevolution of friendship networks and ERI centrality is a novel aspect of this study. Given that adolescents are embedded in multiple relationships, all of which have a potential to transmit peer influence, the innovative nature of our approach is rooted in using analytical techniques that allow us to assess peer influence by using information from all friends (in contrast to considering friendship dyads, as is done in APIM). In addition to moving beyond dyadic conceptualization and estimation of peer influence, SABM is uniquely suited to provide unbiased estimates of peer influence because it allows us to partial out contributions of selection into friendship network and network structural processes. Specifically, accounting for several confounding processes (e.g., structural network processes, network selection on static ethnicity/race attributes, network selection on ERI centrality), we showed that adolescents' levels of ERI centrality changed to become similar to the levels of their friends' ERI centrality (i.e., peer influence). Failure to control for these confounding processes threatens to bias estimates of peer influence on identity development. In sum, examining peer influence processes as unfolding within friendship networks enables us to create a more complete depiction of the complex and reciprocal influences between friendship networks and identity development during adolescence.

Although significant attention has been paid to the development of ERI during adolescence, and given the importance of peers during this developmental period, our understanding of how ERI evolves during this period benefits from a greater focus on the role of peers in shaping ERI. We found that, over time, adolescents' scores on ERI centrality changed to become similar to the ERI centrality scores of their friends. These results underscore the unique opportunity afforded by longitudinal SNA and SABM to explore changes in ERI during adolescence.

Additionally, although scholars have paid greater attention to how family processes and socialization shapes ERI among adolescents (Umaña-Taylor, Bhanot, & Shin, 2006), an important future direction is to consider both family influence as well as peer influence in shaping ERI dynamics. SABM is equipped to analyze both peer network contributions and the role of familial ethnic–racial socialization for ERI development. Finally, future studies may explore dimensions of ERI that are particularly amenable to peer influence (e.g., public regard).

Although our sample is ethnically diverse, slightly more than half of the students were Latino/a. Thus, it is important to note that we explored peer influences in ERI within a school context where members of one ethnic group (i.e., Latinos) were the majority and within a context of a school that serves primarily moderate- to low-income families. Future research adopting a SNA perspective to explore peer influences in ERI may want to consider these processes within the context of schools that vary in their racial/ethnic and socioeconomic composition. For example, peer selection and influence processes may operate differentially for youth who are a numeric racial/ethnic minority within their school because they may have fewer opportunities to form friendships with peers of their own racial/ethnic background. Future research may want to explore how these diverse contexts shape peer selection and influence effects on ERI.

BEST PRACTICES AND RECOMMENDATIONS FOR FUTURE RESEARCH

Applications of SNA to the study of friendships among school-age children and adolescents require friendship nominations data that can be collected by asking students to nominate their closest friends within their classroom, grade, or school. Although there is some variability, friendship nominations of up to 10 friends of either sex are often used to provide adequate representation of complete friendship networks. Students are typically provided with rosters containing names and assigned IDs of all students in their classroom, grade, or school who have agreed to participate in the study. From this roster, study participants nominate their friends and typically only report the ID provided for each friend so as to protect the identity of participants. For researchers who are interested in conducting longitudinal SNA, panel data on friendship networks (e.g., friendship nominations) and individuals' attitudes, beliefs, and behaviors need to be collected. For more information on logistics and choices required of investigators conducting research on friendship networks, readers are encouraged to refer to the following resources: Gest and Kindermann (2012); Kindermann and Gest (2009); Snijders et al., (2010); Valente (2010); Veenstra, Dijkstra, Steglich, and Van Zalk (2013); and Wasserman and Faust (1994).

Additional practical issues to consider when collecting data for SNA analyses include the need to specify an adequate sampling boundary within which networks exist; specifically, a classroom is a sufficient sampling frame for elementary school students, whereas middle school students tend to form their friendships with students within the same grade level (beyond a specific classroom) as the structure of middle school is typically less restricted to one stable classroom (Cairns et al., 1998). Finally, in high schools where students typically have the option of selecting courses that may include peers from multiple grades, and this is the context in which they form friendships, the whole school is a relevant sampling frame. Another issue concerns nonresponse rates and missing data in network studies. In social network research, missing data on friendship ties render the data unusable because this creates "holes" in the network (Kossinets, 2006). Simulation studies have shown that indices of network position in local networks are less affected by missing data compared with those for global network position (Costenbader & Valente, 2003).

Missing data are especially problematic for longitudinal network studies, and simulation studies have shown that SABM estimates appear to be stable with at least 70% of nonmissing network-behavior data per sampling unit (e.g., grade, school; Huisman & Steglich, 2008).

Although SABM offers substantial strengths for the study of coevolution of network and ethnic identity development, several limitations of this method should be noted. SABM assumes that actors have perfect knowledge about all other actors in the network using a rational choice model; thus, it may not appropriate for large networks (e.g., over 1,000 individuals). SABM requires discrete ordinal variables for the dependent behavioral variables; thus, continuous variables must be transformed. Additionally, SABM requires intensive longitudinal data on changing behavior or internal states and complete, or near complete, networks (i.e., all or near most individuals within a specified ecology, such as grade or school, need to complete friendship nominations). Finally, in addition to the time and resources that are needed for data collection, this form of simulation-based inference is computationally intensive.

CONCLUSION

This chapter introduced SNA as a new conceptual and methodological approach to examining the contributions of social context, in particular, peers and friends, to the development of ERI among youth. We described how friendship network position may be associated with ERI development processes. We provided an illustration of how longitudinal SNA can inform ERI research pertaining to peer influence. Specifically, we found that friendship network selection and peer influence had an effect on youths' ERI centrality. In other words, we documented for the first time that adolescents tend to become similar to their friends in terms of ERI centrality over time. This finding supports our assertion that peer influence is an important contributing process to ERI development that requires more careful consideration among ERI scholars.

REFERENCES

Baumeister, R. F., & Leary, M. R. (1995). The need to belong: Desire for interpersonal attachments as a fundamental human motivation. *Psychological Bulletin, 117*, 497–529. http://dx.doi.org/10.1037/0033-2909.117.3.497

Berndt, T. J., & McCandless, M. A. (2009). Methods for investigating children's relationships with friends. In K. H. Rubin, W. M. Bukowski, & B. Laursen (Eds.), *Handbook of peer interactions, relationships, and groups: Social, emotional, and personality development in context* (pp. 63–81). New York, NY: Guilford Press.

Blau, P. M. (1977). *Inequality and heterogeneity.* New York, NY: Free Press.

Borgatti, S. P. (2005). Centrality and network flow. *Social Networks, 27,* 55–71. http://dx.doi.org/10.1016/j.socnet.2004.11.008

Borgatti, S. P., Mehra, A., Brass, D. J., & Labianca, G. (2009). Network analysis in the social sciences. *Science, 323,* 892–895. http://dx.doi.org/10.1126/science.1165821

Brechwald, W. A., & Prinstein, M. J. (2011). Beyond homophily: A decade of advances in understanding peer influence processes. *Journal of Research on Adolescence, 21,* 166–179. http://dx.doi.org/10.1111/j.1532-7795.2010.00721.x

Burt, R. S., Kilduff, M., & Tasselli, S. (2013). Social network analysis: Foundations and frontiers on advantage. *Annual Review of Psychology, 64,* 527–547. http://dx.doi.org/10.1146/annurev-psych-113011-143828

Cairns, R., Xie, H., & Leung, M. C. (1998). The popularity of friendship and the neglect of social networks: Toward a new balance. *New Directions for Child and Adolescent Development, 1998*(81), 25–53. http://dx.doi.org/10.1002/cd.23219988104

Carboni, I., & Gilman, R. (2012). Brokers at risk: Gender differences in the effects of structural position on social stress and life satisfaction. *Group Dynamics: Theory, Research, and Practice, 16,* 218–230. http://dx.doi.org/10.1037/a0028753

Cillessen, A. H. N., & Borch, C. (2008). Analyzing social networks in adolescence. In N. A. Card, J. P. Selig, & T. Little (Eds.), *Modeling dyadic and interdependent data in the developmental and behavioral sciences* (pp. 61–87). New York, NY: Routledge.

Costenbader, E., & Valente, T. W. (2003). The stability of centrality measures when networks are sampled. *Social Networks, 25,* 283–307. http://dx.doi.org/10.1016/S0378-8733(03)00012-1

Crosier, B. S., Webster, G. D., & Dillon, H. M. (2012). Wired to connect: Evolutionary psychology and social networks. *Review of General Psychology, 16,* 230–239. http://dx.doi.org/10.1037/a0027919

de la Haye, K., Robins, G., Mohr, P., & Wilson, C. (2011). Homophily and contagion as explanations for weight similarities among adolescent friends. *Journal of Adolescent Health, 49,* 421–427. http://dx.doi.org/10.1016/j.jadohealth.2011.02.008

de Nooy, W., Mrvar, A., & Batagelj, V. (2005). *Exploratory social network analysis with Pajek.* New York, NY: Cambridge University Press. http://dx.doi.org/10.1017/CBO9780511806452

Dishion, T. J., & Tipsord, J. M. (2011). Peer contagion in child and adolescent social and emotional development. *Annual Review of Psychology, 62,* 189–214. http://dx.doi.org/10.1146/annurev.psych.093008.100412

Faris, R., & Felmlee, D. (2011). Status struggles: Network centrality and gender segregation in same- and cross-gender aggression. *American Sociological Review, 76,* 48–73. http://dx.doi.org/10.1177/0003122410396196

Fuligni, A. J., Witkow, M., & Garcia, C. (2005). Ethnic identity and the academic adjustment of adolescents from Mexican, Chinese, and European backgrounds.

Developmental Psychology, 41, 799–811. http://dx.doi.org/10.1037/0012-1649.41.5.799

Gest, S. D., & Kindermann, T. A. (2012). Analysis of static social networks and their developmental effects. In B. Laursen, T. D. Little, & N. A. Card (Eds.), *Handbook of developmental research methods* (pp. 577–598). New York, NY: Guilford Press.

Goodreau, S. M., Kitts, J. A., & Morris, M. (2009). Birds of a feather, or friend of a friend? Using exponential random graph models to investigate adolescent social networks. *Demography, 46,* 103–125. http://dx.doi.org/10.1353/dem.0.0045

Hamm, J. V. (2000). Do birds of a feather flock together? The variable bases for African American, Asian American, and European American adolescents' selection of similar friends. *Developmental Psychology, 36,* 209–219. http://dx.doi.org/10.1037/0012-1649.36.2.209

Hawley, P. H. (1999). The ontogenesis of social dominance: A strategy-based evolutionary perspective. *Developmental Review, 19,* 97–132. http://dx.doi.org/10.1006/drev.1998.0470

Hughes, D., Way, N., & Rivas-Drake, D. (2011). Stability and change in private and public ethnic regard among African American, Puerto Rican, Dominican, and Chinese American early adolescents. *Journal of Research on Adolescence, 21,* 861–870. http://dx.doi.org/10.1111/j.1532-7795.2011.00744.x

Huisman, M., & Steglich, C. (2008). Treatment of non-response in longitudinal network studies. *Social Networks, 30,* 297–308. http://dx.doi.org/10.1016/j.socnet.2008.04.004

Kenny, D. A., Kashy, D. A., & Cook, W. L. (2006). *Dyadic data analysis.* New York, NY: Guilford Press.

Kiang, L., Peterson, J. L., & Thompson, T. L. (2011). Ethnic peer preferences among Asian American adolescents in emerging immigrant communities. *Journal of Research on Adolescence, 21,* 754–761. http://dx.doi.org/10.1111/j.1532-7795.2011.00750.x

Kiang, L., Witkow, M. R., Baldelomar, O. A., & Fuligni, A. J. (2010). Change in ethnic identity across the high school years among adolescents with Latin American, Asian, and European backgrounds. *Journal of Youth and Adolescence, 39,* 683–693. http://dx.doi.org/10.1007/s10964-009-9429-5

Kindermann, T. A., & Gest, S. D. (2009). Assessment of the peer group: Identifying naturally occurring social networks and capturing their effects. In K. H. Rubin, W. M. Bukowski, & B. Laursen (Eds.), *Handbook of peer interactions, relationships, and groups: Social, emotional, and personality development in context* (pp. 100–121). New York, NY: Guilford Press.

Kornienko, O., Clemans, K. H., Out, D., & Granger, D. A. (2013). Friendship network position and salivary cortisol levels. *Social Neuroscience, 8,* 385–396. http://dx.doi.org/10.1080/17470919.2013.795500

Kornienko, O., & Santos, C. E. (2014). The effects of friendship network popularity on depressive symptoms during early adolescence: Moderation by fear of negative evaluation and gender. *Journal of Youth and Adolescence, 43,* 541–553.

Kossinets, G. (2006). Effects of missing data in social networks. *Social Networks*, 28, 247–268. http://dx.doi.org/10.1016/j.socnet.2005.07.002

Larson, R., & Richards, M. H. (1991). Daily companionship in late childhood and early adolescence: Changing developmental contexts. *Child Development*, 62, 284–300. http://dx.doi.org/10.2307/1131003

Larson, R. W., & Verma, S. (1999). How children and adolescents spend time across the world: Work, play, and developmental opportunities. *Psychological Bulletin*, 125, 701–736. http://dx.doi.org/10.1037/0033-2909.125.6.701

Mehta, C. M., & Strough, J. (2009). Sex segregation in friendships and normative contexts. *Developmental Review*, 29, 201–220. http://dx.doi.org/10.1016/j.dr.2009.06.001

Parker, J. G., Rubin, K. H., Erath, S. A., Wojslawowicz, J. C., & Buskirk, A. A. (2006). Peer relationships, child development, and adjustment: A developmental psychopathology perspective. In D. Cicchetti & D. J. Cohen (Eds.), *Developmental psychopathology: Vol. 1. Theory and methods* (2nd ed., pp. 96–161). New York, NY: Wiley.

Pellegrini, A. D., Roseth, C. J., Van Ryzin, M. J., & Solberg, D. W. (2011). Popularity as a form of social dominance: An evolutional perspective. In A. H. N. Cillessen, D. Schwartz, & L. Mayeux (Eds.), *Popularity in the peer system* (pp. 123–140). New York, NY: Guilford Press.

Phinney, J. S. (1990). Ethnic identity in adolescents and adults: Review of research. *Psychological Bulletin*, 108, 499–514. http://dx.doi.org/10.1037/0033-2909.108.3.499

Phinney, J. S. (2000). Identity formation across cultures: The interaction of personal, societal, and historical change. *Human Development*, 43, 27–31. http://dx.doi.org/10.1159/000022653

Phinney, J. S., Romero, I., Nava, M., & Huang, D. (2001). The role of language, parents, and peers in ethnic identity among adolescents in immigrant families. *Journal of Youth and Adolescence*, 30, 135–153. http://dx.doi.org/10.1023/A:1010389607319

Prinstein, M. J. (2007). Moderators of peer contagion: A longitudinal examination of depression socialization between adolescents and their best friends. *Journal of Clinical Child and Adolescent Psychology*, 36, 159–170. http://dx.doi.org/10.1080/15374410701274934

Ripley, R. M., Snijders, T. A. B., & Preciado, P. (2013). *Manual for RSIENA*. Oxford, England: University of Oxford, Department of Statistics, Nuffield College.

Rivas-Drake, D., Hughes, D., & Way, N. (2009). A preliminary analysis of associations among ethnic–racial socialization, ethnic discrimination, and ethnic identity among urban sixth graders. *Journal of Research on Adolescence*, 19, 558–584. http://dx.doi.org/10.1111/j.1532-7795.2009.00607.x

Rivera, M. T., Soderstrom, S. B., & Uzzi, B. (2010). Dynamics of dyads in social networks: Assortative, relational, and proximity mechanisms. *Annual Review of Sociology*, 36, 91–115. http://dx.doi.org/10.1146/annurev.soc.34.040507.134743

Roberts, R. E., Phinney, J. S., Masse, L. C., Chen, Y. R., Roberts, C. R., & Romero, A. (1999). The structure of ethnic identity of young adolescents from diverse ethnocultural groups. *The Journal of Early Adolescence, 19*, 301–322. http://dx.doi.org/10.1177/0272431699019003001

Rowley, S. J., Burchinal, M. R., Roberts, J. E., & Zeisel, S. A. (2008). Racial identity, social context, and race-related social cognition in African Americans during middle childhood. *Developmental Psychology, 44*, 1537–1546. http://dx.doi.org/10.1037/a0013349

Schaefer, D. R., Haas, S. A., & Bishop, N. J. (2012). A dynamic model of US adolescents' smoking and friendship networks. *American Journal of Public Health, 102*, e12–e18. http://dx.doi.org/10.2105/AJPH.2012.300705

Schaefer, D. R., Kornienko, O., & Fox, A. M. (2011). Misery does not love company: Network selection mechanisms and depression homophily. *American Sociological Review, 76*, 764–785. http://dx.doi.org/10.1177/0003122411420813

Scottham, K. M., Sellers, R. M., & Nguyên, H. X. (2008). A measure of racial identity in African American adolescents: The development of the Multidimensional Inventory of Black Identity—Teen. *Cultural Diversity and Ethnic Minority Psychology, 14*, 297–306. http://dx.doi.org/10.1037/1099-9809.14.4.297

Sijtsema, J. J., Ojanen, T., Veenstra, R., Lindenberg, S., Hawley, P. H., & Little, T. D. (2010). Forms and functions of aggression in adolescent friendship selection and influence: A longitudinal social network analysis. *Social Development, 19*, 515–534. http://dx.doi.org/10.1111/j.1467-9507.2009.00566.x

Snijders, T. A. B., van de Bunt, G. G., & Steglich, C. E. G. (2010). Introduction to stochastic actor-based models for network dynamics. *Social Networks, 32*, 44–60. http://dx.doi.org/10.1016/j.socnet.2009.02.004

Syed, M. (2012). College students' storytelling of ethnicity-related events in the academic domain. *Journal of Adolescent Research, 27*, 203–230. http://dx.doi.org/10.1177/0743558411432633

Syed, M., & Juan, M. J. (2012). Birds of an ethnic feather? Ethnic identity homophily among college-age friends. *Journal of Adolescence, 35*, 1505–1514. http://dx.doi.org/10.1016/j.adolescence.2011.10.012

Tatum, B. D. (2003). *Why are all the black kids sitting together in the cafeteria? And other conversations about race.* New York, NY: Basic Books.

Umaña-Taylor, A. J., Bhanot, R., & Shin, N. (2006). Ethnic identity formation during adolescence: The critical role of families. *Journal of Family Issues, 27*, 390–414. http://dx.doi.org/10.1177/0192513X05282960

Umaña-Taylor, A. J., Quintana, S. M., Lee, R. M., Cross, W. E., Rivas-Drake, D., Schwartz, S. J., . . . Ethnic and Racial Identity in the 21st Century Study Group. (2014). Ethnic and racial identity during adolescence and into young adulthood: An integrated conceptualization. *Child Development, 85*, 21–39. http://dx.doi.org/10.1111/cdev.12196

Valente, T. W. (2010). *Social networks and health: Models, methods, and applications.* New York, NY: Oxford University Press. http://dx.doi.org/10.1093/acprof:oso/9780195301014.001.0001

Van Zalk, M. H. W., Kerr, M., Branje, S. J. T., Stattin, H., & Meeus, W. H. J. (2010). It takes three: Selection, influence, and de-selection processes of depression in adolescent friendship networks. *Developmental Psychology, 46*, 927–938. http://dx.doi.org/10.1037/a0019661

Veenstra, R., Dijkstra, J. K., Steglich, C., & Van Zalk, M. H. W. (2013). Network–behavior dynamics. *Journal of Research on Adolescence, 23*, 399–412. http://dx.doi.org/10.1111/jora.12070

Wasserman, S., & Faust, K. (1994). *Social network analysis: Methods and applications.* Cambridge, England: Cambridge University Press. http://dx.doi.org/10.1017/CBO9780511815478

Way, N., Santos, C., Niwa, E. Y., & Kim-Gervey, C. (2008). To be or not to be: An exploration of ethnic identity development in context. *New Directions for Child and Adolescent Development, 2008*(120), 61–79. http://dx.doi.org/10.1002/cd.216

Yip, T., Douglass, S., & Shelton, J. N. (2013). Daily intragroup contact in diverse settings: Implications for Asian adolescents' ethnic identity. *Child Development, 84*, 1425–1441. http://dx.doi.org/10.1111/cdev.12038

8

ADOLESCENT ETHNIC IDENTITY IN CONTEXT: INTEGRATING DAILY DIARIES, BIANNUAL SURVEYS, AND SCHOOL-LEVEL DATA

SARA DOUGLASS AND TIFFANY YIP

Ethnic identity is a complex phenomenon influencing the social development of adolescents. Over the past few decades, researchers have asked a host of questions, such as: What does ethnic identity include? When and where does ethnic identity matter? For whom and how does ethnic identity develop? The answers to these questions have contributed to our complex, multifaceted understanding of ethnic identity, yet many questions remain unanswered. In particular, integration of the many complex components and influential factors (i.e., the integration of the "what, when, where, for whom, and how") in ethnic identity remains limited, leaving this complex understanding in a fragmented state.

In this chapter, we review what we refer to as the *multilevel integration method* in which experience sampling methods, biannual surveys, and school-level data are used to capture and integrate a broad range of this complexity for adolescents' ethnic identity development. We begin by reviewing a

http://dx.doi.org/10.1037/14618-009
Studying Ethnic Identity: Methodological and Conceptual Approaches Across Disciplines, C. E. Santos and A. J. Umaña-Taylor (Editors)

general conceptualization of ethnic identity that sets forth the need for a multilevel integration method. Next, we turn to the components of the multilevel integration method and the benefits and insights that this approach can provide for our understanding of adolescent ethnic identity. We then provide an empirical example using data from a 3-year longitudinal study of ethnic identity in a diverse sample of youths. Finally, we discuss the implications, strengths, and future directions that this approach supports.

CONCEPTUALIZATION OF ETHNIC IDENTITY

Research on ethnic identity has historically been divided, with one theoretical and empirical approach considering the process related to the development of ethnic identity (Cross, 1971, 1991; Erikson, 1968; Marcia, 1966; Phinney, 1989) and another considering the content of that identity at a given point in time (Sellers et al., 1998; Tajfel, 1981; Tajfel & Turner, 1986). In reality, these approaches are complementary, and in fact, a simultaneous understanding of both process and content is necessary to accurately capture ethnic identity (Syed & Azmitia, 2008; Umaña-Taylor, Yazedjian, & Bamaca-Gomez, 2004). In addition, neither the process nor content of ethnic identity occurs in a vacuum, but rather is deeply contextualized, influenced by a number of outside forces, including families, peers, schools, neighborhoods, and communities (Phinney, Romero, Nava, & Huang, 2001; Supple, Ghazarian, Frabutt, Plunkett, & Sands, 2006; Tatum, 2004; Umaña-Taylor & Fine, 2004; Yip, Douglass, & Shelton, 2013).

Using ecological systems theory and the process-person-context-time model as guiding frameworks, the influence of proximal and distal contexts on the individual, as well as potential relationships between them, can be organized (Bronfenbrenner, 1979; Bronfenbrenner & Morris, 1998). The process-person-context-time model argues that the most primary mechanisms of development are proximal processes, or the ways in which an individual interacts with his or her environment (i.e., proximal contexts) in a direct way and on a regular basis. This is consistent with other theoretical perspectives that place daily activities and daily interactions at the center of development (Chaiklin, Hedegaard, & Jensen, 1999; Tharp & Gallimore, 1988). The *person* includes characteristics that an individual brings to any situation, which can be an active force on that proximal *process*. *Context* refers to any larger, distal environment in which an individual and relevant proximal processes are embedded. For example, the microsystem includes contexts that individuals regularly experience. The final component, *time*, captures both short-term changes in regular experiences and long-term changes in development (Bronfenbrenner & Morris, 1998). Application of this model to the process and content of ethnic identity suggests that ethnic identity is a person-level characteristic that develops over time in relation to both distal contexts and intraindividual proximal contexts, all of which have implications for the content of ethnic identity. The study of ethnic identity within this framework demands a method that can capture the many aspects of ethnic identity, including the intraindividual dynamics of proximal processes, the long-term dynamics of development, and the meaningful characteristics of the context. The multilevel integration method allows each of these aspects to be captured and considered simultaneously. We turn now to an overview of this method and its components.

OVERVIEW OF THE MULTILEVEL INTEGRATION METHOD

The multilevel integration method as proposed here contains three main components: experience sampling method (ESM), biannual surveys, and school-level data. In this section, we outline the unique contributions of each of these components, using existing research to highlight these contributions.

The Experience Sampling Method

The experience sampling method is particularly adept at capturing the proximal contexts that are involved in those proximal processes that are central to development. ESM is a general technique that aims to capture ecologically valid snapshots of experiences using interval-intensive, repeated observations of individuals in everyday life. ESM has been successfully used to yield new discoveries in the area of ethnic identity research (Yip & Douglass, 2013). This chapter highlights the daily diary method in which participants complete surveys once a day, though this is just one particular method within the broader framework of ESM (others include random sampling and event sampling methods, which are not covered herein). In research on ethnic identity, participants are typically asked to complete brief surveys every day prior to going to bed for any interval of time that the researcher sees fit (e.g., 7, 21, or 30 days). These surveys ask participants to complete standard measures on the basis of that particular day's experiences only. The daily diary method offers unique and compelling benefits when compared with standard survey methods. First, the daily diary method limits the time of recall by capturing smaller snapshots of experiences, thereby tempering concerns about retrospective bias in reporting (Bolger, Davis, & Rafaeli, 2003). Therefore, it is particularly accurate at capturing daily experiences and proximal contexts (Csikszentmihalyi & Larson, 1987). For example, using this method, Cross and Strauss (2008) found five unique ethnic identity functions (i.e., daily experiences) that individuals used as a result of daily contact with same- or other-race individuals (i.e., proximal contexts). These include bridging (i.e., making connections across racial or ethnic lines), bonding (i.e., making connections within racial or ethnic groups to cope with stigma), code switching (i.e., highlighting or using one component of identity depending on the demands of the situation), buffering (i.e., use of ethnic identity as a protective factor in stressful interracial or interethnic situations, such as in the face of discrimination), and individualism (i.e., distinguishing oneself in an intraracial or intraethnic interaction on the basis of unique characteristics unrelated to race or ethnicity).

Second, the daily diary method is particularly adept at capturing intra-individual processes. By capturing multiple measures of psychological experiences and proximal contexts for each individual across multiple days, processes within an individual across time can be considered. For example, Cross and Strauss (2008) found that the tendency to engage in any of those ethnic identity functions differed for a given person as a function of how their proximal contexts varied; that is, individuals could alternately engage in bridging, code switching, or individualism on the basis of the demands of their context. The ability to accurately capture daily experiences and proximal contexts and consider how they may vary over time within an individual, is a unique feature of the daily diary method that enables an understanding of how ethnic identity functions in the lived experiences of adolescents (Yip & Douglass, 2013).

Biannual Surveys

Biannual surveys are particularly useful for capturing the person-level and time-varying components of development. This is important for two reasons. First, surveys can gather data on how characteristics of the developing youth influence proximal processes captured by ESM. Additionally, biannual surveys are particularly well-suited to investigate how repeated experiences at the daily level are then associated with person-level phenomenon such as the development of ethnic identity (Yip, 2014; Yip & Douglass, 2013). Biannual surveys involve the collection of standard survey measures twice a year, so that large-scale developmental snapshots are captured every 6 months. This typical use of survey methods captures characteristics that theoretically develop (and therefore change) in adolescence but are not considered to fluctuate on a daily basis and therefore are relatively stable compared with those characteristics captured through ESM. In considering ethnic identity, a single survey represents a snapshot of continuous developmental processes by capturing an individual's characteristics at a single point in time, which in turn allows consideration of how that characteristic influences their experiences.

For example, Umaña-Taylor, Wong, Gonzales, and Dumka (2012) found that ethnic identity affirmation in seventh grade protected Mexican-origin adolescent boys from the negative effects of discrimination on externalizing behaviors 1 year later. Large-scale developmental snapshots can also be captured by returning and measuring the same construct(s) again with the same group of adolescents, thereby allowing individual development (or stability) to be assessed. Although the focus in this chapter is on biannual surveys, collected in intervals of 6 months, alternative measurement intervals may be used depending on how frequently researchers wish to assess the construct (e.g., every 3 months, every 8 months). This procedure can also be repeated over many years, which in fact may be necessary to adequately capture the developmental process as time progresses. For example, French, Seidman, Allen, and Aber (2006) found that ethnic identity exploration increased over 3 years for middle adolescents but remained stable for early adolescents. In sum, biannual surveys are particularly useful for capturing person-level characteristics, interindividual differences, and normative progressions in development.

School-Level Data

School-level data represent distal contexts of the microsystem within which adolescents are embedded. They provide objective measures of structural contexts where adolescents spend a majority of their time and within which proximal processes are embedded (Bronfenbrenner, 1979; Cross & Fhagen-Smith, 2001). Characteristics of schools can be obtained using publicly available information offered by school systems that is typically available online. With regard to ethnic identity, issues of ethnic group representation, student-body diversity, and individual minority/majority status are potential characteristics that are often of interest when studying adolescent ethnic identity (see Budescu & Budescu, 2012, for an overview of possible methods to quantitatively measure such characteristics). For example, Juvonen, Nishina, and Graham (2006) found that African American and Latino youth attending more ethnically diverse schools reported less victimization by their peers, lower levels of loneliness, and higher perceptions of safety in their school than their peers attending less ethnically diverse schools. By incorporating school-level data that measure the composition of the student body, the influence of the microsystem context can be explicitly acknowledged by examining differences in individual experiences across school settings.

ESM, biannual surveys, and school-level data each represent unique methods of capturing process, person, context, and time considerations in ethnic identity. Despite the benefits and insights that can be gained from each method alone, a richer and more dynamic understanding can be gained by combining them, and therefore their true potential lies in their integration.

THE MULTILEVEL INTEGRATION METHOD: EMPIRICAL CONTRIBUTIONS TO INNOVATION

Research has considered piecewise arrangements of daily diaries, biannual surveys, and school-level data. First, we review research that has combined daily diaries with biannual surveys and then turn to research that has combined biannual surveys with school-level data.[1] Though there is less research that has used the full integration of diary surveys with biannual surveys and school-level data, this area is growing (see Yip & Douglass, 2013), and we review the available studies in this emerging area. For each approach that incorporates integration across levels, we outline the empirical strengths and the existing research.

ESM and Biannual Surveys

By considering daily diaries in tandem with biannual surveys, intra-individual differences and interindividual processes can be considered simultaneously (Bolger et al., 2003). That is, the degree to which within-person experiences of proximal contexts may vary for different persons can be captured. For example, Yip and Fuligni (2002) found that the daily association between being aware of one's ethnic identity (i.e., salience) and well-being was stronger for adolescents who had moderate or high ethnic identity in high school than it was for adolescents who had lower ethnic identity in high school. That is, the intraindividual relationship between salience and well-being was different on the basis of their ethnic identity, indicating that ethnic identity includes both stable and fluctuating components, both of which influence adolescents' daily experiences of their contexts. In a study conducted with college students, Yip (2005) found that stable levels of ethnic identity centrality impacted how being surrounded by other Asian individuals was related to daily salience, such that individuals who felt that their ethnicity was very important to them felt higher salience when surrounded by other Asians than individuals who felt that their ethnicity was not very important to them. That is, individual's daily experiences of their proximal contexts varied by individual differences in stable ethnic identity. Once again, this lends evidence to the presence of, as well as the importance of, stable and fluctuating components that make up individuals' ethnic identity. Additionally, Yip (2014) found that developmental stages in the process of ethnic identity formation impacted daily experiences of ethnic identity content; specifically, for individuals who had engaged in some degree of exploration about what

---

[1]Although the combination of ESM and school-level data is another possible subset of the multilevel integration method, to our knowledge there are no studies that take this approach.

their ethnicity meant to them (i.e., were in a moratorium or achieved stage), being aware of one's ethnic identity was related to feeling more positively about one's ethnic identity at that moment. However, for adolescents who had not engaged in exploration (i.e., were in a diffused or foreclosed stage), there was no relationship between being aware of one's ethnicity and feeling positively about it. This research shows that the being aware of ethnicity is a positive experience for some, but not all, individuals, and this experience varies on the basis of where one falls in the larger developmental spectrum. For developmental research in ethnic identity, integrating the daily diary method with biannual surveys is essential to understanding how larger developmental processes impact the lived experiences of adolescents.

Biannual Surveys and School-Level Data

Another subset of the multilevel integration method is combining biannual surveys with school-level data. By considering biannual surveys with school-level data, the impact of distal contexts on development can be examined. Specifically, this integration allows interschool effects on individual development to be considered. For example, Yip, Seaton, and Sellers (2010) found that school diversity impacted how contact with same-race others and same-race friendships impacted identity development. Brittian, Umaña-Taylor, and Derlan (2013) found that as school diversity increased, ethnic identity resolution was linked to better adjustment such that more ethnically diverse schools promoted the positive effects of individuals' ethnic identity resolution. In addition to these interschool effects, the integration of biannual surveys and school-level data also allows consideration of interschool effects in tandem with interindividual effects to show not only how schools may differ, but also how their impact on certain individuals may differ. That is, the degree to which different school contexts may have different meanings for different individuals can be captured. For example, Brown and Chu (2012) found that for Mexican immigrant children, school diversity and ethnic identity impacted the relationship between discrimination from teachers and academic attitudes. Specifically, perceived discrimination was related to poorer academic attitudes for adolescents with less positive ethnic identity who attended predominantly White or moderately diverse schools, but there was no link between discrimination and academic attitudes for adolescents who had more positive ethnic identity in those same school settings. In another example, Benner and Graham (2009) showed that transitioning from middle to high school is most stressful for African American and Latino adolescents when the proportion of same-ethnicity peers in high school decreases significantly. That same experience is less stressful, however, for White and Asian adolescents who experience that same transition. In both of these examples, interschool and interindividual effects were present simultaneously. For developmental research in ethnic identity, integrating biannual surveys with school-level data is essential to understanding the individual impacts of being embedded in certain microsystems and how those microsystems may not have the same meaning for all adolescents.

Three-Level Multilevel Integration

It is also possible (and in many cases, desirable) to consider daily diaries with biannual surveys and school-level data, which together make up the multilevel integration method. In this way, we can comprehensively consider ethnic identity from a person-by-context interaction approach (Magnusson & Stattin, 1998) to understand how distal contexts (captured with school-level data) and individual differences (captured with biannual surveys) may simultaneously influence individuals' experiences and proximal contexts (captured with daily diary data). Though limited, findings from existing work using this full integration method highlight the benefits of this approach over the piecewise methods described previously. For example, Yip et al. (2013) found a three-way cross-level interaction by which the daily effect of ingroup contact on daily private regard varied on the basis of both individual stable ethnic identity and the racial composition of high schools for Asian American adolescents. Specifically, this research found that daily ingroup contact was associated with daily private regard. That is, contact with similar others (i.e., being surrounded by same-ethnic others) was generally associated with positive feelings about one's racial/ethnic group membership; however, the nature of this relationship was moderated by both individual differences (i.e., racial identity centrality) and school-level differences (i.e., school ethnic composition). In schools where the majority of peers were White or where there was no single majority racial population, Asian American adolescents who felt that their racial identity was important to them (i.e., high centrality) reported feeling better about their racial group on days that they were surrounded by other Asians. However, in these same school settings, Asian American adolescents who reported that their racial identity was not important to their sense of self reported feeling worse about their racial group on days that they were surrounded by other Asians. In schools where Asian American adolescents were in the majority, there was no daily-level relationship between being surrounded by other Asians and feelings about their ethnic group. That is, the intraindividual daily-level relationships varied across both individuals and school contexts, thereby allowing a fully dynamic understanding of the lived experiences of individuals in context. By taking this approach, we can move away from a unidimensional or static understanding of ethnic identity and see the influence of ethnic identity as both a developmental process and as a lens through which adolescents experience their environment.

Taken together, daily diaries, biannual surveys, and school-level data can provide insights into how ethnic identity functions on a daily basis, how individual differences in ethnic identity appear in development, and how ethnic identity is influenced by important distal contexts for adolescents. Most important, the multilevel integration method allows for the simultaneous understanding of each of these processes, thereby offering a nuanced, contextualized, and meaningful understanding of the lived experiences of adolescents. In the next section of this chapter we present an empirical study using the multilevel integration method, which enables us to illustrate the benefits of this method.

EMPIRICAL ILLUSTRATION: THE YOUTH EXPERIENCES STUDY

The empirical illustration of the multilevel integration method uses data drawn from the Youth Experiences Study, a longitudinal study conducted in five New York City high schools that collected experience sampling measures, biannual surveys, and school-level data.

Conceptualization

As noted previously, the multilevel integration method can provide unique and meaningful insight into our understanding of adolescent ethnic identity. The current study uses this method to integrate our understanding of the long-term developmental process of ethnic identity with the varying content of that identity, with attention to both proximal and distal contexts. We draw on each of the unique strengths of the components of the multilevel integration method, as well as the cumulative strengths of considering each of the components simultaneously.

The first aim of this study was to examine the daily relationship between actively interacting with same-ethnic others and one's awareness of one's ethnic identity. Focusing on intragroup contact is supported by ecological systems theory, which suggests that proximal contexts are meaningful for adolescents (Bronfenbrenner, 1999), and by empirical evidence that demonstrates the influence of proximal group contact on feelings related to ethnicity (Hamm, 2000; Yip et al., 2010, 2013). Awareness of one's ethnic identity, or salience, has been shown to fluctuate in connection to proximal contexts (Yip, 2005; Yip & Fuligni, 2002). Salience, therefore, highlights one way in which ethnic identity is enacted and becomes meaningful in the lives of adolescents (Cross, Smith, & Payne, 2002; Yip, 2008), which is consistent with a content approach to ethnic identity (Sellers et al., 1998). It is expected that daily intragroup interactions will be positively related to daily salience, as interacting with other-ethnic members increases awareness of one's own ethnicity.

The second aim is to consider the effect of between-person differences on intraindividual experiences by considering how individual differences in ethnic identity development statuses—including diffused, foreclosed, moratorium, and achieved—moderate the daily relationship between intragroup interactions and ethnic identity salience. Based on a process-orientated approach to ethnic identity (Phinney, 1993), these statuses reflect variations in the degree to which individuals have explored their ethnic identity and have made decisions about how important their ethnic identity is to them (Erikson, 1968; Marcia, 1966; Parham, 1989). Emerging research has suggested that such statuses have implications for how aware adolescents are of their ethnic identity adolescents and what it means for them when they are aware (Yip, 2014). Further, intergroup contact theory suggests that contact with similar and different others can provide influential information regarding one's ethnicity (e.g., can influence attitudes and behavior; Pettigrew, 1998), and this information may vary on the basis of the developmental process of forming one's ethnic identity. Therefore, it is expected that ethnic identity statuses will moderate the daily relationship between intragroup contact and ethnic identity salience. Specifically, we expected that intragroup contact would be most influential for adolescents who have low levels of exploration and commitment; for adolescents who have not engaged with their ethnic identity, such contexts may be particularly incongruent for them and therefore increase awareness of their own ethnicity.

The third aim is to consider the effect of more distal contexts on between-person differences in intraindividual experiences by considering how diversity of school settings moderates the influence of ethnic identity development status on the daily relationship between intragroup interactions and ethnic identity salience. Therefore, we consider a three-way interaction of school diversity, ethnic identity status, and daily intragroup contact on ethnic identity salience to capture the complete person-by-context interaction that allows for the most dynamic and nuanced understanding of the lived experiences of adolescents and maximizes the benefits of the multilevel integration method. Given the large amount of time that adolescents spend in school or school-related settings (e.g., after-school activities, sports teams), research has suggested that adolescents' understanding of their ethnic identity is relative to the ethnic composition of school settings in particular (Tatum, 2004; Umaña-Taylor, 2004; Yip et al., 2010, 2013). From an intergroup contact theory perspective, this is consistent with the conceptualization of distal opportunities for group contact (de Souza Briggs, 2007; Pettigrew & Tropp, 2006), which will vary as a direct function of school diversity. Therefore, it is expected that school diversity will interact with ethnic identity statuses to moderate the daily relationship between intragroup contact and ethnic identity salience. Specifically, it is expected that for adolescents in identity statuses for whom intragroup contact and salience are linked, diverse settings will increase this effect. As the opportunities for interacting with same ethnic others are more limited in such settings, diverse settings are expected to render instances when such contact does occur more influential.

METHOD

Participants

Participants were a diverse sample of 306 racial/ethnic minority adolescents (mean age = 14.16, SD = .43, 201 girls). Data for the current illustration were drawn from a larger multiyear study involving two cohorts (Cohort 1, n = 189; Cohort 2, n = 117) that began in ninth grade; participants were excluded from the current analyses if they identified as White or if they did not indicate their primary racial/ethnic identification (n = 99). Of the participants included in the current study, 45% (n = 139) reported that they were Asian or Asian American; 16% (n = 49) reported that they were Black, African American, or West Indian; 33% (n = 102) reported that they were Hispanic or Latino; and 6% (n = 16) reported another race/ethnicity (e.g., American Indian, Native Hawaiian, nonspecified) in an open-ended question about race/ethnicity. A significant portion (19%, n = 57) of adolescents indicated being born outside of the United States. For these adolescents, age of immigration ranged from 6 months to 14 years, and the largest proportion immigrated from China (7%, n = 21), followed by Bangladesh (1%, n = 3), Colombia (1%, n = 3), Ecuador (1%, n = 3), and the Philippines (1%, n = 3). A majority of the students reported not knowing the highest level of education completed by their parents (39%, n = 138) with the most common response being that their parents completed high school (19%, n = 59).

Procedure

Data on the racial composition of all the New York City public high schools were obtained from the Department of Education. On the basis of these data, five similar-sized and academically comparable schools were selected to represent a predominantly Asian school (n = 1, 20% of participants), a predominantly White school (n = 1, 16% of participants), a predominantly Hispanic school (n = 1, 23% of participants), and two racially heterogeneous schools (n = 2, 41% of participants). *Predominantly* is defined by a single group representing at least 40% of the school's student population. In the racially heterogeneous schools, no group represented more than 40% of the school's population. Once the schools agreed to participate in the study, parental consent and youth assent letters were sent home to all ninth graders. Despite targeting certain schools, all students in each school were welcomed to participate. Only students with completed consent and assent forms participated in the study. Participation began in ninth grade, and students were administered the initial biannual survey in groups ranging from 10 to 30 students. After participants completed the survey, they received a cellular phone to access a web-based survey every night for 7 days before going to bed. Participants were provided with detailed instructions on how to use the phones and complete the surveys. On average, participants completed 4.30 (range 1–7) surveys over the course of the week.

Measures

Daily Measures

Daily-level measures were collected each night for 1 week capturing intragroup interaction and racial/ethnic identity salience. To assess the amount of active contact with same-race/ethnicity others, participants responded to the following: "Think about all the people who you interacted with today. How many were the same race/ethnicity as you?" ($M = 2.12$, $SD = 1.18$). Responses included 0 (*none: 0%*), 1 (*about 25%*), 2 (*about 50%*), 3 (*about 75%*), and 4 (*all: 100%*). To assess the degree to which individuals were aware of their race/ethnicity on that day, participants responded to the following: "How much did you feel like a member of your racial/ethnic group today?" ($M = 3.86$, $SD = 1.81$). Responses ranged from 0 (*not at all*) to 6 (*extremely*).

Individual Measures

Ethnic identity exploration and commitment were assessed using the Multigroup Ethnic Identity Measure (MEIM; Phinney, 1992). *Ethnic identity exploration* refers to the extent to which an individual seeks information and experiences relevant to his or her ethnic group membership and includes six items (e.g., "I have spent time trying to find out more about my own ethnic group, such as history, traditions, and customs"). Participants responded to all items using a scale ranging from 1 (*strongly disagree*) to 4 (*strongly agree*) ($M = 2.64$, $SD = .51$, $\alpha = .70$). *Ethnic identity commitment* refers to the extent to which an individual feels attached and personally invested as a member of their ethnic group, and includes seven items (e.g., "I have a strong sense of belonging to my own ethnic group"). Commitment items were assessed using the same response scale ($M = 3.00$, $SD = .43$, $\alpha = .75$).

School Measures

On the basis of data available on the New York Department of Education (DOE) website about the percentages of White, Black, American Indian, Asian, Hispanic, and Other students at each school, we created an objective, school-reported diversity index. Using Simpson's Index (Simpson, 1949), we computed the racial diversity of each student's school on the basis of the percentage of students in each racial group. Using the number of different racial/ethnic groups (g) and the proportion of individuals (p) who are members of each group (i), the index (DC) provides an estimate of the relative probability that two randomly selected students are from different racial/ethnic groups:

$$D_C = 1 - \sum_{i-1}^{g} p_i^2$$

Higher scores (range 0–1) indicate greater diversity ($M = .65$, $SD = .08$, range from .55–.74).

Control Variables

We controlled for several variables in our analyses because of their theoretical and statistical relationships with our primary variables. Given the repeated measures design of the study, it was important to consider any aspects of the method that may have influenced responses, as well as other measures of proximal contexts that may be related to the outcome of interest, daily salience. Because participants in daily diary studies respond to the same question for several days, this can introduce potential method artifacts (Yip & Douglass, 2013). Thus, day of study (range 1–7) was included as a control in all analyses in the current study. Day of study was significantly correlated with intragroup interactions ($r = .21$, $p < .001$) and intragroup contact ($r = .18$, $p < .001$), indicating slight increases in both over the course of the study.

Day type (i.e., weekday, weekend) was also considered as a control. There were significant mean differences by day type for intragroup interactions, $t(1,175) = -12.71$, $p < .001$, and intragroup contact, $t(1,168) = -9.24$, $p < .001$, such that adolescents reported less contact with ingroup members on weekends than weekdays.

Intragroup contact was also included as a control. To isolate the effects of intragroup interactions (e.g., active intragroup contact) independent of intragroup contact that is beyond the adolescent's control, we assessed the amount of passive intragroup contact with same-race/ethnicity others. Participants responded to the following: "Think about all the people who were *surrounding you* today. How many were the same race/ethnicity as you?" ($M = 2.00$, $SD = 1.16$). Responses included 0 (*none: 0%*), 1 (*about 25%*), 2 (*about 50%*), 3 (*about 75%*), and 4 (*all: 100%*).

We also controlled for a number of individual variables in our analyses to account for group differences and to more closely isolate the relationships of interest. In terms of *demographics*, immigrant status was initially considered as an individual control variable. However, t tests indicated that immigrant status was unrelated to all the variables of interest, so it was not included in further analyses. Gender differences were found for intragroup interactions,

$t(267) = -2.83, p < .01$, and intragroup contact, $t(267) = -2.28, p < .05$, such that girls had greater average contact with ingroup members across the 7-day study. Therefore, gender was retained as a control variable in all analyses.

Statistical majority status was also included as an individual control. On the basis of the data gathered from the New York Department of Education website about the percentage of White, Black, American Indian, Asian, Hispanic, and Other students at each school, we created a binary variable that indicated whether adolescents were members of the statistical majority in their school using a cutoff of 40%. That is, if an adolescent self-identified as a member of a group that made up at least 40% of the school's student population, he or she was considered an ethnic majority group member ($n = 88$). Though this variable was created using school-level data, it was considered an individual-level measure because it varied across individuals within schools.

RESULTS

Cluster Analysis

Initially, exploration and commitment subscales of the MEIM were used to conduct cluster analyses to identify identity development statuses of ethnic identity. Both theory and previous empirical research (Marcia, 1966; Seaton, Scottham, & Sellers, 2006; Syed & Azmitia, 2008; Yip, 2014; Yip, Seaton, & Sellers, 2006) have supported four distinct clusters, so k-means analyses were conducted to identify four clusters. These clusters were nearly identical to those found by Yip (2014), of which this study uses a subsample of only ethnic minorities (see Figure 8.1). See Table 8.1 for complete descriptives of these clusters. The smallest group of adolescents ($n = 20$) fell into a cluster that was consistent with a diffused status, with both low exploration and low commitment. The next smallest group of adolescents ($n = 47$) fell into a cluster that was consistent with a foreclosed status, with low exploration and approximately average commitment. The second largest group of adolescents ($n = 82$) fell into a cluster that was consistent with an achieved status, with both high exploration and commitment. Finally, the largest group of adolescents ($n = 157$) fell into a cluster that was consistent with a moratorium status, with average levels of both exploration and commitment.

Descriptive Statistics

We conducted bivariate correlations to examine relationships among daily study variables (see Table 8.2). There were significant, positive correlations among all daily variables of interest. Mean differences between identity clusters were also examined for all daily study variables (see Table 8.1); there

Figure 8.1. Mean levels of exploration and commitment for ethnic identity statuses.

TABLE 8.1
Means and Standard Deviations of Primary Study Variables
by Identity Status

	Diffused *M* (*SD*)	Foreclosed *M* (*SD*)	Moratorium *M* (*SD*)	Achieved *M* (*SD*)
Exploration	1.97 (0.46)	1.92 (0.60)	2.67 (0.51)	3.16 (0.53)
Commitment	2.03 (0.51)	2.91 (0.48)	2.92 (0.43)	3.45 (0.40)
Intragroup interactions	1.67 (0.78)	1.90 (0.95)	2.06 (0.85)	2.04 (0.94)
Intragroup contact	1.73 (0.61)	1.96 (0.84)	1.92 (0.79)	1.92 (0.93)
Salience	2.81 (1.74)	3.32 (1.82)	3.69 (1.53)	4.53 (1.31)

TABLE 8.2
Bivariate Correlations Among Primary Study Variables

	1	2	3	4
1. Intragroup interactions		.70***	.27***	.02
2. Intragroup contact			.28***	.00
3. Salience				.04
4. School diversity				

***$p < .001$.

were significant differences in daily salience, $F(3,265) = 9.17$, $p < .001$, with adolescents in the achieved cluster reporting higher average daily salience than all others. Chi-square analyses indicated that there were no differences from the expected distribution of identity statuses within any of the schools (School 1: $\chi^2[3] = 2.29$, $p = .51$; School 2: $\chi^2[3] = 1.57$, $p = .67$; School 3: $\chi^2[3] = 3.58$, $p = .31$; School 4: $\chi^2[3] = 4.17$, $p = .24$; School 5: $\chi^2[3] = 4.34$, $p = .22$).

Data Analysis Overview

Given the nested structure of the data, we used hierarchical linear models (HLM; Bryk & Raudenbush, 1992). HLM is appropriate for nested data because it allows for simultaneous analyses of data at more than one level. For the current research, it allows investigation into the moderating effects of both person-level (e.g., identity status) and school-level (e.g., diversity) factors on daily experiences. In the current study, Level 1 represents the daily-level experiences, Level 2 represents stable characteristics of the individual, and Level 3 represents characteristics of the school.

Daily Relationships

First, we explored the daily-level relationship between intragroup interactions and ethnic identity salience without individual or school moderators. At Level 1, the method control variables of diary day and weekday were included. Intragroup contact was also included to isolate the effects of active intragroup interactions from passive contact. For the Level 1 model, P0 represents the intercept, and E represents the random component of ethnic identity salience not accounted for in the model.

Level 1 Model:

ETHNIC IDENTITY SALIENCE = P0 + P1 * (DAY OF STUDY)

+ P2 * (DAY TYPE) + P3 * (INTRAGROUP INTERACTIONS)

+ P4 * (INTRAGROUP CONTACT) + E

Results indicated that intragroup interactions were positively related to ethnic identity salience (B30, G300; see Table 8.3). That is, on days when adolescents interacted with more same-ethnic others, they were more aware of their ethnic identity. Intragroup contact was also positively related to ethnic identity salience (B40, G400), such that on days when adolescents were surrounded by more same-ethnic others, they were more aware of their ethnic identity. There was also a significant effect of day type, showing that adolescents were more aware of their ethnic identity on weekdays than weekends.

TABLE 8.3
HLM Estimates of Daily Intragroup Interactions Predicting
Daily Ethnic Identity Salience

		B	SE
Daily ethnic identity salience	B00, G000	3.09***	0.15
Day of study	B10, G100	0.02	0.02
Day type	B20, G200	−0.18*	0.06
Daily intragroup interactions	B30, G300	0.18*	0.06
Daily intragroup contact	B40, G400	0.17*	0.05

Note. SE = standard error.
*p < .05. ***p < .001.

Individual Differences in Daily Relationships

Next, individual differences in these daily-level relationships based on ethnic identity status were considered. At Level 2, the individual control variables of gender and school majority status were included. Ethnic identity statuses were entered as the primary variables of interest, with achieved status as the reference group. Day of study and day type were treated as fixed effects at Level 2, with all other effects being treated as random.

Level 2 Model:

$$P0 = B00 + B01 * (GENDER) + B02 * (SCHOOL\ MAJORITY)$$
$$+ B03 * (DIFFUSED\ STATUS) + B04 * (FORECLOSED\ STATUS)$$
$$+ B05 * (MORATORIUM\ STATUS) + R0$$

$$P1 = B10$$

$$P2 = B20$$

$$P3 = B30 + B31 * (DIFFUSED\ STATUS)$$
$$+ B32 * (FORECLOSED\ STATUS)$$
$$+ B33 * (MORATORIUM\ STATUS) + R3$$

$$P4 = B40 + R4$$

As shown in Table 8.4, results revealed that there were main effects of diffused (B03, G030), foreclosed (B04, G040), and moratorium statuses (B05, G050), indicating differences in daily ethnic identity salience between stable identity statuses. Specifically, individuals with achieved status reported higher daily salience than individuals with diffused, foreclosed, and moratorium status alike. To examine all possible differences between diffused,

TABLE 8.4
HLM Estimates of Daily Intragroup Interactions Predicting Daily Ethnic
Identity Salience Moderated by Ethnic Identity Status

		B	SE
Daily ethnic identity salience	B00, G000	3.99***	0.28
Gender	B01, G010	0.17	0.18
School majority status	B02, G020	0.05	0.22
Diffused status	B03, G030	−2.17*	0.67
Foreclosed status	B04, G040	−1.56*	0.42
Moratorium status	B05, G050	−1.17*	0.33
Day of study	B10, G100	0.02	0.02
Day type	B20, G200	−0.19*	0.09
Daily Intragroup Interactions	B30, G300	0.05	0.08
Diffused status	B31, G310	0.26	0.19
Foreclosed status	B32, G320	0.22	0.13
Moratorium status	B33, G330	0.17	0.09
Daily intragroup contact	B40, G400	0.18*	0.05

Note. SE = standard error.
*$p < .05$. ***$p < .001$.

foreclosed, and moratorium statuses, the reference group was changed in the Level-2 HLM model, but there were no further significant differences. There was no significant interaction of identity status on the daily relationship between intragroup interactions and ethnic salience, indicating that despite differences in daily levels of salience, intragroup interactions were not differentially related to this salience by identity status.

Individual Differences in Daily Relationships in School Contexts

Next, school-level considerations were added to determine whether individual differences in these daily relationships may also vary on the basis of school diversity. Building on the previous model, we included objective school diversity as a Level 3 predictor, including main effects (B00, G001), two-way interactions (B03, G031; B04, G041; B05, G051; B30, G301), and three-way interactions of interest (B31, G311; B32, G321; B33, G331) to examine whether the relationship between identity status, daily intragroup interactions, and daily salience differed by the racial diversity of the school.

Level 3 Model:

B00 = G000 + G001 * (SCHOOL DIVERSITY) + U00

B01 = G010

B02 = G020

B03 = G030 + G031 * (SCHOOL DIVERSITY)

B04 = G040 + G041 * (SCHOOL DIVERSITY)

B05 = G050 + G051 * (SCHOOL DIVERSITY)

B10 = G100

B20 = G200

B30 = G300 + G301 * (SCHOOL DIVERSITY)

B31 = G310 + G311 * (SCHOOL DIVERSITY)

B32 = G320 + G321 * (SCHOOL DIVERSITY)

B33 = G330 + G331 * (SCHOOL DIVERSITY)

B40 = G400

Results revealed no significant three-way cross-level interactions for foreclosed or moratorium statuses (B32, G321; B33, G331), indicating that the daily-level relationship between intragroup contact and ethnic identity salience did not vary by school diversity for adolescents in foreclosed or moratorium statuses. Results did reveal a significant three-way cross-level interaction for diffused status (B31, G311), indicating a difference between diffused and achieved statuses in the effect of school diversity on the daily-level relationships (see Table 8.5). Once again, simple slopes were conducted, and for clarity we present the results by identity status.

For individuals classified as diffused status who attend schools with the highest relative levels of diversity (school diversity = .67 or .74), there was a positive daily-level association between intragroup interactions and salience (see Figure 8.2). For individuals classified as diffused status who attended schools with the lowest relative levels of diversity (diversity = .55 or .59), there was no daily-level association between intragroup interactions and salience; simple slopes tests revealed that the slopes were not significantly different from zero.

For individuals classified as achieved status, there was no daily-level association between intragroup interactions and salience; simple slopes tests revealed that the slopes for all school diversity levels were not significantly different from zero (see Figure 8.3).

SUMMARY

Results from the two-level and three-level model reveal that the influence of school diversity on the relationship between daily intragroup interactions and ethnic identity salience varies by ethnic identity status. That is,

TABLE 8.5
HLM Estimates of Daily Intragroup Interactions Predicting Daily Ethnic Identity Salience Moderated by Ethnic Identity Status and School Diversity

		B	SE
Daily ethnic identity salience	B00, G000	2.86	1.50
School diversity	B00, G001	1.63	3.75
Gender	B01, G010	0.16	0.18
School majority status	B02, G020	0.40	0.28
Diffused status	B03, G030	0.67	5.05
School diversity	B03, G031	−4.45	7.46
Foreclosed status	B04, G040	1.40	3.63
School diversity	B04, G041	−0.30	5.45
Moratorium status	B05, G050	−2.26	2.58
School diversity	B05, G051	1.52	3.88
Day of study	B10, G100	0.02	0.02
Day type	B20, G200	−.21*	0.09
Daily Intragroup Interactions	B30, G300	0.63	0.59
School diversity	B30, G301	−0.84	0.87
Diffused status	B31, G310	−3.86**	1.48
School diversity	B31, G311	6.19**	2.20
Foreclosed status	B32, G320	−0.02	1.12
School diversity	B32, G321	0.36	1.67
Moratorium status	B33, G330	−0.72	0.76
School diversity	B33, G331	1.34	1.13
Daily intragroup contact	B40, G400	0.16*	0.03

Note. SE = standard error.
* $p < .05$. ** $p < .01$.

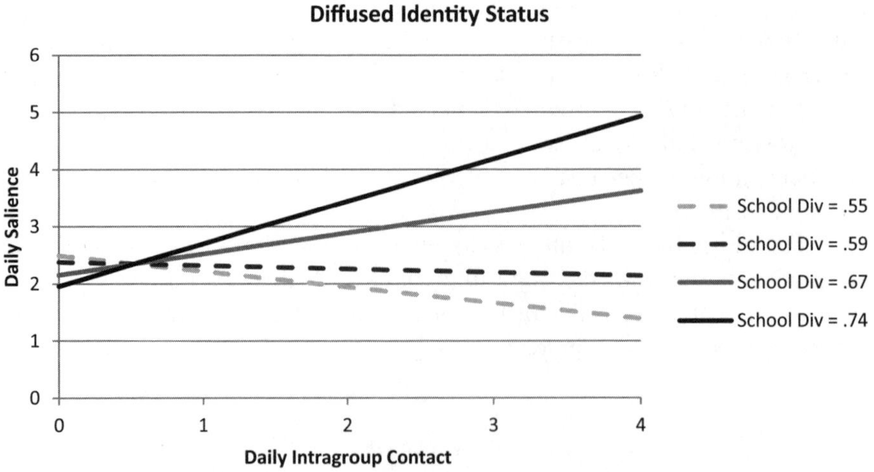

Figure 8.2. Interaction of school diversity and daily intragroup interactions on daily ethnic identity salience for adolescents with diffused identity status. Lines with significant slopes are depicted in solid lines. Lines with nonsignificant slopes are depicted in dotted lines.

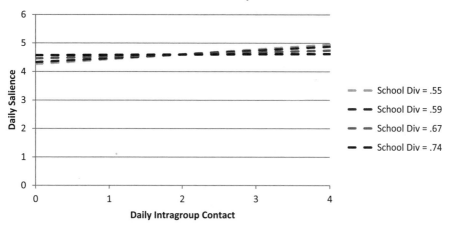

Figure 8.3. Interaction of school diversity and daily intragroup interactions on daily ethnic identity salience for adolescents with achieved identity status. All slopes are nonsignificant.

the intraindividual relationships between proximal contexts and daily experiences varied across both individuals and more distal school contexts. For individuals with foreclosed and moratorium statuses, daily intragroup contact was positively related to ethnic identity salience, regardless of the diversity of the school that they attended. For individuals with achieved status, daily intragroup contact was unrelated to ethnic identity salience, regardless of the diversity of the school that they attended. However, individuals with achieved status also reported the highest ethnic identity salience on a daily basis. Finally, for individuals with diffused status, school diversity mattered; for those who attended schools with the highest relative levels of diversity, there was a positive relationship between daily intragroup interactions and salience. However, for those who attended schools with the lowest relative levels of diversity, there was no relationship between daily intragroup interactions and salience.

DISCUSSION

Using an empirical illustration, this chapter highlights how a multilevel integration method can provide a more comprehensive approach to studying the development of ethnic identity among youth and adolescents. Exploring the daily-, person- and school-level effects on adolescents' ethnic identity adds layers of complexity to developmental processes. In the current chapter, our empirical illustration includes attention to both the process related to ethnic identity development and the content of that identity at a given point in time. Assessing daily-, person- and school-level constructs uniquely contributes to our ability to integrate process and content perspectives. The example provided in this chapter highlights the strengths of a multilevel integration approach in which the addition of a new level of analysis such as adding person-level data to daily-level processes provides unique insight into the phenomenon of interest.

For example, in our first aim, we explored the daily-level association between intragroup interactions and ethnic identity salience. Across the full sample, intragroup interactions were observed to be associated with higher ethnic identity salience. Examined in isolation, one might conclude that the presence of same-ethnic others is associated with increased ethnic identity salience for all adolescents. However, the inclusion of ethnic identity status at the person level led to a slightly different conclusion. Namely, differences in average (i.e., intercept) levels of ethnic identity salience were observed, such that achieved adolescents, reporting high levels of both exploration and commitment, reported higher levels of salience compared with adolescents in the other three ethnic identity statuses. Across days, adolescents reporting the most "developed" ethnic identity status (Erikson, 1968; Phinney, 1989) reported thinking more about their ethnic identity. This particular observation would not have been possible without the inclusion of ethnic identity status as a person-level variable in the daily-level analyses of contact and salience. Interestingly, when exploring the impact of ethnic identity status on the association between intragroup contact and salience, we arrive at conclusions similar to those in the first aim—that for all adolescents, more intragroup contact is associated with higher ethnic identity salience. These within- and between-person distinctions indicate that the development of ethnic identity varies in adolescence, and this individual development has implications for how ethnicity is experienced in general. They also indicate, however, that experiences of ethnic identity are universal, as daily interactions and daily contexts can have the same meaning for all adolescents, regardless of where they are on the developmental spectrum. It is important to note here that differences between racial/ethnic groups were not examined in the current study because of the lack of power to address the multilevel research questions; this would require a larger sample size for each racial/ethnic subsample, with a more equal distribution across school settings.

In our third aim, we included possible effects of school diversity on the daily- and person-level associations examined in the first and second aims. The goal of this aim was to explore if school-level diversity influenced the ways in which adolescents with different ethnic identity statuses experienced the daily association between intragroup contact and ethnic identity salience. The inclusion of school-level diversity qualified the conclusions drawn in the first two aims—namely, that school diversity influences how adolescents with different ethnic identity statuses experience the daily association between contact and salience. Specifically, adolescents who were diffused, reporting low levels of exploration and commitment, reported different levels of ethnic identity salience depending on daily intragroup contact and school diversity. Compared with achieved adolescents, diffused adolescents attending schools with higher diversity, reported higher daily ethnic identity salience on days in which they interacted with more same-ethnicity others. As we observed in the previous set of analyses, achieved adolescents report higher average levels of daily ethnic identity salience, irrespective of levels of intragroup contact. Indeed, adding school-level diversity into the equation further reiterates that achieved adolescents report higher levels of daily ethnic identity salience, irrespective of not only intragroup contact but also school diversity. Hence, considering school diversity leads us to a very different set of conclusions. Rather than intragroup contact appearing to be associated with ethnic identity salience for all adolescents, we observe that both ethnic identity status and school diversity present caveats to this conclusion. We now qualify our previous observations to note that achieved adolescents do not report a daily-level association between intragroup contact and salience. Diffused adolescents, however, do report a positive association between intragroup contact and ethnic identity salience, but only if they attend a racially diverse school. This important finding demonstrates how those individually varying and universal experiences of ethnic identity are sensitive to aspects of the stable context. In line with previous research, this indicates that when examining daily experiences of ethnic identity, it is important to consider for whom and in what context when considering the meaning that individuals ascribe to their ethnic identity (Yip et al., 2013).

DIRECTIONS FOR FUTURE RESEARCH

The integration of these approaches with the growing popularity of multilevel techniques has the potential to advance the literature even further. Here we propose several areas where the application of multilevel integration models has the potential to provide further insight into key areas of ethnic identity development.

First, the incorporation of daily diary and experience sampling techniques has added complexity to our knowledge about identity, stress, and coping processes (Kiang, Yip, Gonzales-Backen, Witkow, & Fuligni, 2006), discrimination (Seaton & Douglass, 2014), biracial identity (Sanchez & Garcia, 2009), and ethnic identity (Yip, 2005; Yip & Fuligni, 2002). Whereas daily diary reports capture experiences at the daily level, experience sampling reports often attempt to capture phenomenon at the level of the specific situation or event. Yet, there is a natural relationship between these two levels that has the potential to reveal interesting data. Researchers interested in the effects of discrimination on youth outcomes could measure discrimination at the level of the specific event (i.e., experience sampling) or at the daily level (i.e., daily diary). Each approach would provide slightly different information and hence answer slightly different research questions. Researchers interested in the immediate physiological response to discrimination may opt for the ESM report, whereas those interested in the cumulative effects of repeated exposure to discrimination may opt for the daily measure. Yet, the combination of the two approaches may be even more illuminating because together, the two approaches could explore how the immediate physiological response to discrimination might have cumulative effects related to repeated exposure over time. Adding yet another level to the analyses, one might then consider individual differences in exposure to lifetime discrimination that might influence adolescents' physiological responses and their cumulative effects. For example, adolescents with higher lifetime exposure to discrimination may develop accompanying coping resources and are therefore less physiologically reactive and show weaker cumulative effects. Adolescents with lower lifetime exposure might have less experience coping with discrimination and therefore show more physiological reactivity and stronger cumulative effects. The addition of lifetime discrimination introduces another level of analysis and complexity to the research question.

Introducing yet another level of analysis and complexity, one could also explore classroom effects. In schools, there may be particular classrooms in which the climate is more or less tolerant of discrimination, leading to classroom-level differences that interact with the effects of lifetime or daily discrimination. Carrying out this illustration, when an adolescent who has had high exposure to lifetime discrimination experiences a discriminatory incident in a classroom that is tolerant of such transgressions, the physiological and cumulative effects of discrimination may be particularly negative compared with when that same adolescent has a similar experience in a less tolerant classroom in which other students or faculty may intervene on his or her behalf. The illustration could continue by adding yet other levels of analyses and complexity, such as school or neighborhood, to the research question presented here. Indeed, there are numerous configurations for creating multilevel integration models that would all address important and novel questions.

Another area we believe is ripe for advances is the integration of multilevel models with longitudinal data. Many multilevel models involve repeated measures, by design. Typically, the repeated measures occur at the "lower" levels of analyses (e.g., daily, monthly). However, incorporating repeated measures at the "higher" levels of analyses has the potential to yield new information. For example, continuing our previous example of daily discrimination and cumulative effects, one might be interested in how daily processes might change as adolescents transition from high school to college. As adolescents enter young adulthood, they have more agency over the classes they take, the friends they make, and with whom they interact (Arnett, 2000); as such, the ways in which schools might influence daily discrimination experiences may differ. Following adolescents as they move into young adulthood and new educational settings could yield information on how physiological reactivity to discrimination may change over time as adolescents are exposed to more discriminatory experiences. Or, it is possible that physiological reactivity may remain constant over time but that the cumulative effects wane. These questions can only be addressed with sufficient repeated measures at the higher levels (e.g., capturing person-level data over long periods of time to capture such transitions), coupled with sufficient repeated measures at the lower levels (e.g., using ESM over long enough periods to capture such physiological reactivity). In sum, there are a host of possibilities for future research using multilevel integration methods to expand our understanding of ethnic identity. However, there are many considerations to be taken into account when designing research that uses the multilevel integration method; next, we discuss a number of issues related to best practices, and tips for avoiding common pitfalls, that may help researchers optimize the potential contributions of the multilevel integration method.

BEST PRACTICES AND AVOIDING COMMON PITFALLS

Use of the multilevel integration method will be unique to each research question, but researchers should refer to a number of basic guidelines as they develop their method and protocols. First and foremost, it is important that the levels of measurement match the conceptual relationships of interest. What aspect of daily experiences is the researcher trying to capture, and does this aspect truly vary on a day-to-day (or perhaps moment-to-moment) basis? What individual factors might influence such daily experiences, and why? What specific aspect of the context would be expected to influence individuals and daily experiences, and why? Using the multilevel integration method will be fruitless unless researchers have clear theoretical or empirical reasons for doing so, and the method will be most fruitful for researchers who have clearly detailed their expectations at every level of the data.

When considering ESM in particular, keeping surveys short enough to avoid participant fatigue is vital to the success of the multilevel integration method. Because of the repeated measures nature of ESM, missing data can plague researchers, a problem that may be compounded if participants find the surveys particularly long and cumbersome. Related to this issue is the use of branching, by which survey questions are only given on the basis of answers to previous questions. Though branching is an effective method for collecting increasingly specific data from participants, it can be related to participants' perceptions of burden (Stone & Shiffman, 2002). In instances in which branching is used, careful attention should be paid to making all possible branches of equal length (e.g., including filler questions equal to the follow-up questions of interest). If participants realize that branching options help them finish the survey more quickly, they may tailor their answers to achieve this aim rather than accurately reporting on their experiences.

Another important point of note is time span, which is relevant for every level of the multilevel integration method. As the most basic level, the time span selected for ESM should be adequate to capture instances of and variability in the construct of interest; if researchers are interested in explicit race-based altercations, they may need to use a longer ESM time frame (e.g., 1 month) than if they are interested in intragroup interactions, which are likely to occur more frequently. Alternatively, the researcher could consider event-based sampling where participants respond to questions when an identified event (e.g., being the target of racial discrimination) occurs. It is also important to consider the time span for collection of person-level measures; such decisions should be influenced by developmental theory to consider how long it may take for the construct of interest to develop. Is 3 months, 6 months, or 1 year adequate to capture such changes? Such decisions should also be influenced by the research question at hand; if transition periods are of particular interest, how long before and how long after the transition takes place should be considered when planning data collection? Although not as obvious, time span should also be considered for school-level data; although schools are often considered a stable context, researchers should be cognizant of the stability of the characteristics of interest. For example, do the demographics of the student body change over the duration of the study? For research studies conducted over multiple years, this may be particularly relevant. Overall, considerations of time span need to inform decisions at every level for the multilevel integration method.

Another potential pitfall to avoid is inadequate variability, particularly at the school level. If school contexts are of interest, it is important to include an adequate number of schools that represent enough variability on the variable of interest so that you have the statistical power to answer the research question. Sample size and variability should be considered in tandem; comparisons between two schools that are drastically different in demographics will not yield adequate power at Level 3 to statistically capture their influence, but nor will 15 schools that are extremely similar in their demographics. Given the logistical difficulties of recruiting multiple schools for studies, sample size and variability need to be at the forefront of researchers' minds as they are designing and assessing feasibility of their research study. Optimal Design, developed by Raudenbush, Spybrook, Congdon, Liu, and Martinez (2011), is a free software program designed to help researchers assess these issues and may be a helpful resource.

Overall, researchers interested in applying the multilevel integration method should first be sure that it conceptually matches their research questions and should think critically about how it will inform their knowledge of the field at every level. Once researchers have attended to those larger questions, specific attention should be paid to how long ESM surveys take to complete, how long all survey methods should be used for, and whether school-level data will be statistically sufficient to address the research questions at hand. Though the multilevel integration method requires many careful points of consideration, successful use can provide unique insights into our understanding of ethnic identity.

CONCLUSION

The goal of this chapter was to illustrate the benefits of integrating daily diaries, surveys, and school-level data to understand how ethnic identity is experienced in the everyday lives of ethnic minority youth. The literature on ethnic identity has blossomed in the past few decades with the availability of measures of ethnic identity development (Phinney, 1992) and content (Sellers et al., 1998), along with ever-expanding methods for analyzing such measures at multiple levels. In addition, technological and analytical advances have facilitated the match between conceptualizing ethnic identity as a dynamic component of self-concept and demonstrating this empirically. By capturing multiple aspects of ethnic identity and contexts that are relevant to ethnic identity in tandem, innovative insights can be gained that push our understanding of the complexity of these experiences even further.

REFERENCES

Arnett, J. J. (2000). Emerging adulthood. A theory of development from the late teens through the twenties. *American Psychologist, 55,* 469–480. http://dx.doi.org/10.1037/0003-066X.55.5.469

Benner, A. D., & Graham, S. (2009). The transition to high school as a developmental process among multiethnic urban youth. *Child Development, 80,* 356–376. http://dx.doi.org/10.1111/j.1467-8624.2009.01265.x

Bolger, N., Davis, A., & Rafaeli, E. (2003). Diary methods: Capturing life as it is lived. *Annual Review of Psychology, 54,* 579–616. http://dx.doi.org/10.1146/annurev.psych.54.101601.145030

Brittian, A. S., Umaña-Taylor, A. J., & Derlan, C. L. (2013). An examination of bi-racial college youths' family ethnic socialization, ethnic identity, and adjustment: Do self-identification labels and university context matter? *Cultural Diversity and Ethnic Minority Psychology, 19,* 177–189. http://dx.doi.org/10.1037/a0029438

Bronfenbrenner, U. (1979). *The ecology of human development.* Cambridge, MA: Harvard University Press.

Bronfenbrenner, U. (Ed.). (1999). *Environments in developmental perspective: Theoretical and operational models.* Washington, DC: American Psychological Association.

Bronfenbrenner, U., & Morris, P. A. (Eds.). (1998). *The ecology of developmental processes.* Hoboken, NJ: Wiley.

Brown, C. S., & Chu, H. (2012). Discrimination, ethnic identity, and academic outcomes of Mexican immigrant children: The importance of school context. *Child Development, 83,* 1477–1485. http://dx.doi.org/10.1111/j.1467-8624.2012.01786.x

Bryk, A. S., & Raudenbush, S. W. (1992). *Hierarchical linear models: Applications and data analysis methods.* Thousand Oaks, CA: Sage.

Budescu, D. V., & Budescu, M. (2012). How to measure diversity when you must. *Psychological Methods, 17,* 215–227. http://dx.doi.org/10.1037/a0027129

Chaiklin, S., Hedegaard, M., & Jensen, U. F. J. (1999). *Activity theory and social practice.* Aarhus, Denmark: Aarhus University Press.

Cross, W. E. (1971). The Negro-to-Black conversion experience: Toward a psychology of Black liberation. *Black World, 20*(9), 13–27.

Cross, W. E. (1991). *Shades of Black: Diversity in African-American identity.* Philadelphia, PA: Temple University Press.

Cross, W. E., & Fhagen-Smith, P. (2001). Patterns of African American identity development: A life span perspective. In C. L. Wijeyesinghe & B. W. Jackson (Eds.), *New perspectives on racial identity development: A theoretical and practical anthology* (pp. 243–270). New York, NY: New York University Press.

Cross, W. E., Smith, L., & Payne, Y. (2002). Black identity: A repertoire of daily enactments. In P. B. Pederson, J. G. Draguns, W. J. Lonner, & J. E. Trimble (Eds.), *Counseling across cultures* (5th ed., pp. 93–107). Thousand Oaks, CA: Sage.

Cross, W. E., & Strauss, L. (2008). The everyday functions of African American identity. In J. K. Swim & C. E. Stangor (Eds.), *Prejudice: The target's perspective* (pp. 267–279). San Diego, CA: Academic Press.

Csikszentmihalyi, M., & Larson, R. (1987). Validity and reliability of the experience-sampling method. *Journal of Nervous and Mental Disease, 175,* 526–536. http://dx.doi.org/10.1097/00005053-198709000-00004

de Souza Briggs, X. (2007). "Some of my best friends are . . .": Interracial friendships, class, and segregation in America. *City & Community, 6,* 263–290. http://dx.doi.org/10.1111/j.1540-6040.2007.00228.x

Erikson, E. (1968). *Identity: Youth and crisis.* New York, NY: Norton.

French, S. E., Seidman, E., Allen, L., & Aber, J. L. (2006). The development of ethnic identity during adolescence. *Developmental Psychology, 42*, 1–10. http://dx.doi.org/10.1037/0012-1649.42.1.1

Hamm, J. V. (2000). Do birds of a feather flock together? The variable bases for African American, Asian American, and European American adolescents' selection of similar friends. *Developmental Psychology, 36*, 209–219. http://dx.doi.org/10.1037/0012-1649.36.2.209

Juvonen, J., Nishina, A., & Graham, S. (2006). Ethnic diversity and perceptions of safety in urban middle schools. *Psychological Science, 17*, 393–400. http://dx.doi.org/10.1111/j.1467-9280.2006.01718.x

Kiang, L., Yip, T., Gonzales-Backen, M., Witkow, M., & Fuligni, A. J. (2006). Ethnic identity and the daily psychological well-being of adolescents from Mexican and Chinese backgrounds. *Child Development, 77*, 1338–1350. http://dx.doi.org/10.1111/j.1467-8624.2006.00938.x

Magnusson, D., & Stattin, H. (1998). Person–context interaction theories. In W. Damon (Series Ed.) & R. M. Lerner (Vol. Ed.), *Handbook of child psychology: Vol. 1. Theoretical models of human development* (5th ed., pp. 685–759). New York, NY: Wiley.

Marcia, J. E. (1966). Development and validation of ego-identity status. *Journal of Personality and Social Psychology, 3*, 551–558. http://dx.doi.org/10.1037/h0023281

Parham, T. A. (1989). Cycles of psychological nigrescence. *The Counseling Psychologist, 17*, 187–226. http://dx.doi.org/10.1177/0011000089172001

Pettigrew, T. F. (1998). Intergroup contact theory. *Annual Review of Psychology, 49*, 65–85. http://dx.doi.org/10.1146/annurev.psych.49.1.65

Pettigrew, T. F., & Tropp, L. R. (2006). A meta-analytic test of intergroup contact theory. *Journal of Personality and Social Psychology, 90*, 751–783. http://dx.doi.org/10.1037/0022-3514.90.5.751

Phinney, J. S. (1989). Stages of ethnic identity in minority group adolescents. *The Journal of Early Adolescence, 9*, 34–49. http://dx.doi.org/10.1177/0272431689091004

Phinney, J. S. (1992). The Multigroup Ethnic Identity Measure: A new scale for use with diverse groups. *Journal of Adolescent Research, 7*, 156–176. http://dx.doi.org/10.1177/074355489272003

Phinney, J. S. (1993). A three-stage model of ethnic identity development in adolescence. In M. E. Bernal (Ed.), *Ethnic identity: Formation and transmission among Hispanics and other minorities* (pp. 61–79). Albany: State University of New York Press.

Phinney, J. S., Romero, I., Nava, M., & Huang, D. (2001). The role of language, parents, and peers in ethnic identity among adolescents in immigrant families. *Journal of Youth and Adolescence, 30*, 135–153. http://dx.doi.org/10.1023/A:1010389607319

Raudenbush, S. W., Spybrook, J., Congdon, R., Liu, X., & Martinez, A. (2011). Optimal Design Software for Multi-level and Longitudinal Research (Version 2.01) [Computer software].

Sanchez, D. T., & Garcia, J. A. (2009). When race matters: Racially stigmatized others and perceiving race as a biological construction affect biracial people's daily well-being. *Personality and Social Psychology Bulletin, 35*, 1154–1164. http://dx.doi.org/10.1177/0146167209337628

Seaton, E. K., & Douglass, S. (2014). School diversity and racial discrimination among African-American adolescents. *Cultural Diversity and Ethnic Minority Psychology, 20*, 156–165. http://dx.doi.org/10.1037/a0035322

Seaton, E. K., Scottham, K. M., & Sellers, R. M. (2006). The status model of racial identity development in African American adolescents: Evidence of structure, trajectories, and well-being. *Child Development, 77*, 1416–1426. http://dx.doi.org/10.1111/j.1467-8624.2006.00944.x

Sellers, R. M., Shelton, J. N., Cooke, D. Y., Chavous, T. M., Rowley, S. A. J., & Smith, M. A. (Eds.). (1998). *A multidimensional model of racial identity: Assumptions, findings, and future directions*. Hampton, VA: Cobb & Henry.

Simpson, E. H. (1949). Measurement of diversity. *Nature, 163*, 688. http://dx.doi.org/10.1038/163688a0

Stone, A. A., & Shiffman, S. (2002). Capturing momentary, self-report data: A proposal for reporting guidelines. *Annals of Behavioral Medicine, 24*, 236–243. http://dx.doi.org/10.1207/S15324796ABM2403_09

Supple, A. J., Ghazarian, S. R., Frabutt, J. M., Plunkett, S. W., & Sands, T. (2006). Contextual influences on Latino adolescent ethnic identity and academic outcomes. *Child Development, 77*, 1427–1433. http://dx.doi.org/10.1111/j.1467-8624.2006.00945.x

Syed, M., & Azmitia, M. (2008). A narrative approach to ethnic identity in emerging adulthood: Bringing life to the identity status model. *Developmental Psychology, 44*, 1012–1027. http://dx.doi.org/10.1037/0012-1649.44.4.1012

Tajfel, H. (1981). *Human groups and social categories: Studies in social psychology.* Cambridge, England: Cambridge University Press.

Tajfel, H., & Turner, J. C. (1986). The social identity theory of inter-group behavior. In S. Worchel & L. W. Austin (Eds.), *Psychology of intergroup relations* (pp. 7–24). Chicago, IL: Nelson-Hall.

Tatum, B. D. (2004). Family life and school experience: Factors in the racial identity development of Black youth in White communities. *Journal of Social Issues, 60*, 117–135. http://dx.doi.org/10.1111/j.0022-4537.2004.00102.x

Tharp, R. G., & Gallimore, R. (1988). *Rousing minds to life: Teaching, learning, and schooling in social context.* Cambridge, England: Cambridge University Press.

Umaña-Taylor, A. J. (2004). Ethnic identity and self-esteem: Examining the role of social context. *Journal of Adolescence, 27*, 139–146. http://dx.doi.org/10.1016/j.adolescence.2003.11.006

Umaña-Taylor, A. J., & Fine, M. A. (2004). Examining ethnic identity among Mexican-origin adolescents living in the United States. *Hispanic Journal of Behavioral Sciences, 26*, 36–59. http://dx.doi.org/10.1177/0739986303262143

Umaña-Taylor, A. J., Wong, J. J., Gonzales, N. A., & Dumka, L. E. (2012). Ethnic identity and gender as moderators of the association between discrimination and academic adjustment among Mexican-origin adolescents. *Journal of Adolescence*, *35*, 773–786. http://dx.doi.org/10.1016/j.adolescence.2011.11.003

Umaña-Taylor, A. J., Yazedjian, A., & Bamaca-Gomez, M. (2004). Developing the Ethnic Identity Scale using Eriksonian and social identity perspectives. *Identity: An International Journal of Theory and Research*, *4*, 9–38. http://dx.doi.org/10.1207/S1532706XID0401_2

Yip, T. (2005). Sources of situational variation in ethnic identity and psychological well-being: A Palm Pilot study of Chinese American students. *Personality and Social Psychology Bulletin*, *31*, 1603–1616. http://dx.doi.org/10.1177/0146167205277094

Yip, T. (2008). Everyday experiences of ethnic and racial identity among adolescents and young adults. In S. M. Quintana & C. McKown (Eds.), *Handbook of race, racism, and the developing child* (pp. 182–202). Hoboken, NJ: Wiley.

Yip, T. (2014). Ethnic identity in everyday life: The influence of identity development status. *Child Development*, *85*, 205–219.

Yip, T., & Douglass, S. (2013). The application of experience sampling approaches to the study of ethnic identity: New developmental insights and future directions. *Child Development Perspectives*, *7*, 211–214. http://dx.doi.org/10.1111/cdep.12040

Yip, T., Douglass, S., & Shelton, J. N. (2013). Daily intragroup contact in diverse settings: Implications for Asian American adolescents' ethnic identity. *Child Development*, *84*, 1425–1441. http://dx.doi.org/10.1111/cdev.12038

Yip, T., & Fuligni, A. J. (2002). Daily variation in ethnic identity, ethnic behaviors, and psychological well-being among American adolescents of Chinese descent. *Child Development*, *73*, 1557–1572. http://dx.doi.org/10.1111/1467-8624.00490

Yip, T., Seaton, E. K., & Sellers, R. M. (2006). African American racial identity across the lifespan: Identity status, identity content, and depressive symptoms. *Child Development*, *77*, 1504–1517. http://dx.doi.org/10.1111/j.1467-8624.2006.00950.x

Yip, T., Seaton, E. K., & Sellers, R. M. (2010). Interracial and intraracial contact, school-level diversity, and change in racial identity status among African American adolescents. *Child Development*, *81*, 1431–1444. http://dx.doi.org/10.1111/j.1467-8624.2010.01483.x

9

CURRENT AND FUTURE DIRECTIONS IN ETHNIC–RACIAL IDENTITY THEORY AND RESEARCH

CARLOS E. SANTOS

The focus on methodological and conceptual advances in ethnic–racial identity research highlighted in the collection of articles presented in this volume advances a number of important perspectives for future research. In this chapter, I (a) summarize the unique perspectives offered by each contributor and (b) discuss directions for future research in ethnic–racial identity. Specifically, I highlight the opportunities and limitations of diverse methods and perspectives to the study of ethnic–racial identity. I explore, for example, the role of examining the intersections of multiple social identities as a way to further elucidate our understanding of ethnic–racial identity. In planning this volume, my coeditor and I hoped that readers would develop and/ or strengthen their openness to, and interest in, interdisciplinary research on ethnic–racial identity. Finally, we hoped that the readers of this volume

I would like to thank my coeditor, Adriana Umaña-Taylor, for her insightful comments on earlier drafts of this chapter.

http://dx.doi.org/10.1037/14618-010

Studying Ethnic Identity: Methodological and Conceptual Approaches Across Disciplines, C. E. Santos and A. J. Umaña-Taylor (Editors)

would consider building on the limitations and opportunities afforded by the novel methods and perspectives presented in each chapter.

With regard to terminology, as outlined next in my description of Umaña-Taylor's chapter, a new metaconstruct, ethnic–racial identity, has been proposed as a way to bridge the literature on ethnic and racial identity (Umaña-Taylor et al., 2014). Contributors to this volume elected to use their own terms. Some opted for the use of *ethnic identity* when describing their research, others opted for the use of *racial identity*, *ethnic–racial identity*, and even *racial–ethnic* identity. This reflects a state in the field of integrating the complementary and unique perspectives emerging from the ethnic and racial identity literature. As a result, in the following discussion, I retain each author's preferred term. However, when discussing my ideas and reflections, I opted for the use of the term *ethnic–racial identity*.

CONTEMPORARY PERSPECTIVES ON ETHNIC–RACIAL IDENTITY

In Chapter 1, Umaña-Taylor presents a detailed account of how conceptualizations of ethnic–racial identity have evolved over time, as well as opportunities afforded by measurement and methodological advances in research on ethnic and racial identity. As a scholar in the field of ethnic–racial identity, I find Umaña-Taylor's description of the integration of diverse perspectives and her account of the trajectory of research on ethnic and racial identity to be helpful and insightful. This account sets up unique opportunities for scholars to think about innovations and novel directions (e.g., the role of context in shaping ethnic–racial identity, the dynamic and/or relational nature of ethnic and racial identity), but more important, to do so with an eye toward how these processes infuse variability into existing research on the process and content of ethnic and racial identity. By doing so, a new generation of scholars can build on an established body of work and lead us to new and unique directions. Indeed, it is an exciting time to conduct research on ethnic and racial identity, not only because of methodological and conceptual innovations but especially because we already have an established body of research underscoring the importance of ethnic and racial identity to human development and psychological health.

In Chapter 2, Syed underscores methodological opportunities, but he also addresses limitations resulting from an overreliance on a small number of rating scales designed to capture ethnic identity. He then presents a narrative approach to the study of ethnic identity and uncovers voices and stories of individuals related to the experience of ethnicity and race. Syed's narrative method for studying ethnic–racial identity has several strengths. One that I find particularly promising is the ability to examine how experiences related to ethnic and racial identity occur when individuals recount experiences in domains on which we would not typically focus when asking about ethnic–racial identity—for example, in rating scales. In my experience collecting and analyzing qualitative data, individuals often offer revealing nuances to complex topics when narratives emerge naturally in stories they tell about domains and experiences that may seem at first unrelated to the question of interest. For example, when early adolescent Latino youth were interviewed about experiences of ethnic discrimination, they often seemed reluctant to volunteer such information (when asked directly) because at times it seemed as if they were not clear whether certain experiences qualified as an experience of ethnic discrimination. However, invariably, when speaking about other experiences in other domains, narratives about ethnic discrimination would sometimes naturally emerge (e.g., when speaking about being treated by authority figures in a different way than a peer of a different race/ethnicity). These narratives often served as a starting point for discussing a time when youth thought about their race or ethnicity. Narrative methods offer a unique opportunity to examine ethnic and racial identity experiences within contexts and domains of development that may not always seem readily overlapping.

In Chapter 3, Ortiz et al. present a historical account of ethnographic methods and their application to the study of ethnic identity. The authors present a critical ethnography of an intercultural bilingual education classroom that aims to promote indigenous knowledge as well as traditional schooling within the context of a Chilean elementary school serving rural indigenous Mapuche children. There are various strengths in using ethnographic methods to explore how instructional practices and curriculum can provide opportunities for ethnic–racial identities to develop. Within the U.S. context, there has been little empirical attention paid among psychologists to the effects of, for example, ethnic studies programs and curriculum in promoting and reconstructing ethnic–racial identities. Yet, there are many reasons to expect that these experiences might have an impact on one's understanding and sense of ethnic–racial identity. As evidenced in Ortiz et al.'s chapter, ethnographic methods may be particularly well suited to capture this transformative experience.

In Chapter 4, using photo elicitation techniques, Roth challenges the emphasis on identity and instead emphasizes the cognitive structures, or ethnic and racial schemas individuals have in dividing themselves and others into racial and ethnic groups. I find Roth's emphasis to be thought provoking. In other realms of identity research, schemas are seen as central to the development of, for example, gender identity. Dominant theories in gender development, which includes identity, such as gender schema theory (Bem, 1981) and social cognitive theories of gender development and differentiation (Bussey & Bandura, 1999) have paid considerably more attention to schemas, as well as the timing and sequence of when gender identity first develop in children.

Such emphasis has not been as apparent in the study of ethnic–racial identity. Additionally, I find the agentic quality of Roth's approach (i.e., participants actively classify photos of individuals of diverse race and ethnicities and discuss their classification) a reminder of work on identity that emphasizes how individuals "make" and enact identities. For example, Moje's (2000, 2004) research reveals how youth "do" and "enact" identities through literacy, ethnic, popular, and school cultures.

Like Roth, in Chapter 5, López et al. explore the visual experience of ethnicity, but in relation to phenotype. In particular, the authors explore the association between phenotype and ethnic identity among Puerto Rican women. Using quantitative as well as a mixed method approach in three different studies, the authors show that how one looks affects how accepted and embedded one might feel in one's ethnic group. They also show that others' reactions to how one looks can influence how one labels and sees oneself in terms of ethnicity. López et al.'s approach to the study of ethnic identity underscores a striking omission in the existing body of work on ethnic–racial identity. Little attention has been paid to how individuals look and the role that appearance and phenotype may play in shaping ethnic–racial identity. Building on this work, my colleagues and I have coded physical appearance using observational methods, and we have explored the dialectic between feeling typical and looking typical and its association with ethnic identity dimensions (Santos & Updegraff, 2014). Our work supports assertions made by López and colleagues that ethnic–racial identity scholars can and should be paying attention to the role that phenotype plays in shaping ethnic–racial identity.

In Chapter 6, Rogers and Way use qualitative methods, but they focus on the use of semistructured interviews to examine ethnic–racial identity development among African American boys. The authors highlight, similar to Syed's narrative approach, that semistructured interviews privilege the knowledge and perspective of participants (Marecek, Fine, & Kidder, 2001). One element about this research that is particularly exciting is that through the use of semistructured interviews, Rogers and Way reveal how multiple social identities intersect in the lives of African American males. Their research shows that one cannot fundamentally understand the experience of being an African American male without exploring both African American males' racial identity and their gender identity, and how these aspects of the self intersect. In addition, their research underscores the role of stereotypes in shaping ethnic–racial identity experiences and development. Scholars of ethnic–racial identity have paid little empirical attention to stereotype awareness and how stereotype endorsement may influence dimensions of ethnic–racial identity. Rogers and Way's chapter is an important reminder that more work is needed in this area.

In Chapter 7, Kornienko, Santos, and Updegraff also emphasize context, but here they emphasize the peer context of how ethnic–racial identities develop. Their approach relies on advances afforded by social network analysis to the study of peer selection and influence. In their study, they focus on friendships formed within the ecology of a middle school. Much has been said about the importance of peers in shaping developmental processes (Harris, 1998). Not surprisingly, a growing number of scholars have noted both, the significant role that peers play in shaping ethnic–racial identity processes, as well as the limited body of research in this area (Way, Santos, Niwa, & Kim-Gervey, 2008; Syed, Chapter 2). Thus, I find particularly exciting the advances in methodology (i.e., social network analysis) that enable us to capture peer influence, while accounting for selection, with regard to ethnic–racial identity development. This approach has the potential of revolutionizing our understanding of how peers influence ethnic–racial identity and furthering the debate on how the peer context is a critical one within which youth and adults engage with the construction of their ethnic–racial identity.

Similarly, in Chapter 8, Douglass and Yip also highlight the role of context in shaping ethnic identity processes by using quantitative methods. In this chapter, however, the authors introduce the multilevel integration method, which consists of the integration of daily diaries, longitudinal surveys, and large-scale data (e.g., school-level data) to understand ethnic identity development among youth. As a scholar conducting research on ethnic–racial identity, I find several aspects of this research exciting. First, Yip's (2005) pioneering use of experience sampling methods to study situational variation in ethnic identity has moved the field in important new directions that allow for dynamic assessments of how ethnic–racial identity varies daily. Second, Douglass and Yip's chapter reveals the opportunities afforded by multilevel modeling and how future research can take advantage of their proposed method in diverse ways. For example, the authors explore ethnic identity using daily dairies and longitudinal surveys combined with data on ethnic/racial composition of schools; future studies may want to explore other combinations—for example, moment-to-moment variation (rather than daily variation), longitudinal surveys timed in a shorter or longer time span, and ethnic/racial composition of other settings in which youth are embedded (e.g., neighborhoods). Indeed, it is an exciting time to conduct research on ethnic–racial identity because we have several new tools and methods that allow us to address complex questions.

DIRECTIONS FOR FUTURE RESEARCH
IN ETHNIC–RACIAL IDENTITY

As the chapters in this volume illustrate, scholars from a range of disciplines are conducting innovative research on ethnic–racial identity that is pushing the discipline forward and challenging existing paradigms and perspectives. In highlighting such work, this volume serves as a link between cutting-edge research and theory on ethnic–racial identity. In the paragraphs that follow, I discuss directions for future research that draws on the research presented in this volume. These include (a) a discussion of the role of examining the intersections and additive effects of multiple social identities to elucidate ethnic–racial identity processes, (b) a discussion of the opportunities afforded by diverse methodological and disciplinary perspectives, (c) a brief overview of integrative theory and research on ethnic–racial identity, and (d) limitations and future directions in ethnic–racial identity research.

Intersections and Additive Effects of Multiple Social Identities

One important future direction for the study of ethnic–racial identity is a greater focus on how ethnic–racial identity intersects with other social identities to shape development and influence outcomes. Considering the significant advances in measurement and perspectives on ethnic–racial identity in recent years, the time is ripe for the field to grapple with the intersections and additive effects of multiple social identities, as social identities do not develop and are not experienced in isolation. Social identities intersect, influence one another and one's experience of ethnic–racial identity, and consequently play a unique role when examined in conjunction with shaping associations between ethnic–racial identity, its correlates, and related outcomes. Not surprisingly, the intersections or additive effects of social identities, such as how ethnic identity intersects with racial schemas (Roth, Chapter 4, this volume), or gender identity (Rogers & Way, Chapter 6, this volume) are themes in some of the chapters presented in this volume. Furthermore, research on collective identities (Ashmore, Deaux, & McLaughlin-Volpe, 2004) can aid this process by emphasizing connections between multiple bodies of research on different social identities.

It is important to note a key distinction that has emerged in the field of intersectionality. Dill and Kohlman (2011) highlighted that there are weak as well as strong forms of intersectionality. *Weak* intersectionality is characterized by approaches that highlight individual differences, rather than critique systems, for example, by the incorporation of multiple social identities as variables of interest within a study. This approach has also been described as additive, rather than intersectional (Bowleg, 2008). *Strong* intersectionality, however, is concerned with producing counterhegemonic knowledge that challenges systems of oppression, inequality, power, and privilege, for example, by analyzing how these systems influence one another (see Grzanka, 2014).

Although it is important for researchers to frame their research within this larger debate on intersectionality, the notion that social identities intersect need not be seen as a framework guiding research by a reserved group of sociologists, legal scholars, critical race theorists, or a few psychologists who value this perspective. Rather, the additive effects and intersections of ethnic–racial identity with other social identities is a central issue that needs to be considered in the context of research on ethnic–racial identity across disciplinary lines and theoretical perspectives—even if one has not systematically adopted an intersectional perspective as a guiding framework. Contributions from this perspective can, and perhaps should, be addressed, for example, in the limitations and directions for future research of studies that do not adopt intersectionality as a guiding framework. Thus, an intersectional and additive perspective on social identities may prove beneficial not only in the planning of research (for those who wish to adopt this perspective at the onset of their studies) but also in the interpretation of research that may not consider this perspective as a guiding framework from its inception. The contributions of this perspective are too valuable for researchers to overlook, as intersectionality perspectives carry fundamental implications for the advancement of identity research more broadly and ethnic–racial identity research in particular.

Toward an Integrative Dialogue in Ethnic–Racial Identity Research

Psychological research has been slow to catch on to a larger movement in the social sciences that sees the intersections and additive effects of multiple social identities as a critical level of analysis (Shields, 2008). Perhaps an assumed reason for this lack of emphasis has been a focus on quantitative methods within the field. The assumption perhaps has been that a quantitative focus does not lend itself to an analysis of the complexities required to understand the intersections of ethnic–racial identity with other social identities, which are typically woven into a discussion of the role of context, power, and intergroup dynamics. This perspective, however, is increasingly challenged by a growing number of scholars who have used quantitative methods (e.g., Santos, Rodríguez, & Updegraff, 2013), as well as mixed method approaches (e.g., Rogers, 2012) to capture the additive effects of ethnic–racial identity with other social identities.

Similarly, scholars often draw attention to the limitations of a particular method as a rationale for preferring a different method or perspective. A qualitative scholar may espouse the view that quantitative research on ethnic–racial identity does not capture the context of how identities are experienced. Conversely, a quantitative scholar may espouse the perspective that qualitative research is limited in its application because of smaller sample sizes and lack of standardization. The view that one methodological perspective should be emphasized on the basis of presumed limitations of the other, although at times useful, could also, perhaps inadvertently, limit advancement. These methodological divisions, when drawn, may sometimes blind us from acknowledging the ways in which, for example, scholars who develop scales of ethnic and racial identity (including ones that are widely used in quantitative research) draw on grand theories, narratives (even if their own), and common sense to inform the creation of the very items that constitute these rating scales. Conversely, we sometimes use quantitative methods (e.g., via cluster analysis) to inform sample selection in studies with a mixed method design and, coincidently, return to the very qualitative methods that may have aided the production of quantitative scales in the first place. Aside from grand epistemological assertions, in actual practice there seems to be more evidence of circularity in how these perspectives inform one another and how they inform our understanding of ethnic–racial identity than is suggested by the divisive debate one often hears.

It is also important to consider the biases and assumptions that are commonly held by both quantitative and qualitative scholars. For example, qualitative scholars who advance the perspective that quantitative methods have contributed to a static treatment of context and how it shapes ethnic–racial identity should be mindful of the fact that advancements in quantitative research have allowed us to move beyond such simplistic assessments. Perhaps if quantitative assessments were limited to statistical tests of mean differences, or simple correlations between study variables, these perspectives might bear some truth. However, advances in quantitative research, such as those afforded by multilevel modeling approaches (see Douglass & Yip, Chapter 8, this volume), coupled with an accepted emphasis in the field that the action lies in the exploration of mediators and moderators (including types of context) of associations between ethnic–racial identity and its correlates, render these assertions as too simplistic and reductionist. We must develop an inclusive dialogue, one that values the strengths and contributions of each perspective, especially given the tendency in the field to emphasize the limitations of one methodological approach as the rationale for using another (i.e., a tendency to pit these perspectives against each other rather than as complementary). Although there is truth to the argument that quantitative approaches have not always been attentive to how context shapes ethnic–racial identity, as this volume shows, several scholars are expanding our thinking about context across diverse methods and disciplinary lenses, including via the use of advanced quantitative techniques. It is time to move beyond such generalizations.

Quantitative and qualitative perspectives benefit from one another, and methodological divisions between the two limit our understanding and prevent programs of training and outlets of publication from fully embracing the extent to which these perspectives complement one another and are critical to the development and pursuit of quality research on ethnic–racial identity. To challenge these perspectives, my coeditor and I set out to include and bring together diverse methodologies in ethnic–racial identity research (e.g., ethnography, semistructured interviews, multilevel modeling, social network analysis) and contributions by authors with training in diverse disciplines (e.g., sociology, anthropology, education, psychology) within this volume. It is time to move beyond divisions, promote an inclusionary dialogue, and build on what we know from these diverse perspectives and lines of research.

Toward an Integrative Theory of Ethnic–Racial Identity Research

As noted in Chapter 1 of this volume, ethnic and racial identity scholars have joined forces by proposing an integrative approach to their field of study. Umaña-Taylor and colleagues (2014) outlined the shared components of racial identity (e.g., Cross, 1971; Sellers, Smith, Shelton, Rowley, & Chavous, 1998) and ethnic identity perspectives (e.g., Bernal, Knight, Garza, Ocampo, & Cota, 1990; Phinney, 1990; Quintana, 1994; Umaña-Taylor, Yazedjian, & Bámaca-Gómez, 2004). This direction provides a unique opportunity for the field to come together and achieve new advances. This integration can further capitalize on the opportunities and advances presented in this volume. As a new generation of scholars increasingly considers ecological models of development (Bronfenbrenner, 1979), and how ethnic–racial identity fits within this perspective, we are now entering a phase in which we can expand our range of methods and hence our understanding of ethnic–racial identity. For example, by considering how the experience of ethnic–racial identity is shaped by physical characteristics (e.g., phenotype, López et al., Chapter 5), internal processes (e.g., ethnic and racial schemas, Roth, Chapter 4; self-narratives, Syed, Chapter 2), proximal relationships (e.g., peers, Kornienko et al., Chapter 7), micro/macro contexts (e.g., school ethnic/racial composition, Douglass & Yip, Chapter 8); school programs designed to raise critical consciousness among marginalized youth (Ortiz et al., Chapter 3), macro/distal contexts (e.g., cultural stereotypes about race, ethnicity, and gender, Rogers & Way, Chapter 6); and sociohistorical stereotypes and barriers (Ortiz et al., Chapter 3). Thus, we are uniquely poised to expand our repertoire of methods for understanding ethnic–racial identity and its impact on the development of individuals.

Finally, as we now have several established measures of ethnic–racial identity and a growing body of research revealing patterns of association between ethnic–racial identity and related outcomes, it is important to emphasize the role of replication and validation of the studies we already have. The field of psychology, for example, has been notoriously slow in valuing the importance of replication and validation of published findings (e.g., as evidenced by the limited number of published replication and validation studies; see Duncan, Engel, Claessens, & Dowsett, 2014, for a thorough discussion of this issue).

Limitations and Future Directions

In putting together this volume, my coeditor and I confronted some striking limitations. One was the lack of use of experimental and quasi-experimental methods to study ethnic–racial identity (see Yoo & Lee, 2005, for an exception). There continues to be an overreliance on self-report methods in both quantitative and qualitative methods, and some have raised skepticism over the value of self-reports in the study of identity (Schwartz, Vignoles, & Luyckx, 2011). Experimental approaches may be particularly useful, for example, in furthering our understanding of intersectionality by the use of designs that prime one identity over another, or in conjunction. Another direction may be the applicability of actor–partner interdependence modeling techniques (Cook & Kenny, 2005) in the context of friendship dyads, for example. Expanding on Kornienko et al.'s (Chapter 7, this volume) exploration of peer network influences in identity development, this approach may afford opportunities to address questions about how friendship dyads (or even couples) influence each member's ethnic–racial identity overtime. A striking limitation is the limited use of mixed methods in the study of ethnic–racial identity (see López et al., Chapter 5, this volume, for an exception). It is time to move beyond generalizations, such as "it's hard to do" or "qualitative research isn't rigorous enough," because these generalizations reiterate divisions and prevent us from moving forward in the field of ethnic–racial identity. Given the advances outlined in this volume in quantitative as well as qualitative approaches to the study of ethnic–racial identity, it is time for the field to move beyond the characterization of either approaches as unscientific.

Finally, an important future direction for research on ethnic–racial identity is to expand the populations that are typically studied. Much of the focus on ethnic–racial identity research has been on groups such as African Americans; Latinos; and to a lesser degree, Asian Americans, Native Americans, and European Americans. Religious minorities, for example, such as Muslim Americans, among many others, have been vastly understudied, particularly in the United States (see Sirin & Fine, 2008, for an exception). A focus on intersectionality should inevitably lead scholars of ethnic–racial identity to explore how other social identities, such as religious identity, may impact the experience of ethnic–racial identity.

CONCLUSION

The goals of this edited volume were to highlight methodological and conceptual advances in the study of ethnic–racial identity across disciplinary and methodological lines and to reveal new findings derived from these approaches. An edited book on this topic was needed because, despite a number of important advances in the field of ethnic–racial identity, no volume brings together these contributions in one place. The chapters in this volume describe diverse perspectives that are emerging across methodological and disciplinary lines and highlight ways in which scholarship is "pushing the envelope" of how we measure and think about ethnic–racial identity.

REFERENCES

Ashmore, R. D., Deaux, K., & McLaughlin-Volpe, T. (2004). An organizing framework for collective identity: Articulation and significance of multidimensionality. *Psychological Bulletin, 130,* 80–114. http://dx.doi.org/10.1037/0033-2909.130.1.80

Bem, S. L. (1981). Gender schema theory: A cognitive account of sex typing. *Psychological Review, 88,* 354–364. http://dx.doi.org/10.1037/0033-295X.88.4.354

Bernal, M. E., Knight, G. P., Garza, C. A., Ocampo, K. A., & Cota, M. K. (1990). The development of ethnic identity in Mexican American children. *Hispanic Journal of Behavioral Sciences, 12,* 3–24. http://dx.doi.org/10.1177/07399863900121001

Bowleg, L. (2008). When Black + lesbian + woman ≠ Black lesbian woman: The methodological challenges of qualitative and quantitative intersectionality research. *Sex Roles, 59,* 312–325. http://dx.doi.org/10.1007/s11199-008-9400-z

Bronfenbrenner, U. (1979). *The ecology of human development: Experiments by nature and design.* Cambridge, MA: Harvard University Press.

Bussey, K., & Bandura, A. (1999). Social cognitive theory of gender development and differentiation. *Psychological Review, 106,* 676–713. http://dx.doi.org/10.1037/0033-295X.106.4.676

Cook, W. L., & Kenny, D. A. (2005). The actor–partner interdependence model: A model of bidirectional effects in developmental studies. *International Journal of Behavioral Development, 29,* 101–109. http://dx.doi.org/10.1080/01650250444000405

Cross, W. E., Jr. (1971). The Negro-to-Black conversion experience: Toward a psychology of Black liberation. *Black World, 20*(9), 13–27.

Dill, B. T., & Kohlman, M. H. (2011). Intersectionality: A transformative paradigm in feminist theory and social justice. In S. N. Hesse-Biber (Ed.), *The handbook of feminist research: Theory and praxis* (pp. 154–174). Thousand Oaks, CA: Sage.

Duncan, G. J., Engel, M., Claessens, A., & Dowsett, C. (2014). Replication and robustness in developmental research. *Developmental Psychology.* Advance online publication. http://dx.doi.org/10.1037/a0037996

Grzanka, P. (Ed.). (2014). *Intersectionality: A foundations and frontiers reader.* Boulder, CO: Westview Press.

Harris, J. R. (1998). *The nurture assumption: Why children turn out the way they do*. New York, NY: Free Press.

Marecek, J., Fine, M., & Kidder, L. (2001). Working between two worlds: Qualitative methods and psychology. In D. L. Tolman & M. Brydon-Miller (Eds.), *From subjects to subjectivities: A handbook of interpretive and participatory methods* (pp. 29–41). New York, NY: New York University Press.

Moje, E. B. (2000). "To be part of the story": The literacy practices of "gangsta" adolescents. *Teachers College Record*, *102*, 652–690. http://dx.doi.org/10.1111/0161-4681.00071

Moje, E. B. (2004). Powerful spaces: Tracing the out-of-school literacy spaces of Latino/a youth. In K. Leander & M. Sheehy (Eds.), *Spatializing literacy research and practice* (pp. 15–38). New York, NY: Peter Lang.

Phinney, J. S. (1990). Ethnic identity in adolescents and adults: Review of research. *Psychological Bulletin*, *108*, 499–514. http://dx.doi.org/10.1037/0033-2909.108.3.499

Quintana, S. M. (1994). A model of ethnic perspective-taking ability applied to Mexican-American children and youth. *International Journal of Intercultural Relations*, *18*, 419–448. http://dx.doi.org/10.1016/0147-1767(94)90016-7

Rogers, O. (2012). *Young, Black, and male: Exploring the intersections of racial and gender identity in an all-Black, all-male high school*. ProQuest Dissertation Abstracts. (UMI No. 10197)

Santos, C., Rodríguez, S. A., & Updegraff, K. (2013, April). *The overlapping nature and correlates of gender and ethnic identity among Latino youth*. Paper presented at the biennial meeting of the Society for Research in Child Development, Seattle, WA.

Santos, C. E., & Updegraff, K. A. (2014). Feeling typical, looking typical: Physical appearance and ethnic identity among Mexican-origin youth. *Journal of Latina/o Psychology*. Advance online publication. http://dx.doi.org/10.1037/lat0000023

Schwartz, S. J., Vignoles, V. L., & Luyckx, K. (2011). Epilogue: What's next for identity theory and research? In S. J. Schwartz, K. Luyckx, & V. L. Vignoles (Eds.), *Handbook of identity theory and research* (pp. 933–938). New York, NY: Springer. http://dx.doi.org/10.1007/978-1-4419-7988-9

Sellers, R. M., Smith, M. A., Shelton, J. N., Rowley, S. A. J., & Chavous, T. M. (1998). Multidimensional model of racial identity: A reconceptualization of African American racial identity. *Personality and Social Psychology Review*, *2*, 18–39. http://dx.doi.org/10.1207/s15327957pspr0201_2

Shields, S. A. (2008). Gender: An intersectionality perspective. *Sex Roles*, *59*, 301–311. http://dx.doi.org/10.1007/s11199-008-9501-8

Sirin, S., & Fine, M. (2008). *Muslim American youth: Understanding hyphenated identities through multiple methods*. New York, NY: New York University Press.

Umaña-Taylor, A. J., Quintana, S. M., Lee, R. M., Cross, W. E., Rivas-Drake, D., Schwartz, S. J., . . . Ethnic and Racial Identity in the 21st Century Study Group.

(2014). Ethnic and racial identity during adolescence and into young adulthood: An integrated conceptualization. *Child Development, 85,* 21–39. http://dx.doi.org/10.1111/cdev.12196

Umaña-Taylor, A. J., Yazedjian, A., & Bámaca-Gómez, M. Y. (2004). Developing the Ethnic Identity Scale using Eriksonian and social identity perspectives. *Identity: An International Journal of Theory and Research, 4,* 9–38. http://dx.doi.org/10.1207/S1532706XID0401_2

Way, N., Santos, C., Niwa, E. Y., & Kim-Gervey, C. (2008). To be or not to be: An exploration of ethnic identity development in context. *New Directions for Child and Adolescent Development, 2008*(120), 61–79. http://dx.doi.org/10.1002/cd.216

Yip, T. (2005). Sources of situational variation in ethnic identity and psychological well-being: A Palm Pilot study of Chinese American students. *Personality and Social Psychology Bulletin, 31,* 1603–1616. http://dx.doi.org/10.1177/0146167205277094

Yoo, H. C., & Lee, R. M. (2005). Ethnic identity and approach-type coping as moderators of the racial discrimination–well-being relation in Asian Americans. *Journal of Counseling Psychology, 52,* 497–506. http://dx.doi.org/10.1037/0022-0167.52.4.497

INDEX

Pituc, S. T., 43
Postmodern critical theory, 58–60
Poststructuralism, 58, 60
Primary cultural characteristics, xiii
Proactive coping, 164
Process-person-context-time model,
    204–205
Puerto Ricans
    narrative research on, 37
    phenotypes research with, 125–138
    photo elicitation research with,
        97–108
    stereotypes of, 154

Qualitative research, 242–243
Quantitative research, 242–243
Quintana, S. M., 14

Race, 92, 152–153
Racial acculturation, 98, 108
Racial classification, 91, 93–97, 123–124
Racial–ethnic identity. See Ethnic–racial
        identity (ERI)
Racial identity
    measurement of, 16–17
    overlap between ethnic identity and,
        16–18
Raudenbush, S. W., 229
Reflexivity (research), 81–82
Reliability, interrater, 45
Resistance (stereotype response), 156
Rivas-Drake, D., 181
Roberts, J. E., 181
Robinson, T., 164
Rogers, L. O., 155
Romero, I., 181
Rosenberg Self-Esteem Scale, 129
Rowley, S. J., 181

SABM. See Stochastic actor-based
        modeling
Sanjek, R., 97
School diversity, 209, 224–225
School ethnographers, 60
School-level data, 207, 209–210
Secondary cultural characteristics, xiii
Seidman, E., 207
Self-esteem, 129–132
Sellers, R. M., 17, 28

Semistructured interviews (SSIs),
        149–170
    analysis of, 152–153
    challenges with, 165–166
    in critical ethnography, 57, 80
    empirical example, 155–162
    future research, directions for, 166
    protocol for, 167–170
    researching using, 153–155
    strengths of, 164–165
    studying ethnic identity with,
        150–152, 162–164
Shelton, J. N., 180
Sherma, S. J., 95
Sherman, J. W., 95
Shorter-Gooden, K., 154
Simpson's Index, 214–215
Skin color preference, 123
SNA. See Social network analysis
Social contexts, 36–39
Social group perspectives, 17
Social identities
    elements of, 3
    intersections of multiple, 240–241
Social identity theory, 14
Socialization, 140. See also Peer influence
        effects
Social network analysis (SNA),
        177–197
    best practices for, 196–197
    empirical illustration, 188–196
    existing research using, 180–182
    future research, directions for,
        196–197
    methodological contributions of,
        178–179, 182–188
    network positions in, 182–186
    peer influence effects in, 177–182,
        186–196
Somatic norm images, 91
Spencer, M. B., 12, 164
Spybrook, J., 229
SSIs. See Semistructured interviews
Steele, M. B., 151, 163
Stereotypes, 154, 156, 161–163
Stereotype threat, 163
Stochastic actor-based modeling
        (SABM), 179, 186, 190–195
Strauss, L., 205–206

ABOUT THE EDITORS

Carlos E. Santos, PhD, is an assistant professor at Arizona State University in the Counseling & Counseling Psychology program. Prior to his current appointment, Dr. Santos was a Research Fellow at Harvard University's Malcolm Wiener Center for Social Policy and a Mainzer Junior Fellow at the University of Cambridge's Centre for Gender Studies. He received his undergraduate degree and doctoral degree in developmental psychology from New York University and a master's degree in education from Harvard University.

Drawing on ecological theories of development, Dr. Santos's research explores how ethnic and gender identities intersect and form within the individual; how these social identities are influenced by peers as well as cultural stereotypes; and how these processes predict psychological adjustment among adolescents, particularly Latino and immigrant youth. He draws on a variety of disciplines including developmental, social, and cultural psychology; family studies; anthropology; and sociology. His research has been funded by the National Science Foundation and has been published in a variety of outlets.

Dr. Santos was a member of the governing council of the Society for Research in Child Development and was selected as a Faculty Fellow by the Ford Foundation and the American Association of Hispanics in Higher

Education. He is a consulting editor of the *Journal of Counseling Psychology* and *Cultural Diversity and Ethnic Minority Psychology*, and he is a member of the College of Reviewers at the National Science Foundation.

Adriana J. Umaña-Taylor, PhD, is a Foundation Professor at Arizona State University in the T. Denny Sanford School of Social and Family Dynamics. She received her PhD in human development and family studies from the University of Missouri–Columbia.

Dr. Umaña-Taylor's research focuses on ethnic identity formation, familial socialization processes, and culturally informed risk and protective factors. Her expertise lies primarily in the developmental period of adolescence, and her work is largely influenced by an ecological framework, with an emphasis on understanding how individual and contextual factors interact to inform adolescent development and adjustment. A large body of her work has focused on the development and psychosocial adjustment of Latino youth and families living in the United States.

Dr. Umaña-Taylor approaches her research from an interdisciplinary perspective, drawing largely from developmental psychology, social psychology, cultural psychology, family studies, and sociology. Her work, funded by the National Institutes of Health, has been featured in notable journals in the family, cultural, and developmental sciences. Dr. Umaña-Taylor currently serves on multiple editorial boards and a Study Section for the National Institutes of Health. She has served as a member of the executive council of the Society for Research on Adolescence and as a member of the board of directors for the National Council on Family Relations.